CW00832517

Routledge Philosop

Nietzsche on Art

Nietzsche is one of the most important modern philosophers and his writings on the nature of art are amongst the most influential of the Nineteenth and Twentieth centuries. *Nietzsche on Art* introduces and assesses:

- Nietzsche's life and the background to his writings on art
- the ideas and texts of his works which contribute to art, including *The Birth of Tragedy*, *Human, All Too Human* and *Thus Spoke Zarathustra*
- Nietzsche's continuing importance to philosophy and contemporary thought.

Nietzsche on Art will be essential reading for all students coming to Nietzsche for the first time.

Aaron Ridley is Professor of Philosophy at the University of Southampton, UK.

ROUTLEDGE PHILOSOPHY GUIDEBOOKS

Edited by Tim Crane and Jonathan Wolff

University College London

Plato and the Trial of Socrates Thomas C. Brickhouse and Nicholas D. Smith
Aristotle and the Metaphysics Vasilis Politis
Rousseau and the Social Contract Christopher Bertram
Plato and the Republic, Second edition Nickolas Pappas
Husserl and the Cartesian Meditations A.D. Smith
Kierkegaard and Fear and Trembling John Lippitt
Descartes and the Meditations Gary Hatfield
Hegel and the Philosophy of Right Dudley Knowles
Nietzsche on Morality Brian Leiter
Hegel and the Phenomenology of Spirit Robert Stern
Berkeley and the Principles of Human Knowledge Robert Fogelin
Aristotle on Ethics Gerard Hughes
Hume on Religion David O'Connor
Leibniz and the Monadology Anthony Savile
The Later Heidegger George Pattison
Hegel on History Joseph McCarney
Hume on Morality James Baillie
Hume on Knowledge Harold Noonan
Kant and the Critique of Pure Reason Sebastian Gardner
Mill on Liberty Jonathan Riley
Mill on Utilitarianism Roger Crisp
Wittgenstein and the Philosophical Investigations Marie McGinn
Spinoza and the Ethics Genevieve Lloyd
Heidegger on Being and Time, Second Edition Stephen Mulhall
Locke on Government D.A. Lloyd Thomas
Locke on Human Understanding E.J. Lowe
Derrida on Deconstruction Barry Stocker
Kant on Judgement Robert Wicks
Nietzsche on Art Aaron Ridley

Routledge Philosophy Guidebook to

Nietzsche on Art

Aaron
Ridley

Routledge
Taylor & Francis Group

LONDON AND NEW YORK

First published 2007
by Routledge
2 Milton Park Square, Milton Park, Abingdon, OX14 4RN

Simultaneously published in the USA and Canada
by Routledge
711 Third Avenue, New York, NY 10017, USA

*Routledge is an imprint of the Taylor & Francis Group, an informa
business*

© 2007 Aaron Ridley

Typeset in Aldus and Scala by Taylor & Francis Books

British Library Cataloguing in Publication Data
A catalogue record for this book is available from the British Library

Library of Congress Cataloging in Publication Data
A catalog record for this book has been requested

ISBN 10: 0-415-31590-5;   ISBN 13: 978-0-415-31590-6 (hbk)
ISBN 10: 0-415-31591-3;   ISBN 13: 978-0-415-31591-3 (pbk)
ISBN 10: 0-203-96485-3;   ISBN 13: 978-0-203-96485-9 (ebk)

To the memory of Larry Wakefield, painter

Contents

PREFACE   IX
SOURCES AND ABBREVIATIONS   XI

Introduction   1

1   Redemption through Art: *The Birth of Tragedy*   9
    Introduction   9
    1. An outline   13
    2. Dionysus   17
    3. The metaphysical position   21
    4. Between psychology and metaphysics   27
    5. Child's play   31

2   Redemption through Science: *Human, All Too Human*   34
    Introduction   34
    1. The metaphysical position   37
    2. Art and science   41
    3. Genius and inspiration   46
    4. 'Monumental' art   51
    5. Art and the self   58

3   Art to the Rescue: *The Gay Science*   61
    Introduction   61
    1. The metaphysical position   64
    2. Suffering and the intellectual conscience   72
    3. The need for art   78
    4. Art and the self   84

4   Philosophy as Art: *Thus Spoke Zarathustra*   89
    Introduction   89
    1. The teaching of ideals   91
    2. The power of art   97
    3. Zarathustra as exemplar   100
    4. Eternal recurrence   102
    5. Art and the love of fate   108

5   The Art of Freedom: After *Zarathustra*   112
    Introduction   113
    1. The metaphysical position   115
    2. The art of works of art   117
    3. Romanticism   122
    4. Becoming who you are   128
    5. Art and the self   134

    Appendix: Nietzsche on Wagner   141

    NOTES   156
    BIBLIOGRAPHY   172
    INDEX   175

PREFACE

Several people have helped me significantly in writing this book, but the lion's share of thanks is owed, not for the first time, to Alex Neill and David Owen, both of whom were characteristically generous and penetrating in their comments on earlier drafts of everything that appears here. For equally valuable assistance of a more episodic kind I am indebted to Chris Janaway and to two anonymous readers for Routledge: each of them pointed out some real shortcomings, and made helpful suggestions for improvement. And for what one might term environmental support, I am, as ever, grateful to the proprietors and staff of the Avenue Bar, Padwell Road, where this book was largely written. At Routledge, I would like to thank Tony Bruce Priyanka Pathak and Jean Rollinson, whose efforts in seeing the project to completion were as whole-hearted and as smoothly orchestrated as one could wish.

Versions of parts of this book have previously appeared elsewhere. Sections 4 and 5 of Chapter Four draw on an essay, 'Nietzsche's Greatest Weight', first published in the *Journal of Nietzsche Studies* (1997); sections 4 and 5 of Chapter Five are reworkings of pages from my introduction to the Cambridge Texts in the History of Philosophy edition of Nietzsche's last writings

(2005); and parts of the Appendix derive from the same source, as well as from an entry, 'Wagner', contributed to M. Kelly, ed., *The Encyclopedia of Aesthetics* (Oxford: Oxford University Press, 1998). My thanks to those concerned for allowing me to make use of the relevant material here.

Aaron Ridley
Southampton, 2006

Sources and Abbreviations

With the exception of TL, where references in the text are to page-numbers, all references are to sections. So, for example, HH I.314 refers to section 314 of the first volume of *Human, All Too Human*; GM II.12 to section 12 of the second essay of *On the Genealogy of Morals*; D P.5 to section 5 of the preface to *Daybreak*; TI IX.31 to section 31 of the part of *Twilight of the Idols* called 'Expeditions of an Untimely Man'.

AC – *The Anti-Christ*, trans. R.J. Hollingdale, Harmondsworth, Penguin, 1968.

ASC – 'Attempt at a Self-Criticism', trans. W. Kaufmann, in *The Birth of Tragedy* and *The Case of Wagner*, New York, Vintage, 1967, pp.17–27.

BGE – *Beyond Good and Evil*, trans. W. Kaufmann, New York, Vintage, 1966.

BT – *The Birth of Tragedy*, trans. W. Kaufmann, in *The Birth of Tragedy* and *The Case of Wagner*, New York, Vintage, 1967.

CW – *The Case of Wagner*, trans. J. Norman, in *The Anti-Christ, Ecce Homo, Twilight of the Idols* and other writings, Cambridge, Cambridge University Press, 2005.

D – *Daybreak*, trans. R.J. Hollingdale, Cambridge, Cambridge University Press, 1997.

EH – *Ecce Homo*, trans. J. Norman, in *The Anti-Christ, Ecce Homo, Twilight of the Idols* and other writings, Cambridge, Cambridge University Press, 2005.

GM – *On the Genealogy of Morals*, trans. W. Kaufmann and R.J. Hollingdale, New York, Vintage, 1969.

GS – *The Gay Science*, trans. W. Kaufmann, New York, Vintage, 1974.

HH – *Human, All Too Human*, trans. R.J. Hollingdale, Cambridge, Cambridge University Press, 1996.

NCW – *Nietzsche contra Wagner*, trans. J. Norman, in *The Anti-Christ, Ecce Homo, Twilight of the Idols* and other writings, Cambridge, Cambridge University Press, 2005.

OS – 'On Schopenhauer', trans. C. Janaway, in Janaway, ed., *Willingness and Nothingness: Schopenhauer as Nietzsche's Educator*. Oxford: Oxford University Press, 1998, pp.258–65. (This essay is also available in K. Ansell-Pearson and D. Large, eds., *The Nietzsche Reader*. Oxford: Blackwell, 2006, pp.24–29.)

TI – *Twilight of the Idols*, trans. R.J. Hollingdale, Harmondsworth, Penguin, 1968.

TL – 'On Truth and Lies in a Nonmoral Sense', trans. D. Breazeale, in Breazeale, ed., *Philosophy and Truth*, Atlantic Highlands, Humanities Press International, 1990, pp.79–100.

UM – *Untimely Meditations*, trans. R.J. Hollingdale, Cambridge, Cambridge University Press, 1997.

WP – *The Will to Power*, trans. W. Kaufmann, New York, Vintage, 1968.

Z – *Thus Spoke Zarathustra*, trans. R.J. Hollingdale, Harmondsworth, Penguin, 1969.

INTRODUCTION

Nietzsche was bowled over by art, perhaps more so than any other philosopher of comparable stature.[1] His first book, *The Birth of Tragedy* (1872), is devoted to it, and shows his youthful enthusiasm at full flood. Art then features prominently in each of his subsequent books – lit from a variety of angles, playing a variety of roles in the larger movement of his thought – until, in 1888, the final year of his productive life, he completed two further books devoted exclusively to art, *The Case of Wagner* and *Nietzsche contra Wagner*. If we add to this the fact that one of his books – *Thus Spoke Zarathustra* – is intended to *be* a work of art; the fact that the style and construction of all of his books is self-consciously artistic to a degree approached only, perhaps, among philosophers, by Plato and the early Wittgenstein; and the fact that throughout his life Nietzsche regarded himself as a serious composer, despite the evidence of his actual compositions to the contrary – and we have a quick sketch of the most art-fixated of all of the major philosophers. This sketch also indicates a difficulty in saying what Nietzsche's 'philosophy of art' might have been. His engagement with art was multi-dimensional, and it lasted throughout his productive life – a relatively brief period, but long enough for his thought to have developed in some quite dramatic ways. And this means that the search for any single position describable as 'Nietzsche's philosophy of art' is more or less doomed to failure. It is true that he says some things at the beginning of his career that he also says at the end; it is true, too, that his sense of the significance of art barely wavered; but – because of the evolution of his thought as a whole – the apparent sameness of those 'things' and of that 'significance' cannot be taken as a sign that he cleaved throughout to any settled view. Rather, Nietzsche's thinking about art must be seen as standing in a dynamic and reciprocal relation to his thoughts about everything else; and this means that any worthwhile attempt at a reconstruction of his 'philosophy of art' must be both developmental and contextual – that it must, in effect, be an attempt to understand Nietzsche's intellectual biography through the prism of art.

I   Born in 1844 to Karl Ludwig Nietzsche, a Lutheran pastor who died when his son was four, and Franziska Nietzsche, who died in 1897, Friedrich Wilhelm Nietzsche was taught first in Naumberg and then at Schulpforta, Germany's leading Protestant boarding school, from which he received a first class classical education. At the age of twenty, he entered the University of Bonn as a classics student, before moving in the following year to the University of Leipzig (where he first encountered Schopenhauer's philosophy). He proved an extremely precocious scholar: he published his first learned essays in 1867, and was appointed to a professorship in classical philology at Basel two years later, at the absurdly early age of twenty four.

The speed of his advancement is all the more remarkable when one notes two further points. First, he lost six months of study in 1867–68 to military service, before injuring himself getting on to a horse. Second, and more strikingly, he seems very quickly to have come to doubt the real value of philology as an intellectual pursuit: a letter of 1868 sees him fretting about the indifference of philologists to 'the true and urgent problems of life'.[2] And his sense that philology failed to engage with the big questions was surely exacerbated by his first meeting, in the same year, with Richard Wagner, in whom Nietzsche found someone with a truly gargantuan appetite for the big questions – the bigger the better.

Certainly he seems not to have committed himself very whole-heartedly to professorial life: in 1870 he volunteered as a medical orderly in the Franco-Prussian war, and then spent much of the following year on sick-leave in the Alps. By the mid-1870s he was dividing his time between taking cures in spas, travelling in the mountains, and being in Basel when he had to: he finally resigned his post, on grounds of ill-health, in 1879.

The remainder of his life was spent on the move. Supported by a small pension, he took lodgings wherever the climate and environment seemed to promise some respite from his steadily worsening physical condition. In 1880, for instance, he stayed in Bolzano, Venice, Marienbad, Frankfurt, Heidelberg, Locarno, Stresa and Genoa. Italy became increasingly important to him; and it was there, in Turin, that his health finally gave out. On January 3rd 1889 he suffered a complete mental and physical breakdown, from which he never recovered. He died eleven years later, in 1900.[3]

Nietzsche may have ceased officially to be a classical philologist in 1879, when he resigned from Basel, but he had stopped being one in spirit pretty well from the moment of his appointment, ten years earlier. The books that he published during the period of his employment – *The Birth of Tragedy*, *Untimely Meditations* and *Human, all too Human* – are all works of philosophy, and they are motivated by precisely the sorts of big question for which philology, he had come to feel, had no room. Nietzsche began the decade under the twin spells of Schopenhauer and Wagner, and his early work took its bearings from them; but by the end of the decade he had largely broken free of these influences, and had found a voice and a set of problems that were distinctively his own – a set of problems glossed rather neatly in the subtitle to his next book, *Daybreak: thoughts on the prejudices of morality* (1881).

Nietzsche had become convinced that, in an increasingly secular era, our right to our accustomed values has become questionable. Christianity has bequeathed to us a whole style of moral thinking that we are so used to, and which is so ingrained in the fabric of our culture, that we take it as read, and continue to regard it as authoritative despite our loss of faith in the presuppositions that originally underwrote that authority. We don't, as modern products of the Enlightenment, believe in God or heaven or hell any more, and yet we hang on to the values of selflessness and altruism as if we did; and we persist in regarding qualities such as happiness, beauty and luck as, if not quite vices, then at least as thoroughly irrelevant to a proper understanding of ourselves as ethical beings. In Nietzsche's view, this is simply irresponsible. The decline of Christianity presents us with a remarkable opportunity – alarming perhaps, and maybe dangerous, but also rich with promise. For the first time in two millennia we have the chance to take responsibility for our values, to create them and make them our own, rather than merely inherit them from the dominant culture. And this is a chance that we must seize: our future humanity depends upon it, and there is no more urgent task.

Nietzsche's later work is thus devoted to various attempts both to motivate a 're-evaluation of values', as he called it, and to begin to engage in such a re-evaluation – most notably, perhaps, in *On the Genealogy of Morals* (1887). And to these attempts, his thoughts about art are central. Nietzsche had found his big question; and – given his tastes – it is unsurprising that he should have thought that a proper answer to it must have an aesthetic dimension, a dimension that it is a large part of the business of the present book to explore.

II In a famous unpublished note of 1888, Nietzsche remarks that 'we possess *art* lest we *perish of the truth*' (WP 822); and it is possible to track the development of his aesthetics, in broad outline at least, through the different senses that might be attached to this dictum at different periods in Nietzsche's life.

In *The Birth of Tragedy*, his first book, there are several truths at issue, one of which is that individual human lives are not worth living, and that it would have been better – for any given individual – not to have been born. For complicated reasons, however, this is a truth that we need to get at least a glimpse of – but no more than that: face it head on, Nietzsche tells us, and we would be destroyed. So in tragedy, which allows us that glimpse, we are also shielded from its full impact by a variety of aesthetic devices, including character and plot. Here, then, although we need the truth – and the art of tragedy makes it available – we are saved from perishing of it by that very same art. And in performing this indispensable double role, Nietzsche holds, tragedy is vital to the formation and sustenance of a healthy culture.

By the later 1870s, when he wrote the first volume of *Human, All Too Human*, Nietzsche had changed his mind about all of this. He now believed that the truth about the world, as progressively revealed by modern science, is something to be embraced: the truth may be disconcerting and even painful, but by working with and through it great things are to be achieved – for instance, the overcoming of human suffering. And as we come to recognize this, he holds, our need for the palliative fantasies supplied by art (and religion) should wither away. But we are cowards: we continue to use art to soften the impact of the truth, even if we shouldn't. So we possess art because we fear, wrongly, that we would perish otherwise. Art is therefore something that we need to grow out of – again for the sake of a healthy culture.

This is not a view that Nietzsche cleaved to for long. Partly this is because he came to think that the world revealed by science is chaotic, arbitrary and meaningless; and partly it is because he became convinced that human suffering is not merely not about to go away, but that it is in fact integral and essential to any fully human way of living. So the task now is not so much to overcome the human condition, as he had effectively thought in *Human, All Too Human*, as to find ways of making it bearable, of accommodating oneself to its character; and from this point of view, some things may be simply impossible to face. By 1882, then, when he published the first four books of *The Gay Science*, he regarded the function of art – its indispensable function – as taking the edge off realities that we cannot bear, as providing, that is, precisely the sorts of palliative measure that, just a few years earlier, he had viewed with such disdain. In a quite ordinary, everyday sense, therefore, 'we possess *art* lest we *perish of the truth*.'

Nietzsche never moved away from this position. In 1886, for instance, he says this: 'the strength of a spirit should be measured according to how much of the "truth" one could still barely endure – or to put it more clearly, to what degree one would *require* it to be thinned down, shrouded, sweetened, blunted, falsified' (BGE 39) – which is to say, to what degree one would *require* art. And the late aesthetics is largely devoted to exploring the various artistic moves that might (in good conscience) be made, given these facts about ourselves, to render life bearable.

With the exception of a brief period in the late 1870s, then, a constant in Nietzsche's position is that the truth, or certain truths, are impossible to face up to squarely, and that they call for aesthetic counter-measures. Nietzsche may have changed his mind about the precise character of these truths, but this much at least is fairly stable. And there is another theme that acquires a degree of stability, first aired in the second volume of *Human, All Too Human*, and then developed in *The Gay Science* and subsequently. This is the idea that the exercise of palliative artistry, as it were, is to be focused not so much on the production of actual works of art, ordinarily so-called, as on the production of one's self, on self-creation. The thought, in other words, is that a central recourse against unmanageable truths, especially truths about oneself, is to transform them, so that they are either no longer true or are no longer unmanageable. Nietzsche took this idea sufficiently seriously as to construct *Ecce Homo*, his autobiography, entirely in its terms, so that he presents his life, in effect, as an aesthetic masterpiece – and as one that shows, moreover, how the difficult truths of which he hasn't perished have, thanks to his artistry, made him stronger. Nietzsche's aesthetics thus leeches increasingly into his ethics; and I have made no effort, in what follows, to prevent the two from coalescing wherever the texts require.[4]

III   In keeping with the development just outlined, this book is arranged chronologically. Chapter One is devoted to Nietzsche's earliest work – primarily *The Birth of Tragedy*, but also, where relevant, a couple of his youthful essays. Chapter Two covers Nietzsche's so-called 'positivist' period – *Human, All Too Human* (1878–80) first and foremost, but bits of *Untimely Meditations* (1873–76) too. Chapter Three is given over to the first four books of *The Gay Science* (1882). Chapter Four investigates that self-alleged artwork, *Thus Spoke Zarathustra* (1883–85). And Chapter Five is focussed on the late writings – from *Beyond Good and Evil* (1886) through to *Ecce Homo* (1888), a series of mostly shortish books that show where Nietzsche ended up.[5] There is then an Appendix devoted to Wagner.

I should say a word about this last decision, which may seem strange. After all, Nietzsche's three explicitly art-centred books –

The Birth of Tragedy, The Case of Wagner and *Nietzsche contra Wagner* – are largely or exclusively about Wagner. My reason for sidelining or postponing him in this way, however, is to prevent the present book from seeming unduly narrow in focus. It is true that Wagner was the single most important artistic phenomenon in Nietzsche's life. But Nietzsche's thoughts about art are, or should be, of interest even to those for whom Wagner is unexplored or under-appreciated territory; so I don't propose to make a pointful acquaintance with Wagner's work a precondition of following the things that I want to say here.

The structure of the book is therefore quite similar to that of Julian Young's generally admirable *Nietzsche's Philosophy of Art* (1992): Young has more on Schopenhauer than I do, I have more on *Zarathustra* and Wagner. But the basic sense that Nietzsche's aesthetics needs to be understood as a story rather than as a position is something that we share. We don't always agree how that story goes; nor do we agree about what matters most in it. But significant parts of this book would not be as they are were it not for Young's, and I would urge anyone with a serious interest in Nietzsche's thoughts about art to read it – if only to get the other side of a (sometimes implicit) dialogue. Other things to read, although I've not drawn on them directly, include Alexander Nehamas's *Nietzsche: Life as Literature* (1985) and Philip Pothen's *Nietzsche and the Fate of Art* (2002) – good books both, but neither as helpful as Young's, in my view, in bringing out the main strands in Nietzsche's aesthetics.

A word in conclusion about sources. In general, it seems best to give interpretative priority to those texts that Nietzsche either published or had prepared for publication by the time of his final collapse. These, after all, are where Nietzsche himself thought the real meat was, and they must surely take precedence over his voluminous notebooks in any attempt to arrive at an understanding of his views. The unpublished material does have its uses, however. For instance, he sometimes said things there more pithily than he ever did in print – the dictum that 'We possess *art* lest we *perish of the truth*' being a prime case in point. With this exception, though, I have not, in what follows, drawn on Nietzsche's notebooks for their neat encapsulation of his published views. I *have* drawn on them, however, in another context, namely, in my discussion of Nietzsche's first published work, *The Birth of Tragedy*. Here, since there simply aren't the surrounding works to appeal to for elucidation, I have tried to shed some light by going to a couple of quite substantial essays, 'On Schopenhauer' and 'On Truth and Lies in a Nonmoral Sense', which, although unpublished, do at least show the general sort of thing that Nietzsche was thinking at the time. And this helps to make better sense, I believe, of *The Birth of Tragedy* than would be possible through an austere, if perfectly justifiable, insistence on treating that text as self-sufficient. Otherwise, though, I have stuck to the letter of what Nietzsche himself thought worth reading, and have appealed only to the published writings.[6]

1

REDEMPTION THROUGH ART:
THE BIRTH OF TRAGEDY

Profound, hostile silence about Christianity throughout the book. Christianity is neither Apollonian nor Dionysian; it negates all aesthetic values – the only values recognized in *The Birth of Tragedy*: it is nihilistic in the most profound sense, while in the Dionysian symbol the ultimate limit of affirmation is attained.

(Nietzsche, *Ecce Homo*, 'The Birth of Tragedy')

Introduction

Nietzsche's first book, *The Birth of Tragedy* (1872), is a striking debut and an arresting example of German Romanticism at its headiest. Tragedy, as an art form, has long captivated the philosophical imagination – not surprisingly, given that tragic works of art can seem to offer richer and more profound insights into the human condition than works in any other genre. And Nietzsche's early engagement with the topic certainly represents an attempt to do justice to that fact. Tragedy, in his eyes, tells us the deepest and most horrifying truths about ourselves, but does so in a way that makes the news not merely bearable, but welcome, enlivening, and even intoxicating; so that against the backdrop of a fundamentally pessimistic take on existence (the deepest truths *are* horrifying), tragedy offers us a paradoxical form of redemption. This is a very dramatic thought: to many readers, indeed, it has seemed to encapsulate a peculiarly powerful approach not only to tragedy as an art form, but to a proper understanding of our own most fundamental needs. The devil, though, is in the detail; and we will see in what follows that the task of arriving at a sustainable interpretation of Nietzsche's position is a vexed – indeed in my view an unfulfillable – one, however fascinating some of the details might be, and however much it might be true that there is at least *something* seductive about the central vision. But it is an elusive vision; and I don't pretend to have put my finger on it here. Instead, I try to clear some ground, and to identify the kinds of commitment that must be attributed to Nietzsche if his youthful ideas about tragedy are to have a chance, at any rate, of making sense.[1]

The Birth of Tragedy didn't appeal (even this much) to most of its earliest readers. It was denounced, ironically, as an exercise in 'the philology of the future' (Wagner's music, which Nietzsche championed in the book, was at that time referred to as 'the music of the future'); it was castigated for its 'ignorance and lack of love of truth', and its author, described as a 'rotted brain', was taken to task for his 'inanities and wretchednesses' (Kaufmann 1967: 5–6). Nietzsche seems not to have been very perturbed by these responses, but his professional reputation never fully recovered from them; and this, together with his increasingly bad health, contributed to his decision to quit academic life seven years later, in 1879.

It is not very surprising that *The Birth of Tragedy* went down badly. As a work in classical philology it is, at best, eccentric; and as an exercise in philosophy it is unfocused, verbose and frequently obscure. Moreover, it is – in one of its primary motivations – very blatantly a piece of propaganda, a hailing of Wagner as the saviour and redeemer of contemporary culture. In it, Nietzsche gives an account of the origins of Ancient Greek tragedy, and of its death at the hands of Socratic rationalism – a tendency that led, in the end, to Christianity; and he suggests that now, in an age over which this tendency has at last lost its strangle-hold, the possibility of a rebirth of tragedy has not only become imaginable, but has in fact been realised, in Wagner's music dramas. Greek tragedy was the expression of, and the sustaining force behind, a healthy, vibrant culture. In the work of Wagner, therefore, we may hope, he suggests, for a dramatic renewal of our own culture.

When Nietzsche came to reflect on *The Birth of Tragedy* some fourteen years later, in the 'Attempt at a Self-Criticism' included in the second edition of the book, he was chiefly concerned to highlight continuities between his earliest thoughts and his later ones – to suggest, in other words, that *The Birth of Tragedy* was already a premonition of his own mature philosophical position. And it is certainly true that there are pre-echoes. The later Nietzsche is much exercised by *'the problem of science'*, for example, by 'science considered . . . as problematic, as questionable'; and *The Birth of Tragedy*, in its discussion of Socratic rationalism, undoubtedly prefigures that concern – 'for the first time', as Nietzsche has it (ASC 2).[2] The later Nietzsche is, further, committed to fighting 'at any risk whatever the *moral* interpretation and significance of existence', a commitment that he not implausibly claims to detect in his first book, in which 'art, and *not* morality, is presented as the truly *metaphysical* activity of man' (ASC 5). Also, finally, the later Nietzsche, like the earlier, is wedded to the view that the fundamental value of something is to be determined by its value *for life*: in *The Birth of Tragedy*, he says, his 'instinct . . . aligned itself with life', and 'discovered for itself' a radically new 'doctrine and valuation of life – purely artistic and *anti-Christian*' (ibid.). Indeed, the 'task' of the book was *'to look at science in the perspective of the artist, but at art in that of life'*, a task to which the later Nietzsche, as he accurately informs us, 'has not become a stranger' (ASC 2).

These continuities are real, even if Nietzsche does occasionally overstate them. But it is easy to feel that it is the discontinuities that matter more; and of these, Nietzsche accords most prominence to three. The first concerns the younger Nietzsche's metaphysical commitments. Where the later Nietzsche is generally highly critical of metaphysics, regarding it as a hang-over of Christianity, in *The Birth of Tragedy* he had peddled an 'artists' metaphysics' – 'arbitrary, idle, fantastic' (ASC 5) – and had sought to express himself 'by means of Schopenhauerian and Kantian formulas' (ASC 6). He had, moreover – and this is the second discontinuity – argued that it would be *'necessary'* for a man of a vibrant culture 'to desire

a new art, the *art of metaphysical comfort'* (ASC 7, BT 18); to
which the Nietzsche of 1886 replies: 'No, thrice no! . . . it would
not be necessary! But it is highly probable that it will *end* in that
way – namely, "comforted", . . . "comforted metaphysically" – in
sum, as romantics end, as *Christians* . . . No! You ought to learn
the art of *this-worldly* comfort first; you ought to learn to laugh'
(ASC 7). Finally, the earlier Nietzsche had *'spoiled'* his project by
'append[ing] hopes where there was no ground for hope', by
'rav[ing] about "the German spirit"' and imagining that, through
Wagner, this spirit might redeem contemporary culture – when in
fact 'the German spirit' was 'just [then] making its last testament
and *abdicating* forever' (ASC 6). The later Nietzsche no longer
pinned hopes of any sort to Wagner, let alone such grandiose ones;
and in the 'Attempt' he reserves his affection exclusively for those
parts of *The Birth of Tragedy* that have nothing to do with Wagner
at all.

These continuities and contrasts suggest two thoughts. The first
is that the book itself might be divided into two – into those parts
of it that champion Wagner, and those that do not. And the second
thought is that this division might shadow a distinction between
those parts of *The Birth of Tragedy* that are encumbered with
unnecessary metaphysical commitments and aspirations, and those
that are not. Certainly this is the interpretative stance that the
'Attempt' encourages. It encourages one, that is, to read *The Birth
of Tragedy* as if it consisted of an account of the birth and death of
Attic tragedy – some of it misleadingly, but in the end innocently,
couched in Schopenhauerian 'formulas' – onto which has been
grafted a metaphysically compromised, and essentially baseless,
account of the rebirth of tragedy in the works of Wagner. And it is
a reading much like this that has, with the later Nietzsche's blessing, become, if not perhaps the orthodoxy, then at least a conspicuous (and potentially powerful) interpretative option.[3] I shall refer
to this reading as the 'bipartite' reading.

It is one of the principal purposes of this chapter to ask whether
such a reading is sustainable – to ask, in other words, whether the
final ten sections of *The Birth of Tragedy*, which is where the
Wagnerianism is, can be quite so easily pared away, so as to leave
behind a discussion of classical culture that has been purged, in

effect, not only of Nietzsche's (subsequently rescinded) commitment to Wagner, but also of his (perhaps only apparent) commitment to Schopenhauerian metaphysics. To this end it will be most
helpful, I think, to begin with a brief outline of the book that is as
neutral as possible between the bipartite reading and any rivals to
it that might emerge, so that the bones of possible contention are
laid as bare as they feasibly can be.

1. An outline

Nietzsche's central thought about Ancient Greek tragedy has it
shaped a bit like an onion, whose successive layers act as partial
mirrors on their convex sides and as partial filters on their concave
sides. At the heart of the onion is the idea that human
individuality – the separate existence of individual human selves –
is, in some sense, an illusion. Reflected in the outer layer is the (in
some sense) illusory 'self' of the spectator. And it is in the inter-
vening layers, some of which are more reflective and/or permeable
than others, that the actual tragedy – the drama – is played out.

The effect of the drama upon the spectator is, essentially, to
allow him a glimpse of the (alleged) truth that lies at the heart of
it – that human individuality is an illusion – while also shielding
him from the full impact that, without the filtering and mirroring,
this truth would have upon him. Unshielded, Nietzsche holds, the
spectator would be destroyed. So the drama conceals and softens
the truth even as it reveals it. Nietzsche associates the truth at the
heart of the tragedy with the god Dionysus – who, in Greek
mythology, was dismembered by the Titans – and calls the state
induced in the spectator by his glimpse of that truth 'Dionysian', a
state of intoxicated ecstasy. The other aspect of tragedy, which is
responsible for shielding the spectator from the full impact of the
truth, Nietzsche associates with the god Apollo. Apollo sustains the
illusion of individuality – of the intelligibility and, indeed, the
beauty of things, including human beings – and induces in the
spectator the 'Apollonian' state that Nietzsche often describes as
'dream-like'. Both the Dionysian and the Apollonian principles are
therefore essential to tragedy as Nietzsche conceives it. Without

Dionysus, the drama would merely sustain and reinforce the illusion of human individuality. Without Apollo, the drama would destroy (i.e. dismember) its spectators, at any rate psychologically.

But why, on this model, might tragedy be thought to be worth having at all?[4] And still more: why might it be held to be necessary to the sustenance of a healthy culture? If the truth at the heart of tragedy – that human individuality is in some way illusory – is fundamentally destructive, after all, it might seem better not to get even a glimpse of it. Whereas if, on the other hand, that truth really is worth knowing, why wouldn't dream-like illusions – illusions that obscure precisely what the heart of tragedy reveals – be better done without, and the truth faced?

Convincing answers to these questions are extremely difficult – perhaps impossible – to give, although I'll canvas some suggestions presently. For the moment, though, and sticking at the level of generality that an outline of this sort requires, the story is this. Man requires (the illusion of) individuality in order to act and function in the world. He must experience himself not only as numerically distinct from others (I am I, you are you), but as qualitatively distinct: I, but not you, am father of this child, have responsibility for milking the cows, need to distinguish myself at darts, am giving a lecture first thing in the morning, etc. And for these things to be possible, he must experience the world in which he acts and functions as relevantly orderly, as patterned in the various ways that those actions and functions presuppose, so that the world is experienced as intelligible and, at least in principle, as amenable to his purposes. The world, that is, together with the overlapping and interlocking endeavours of its 'individual' inhabitants, must appear capable of sustaining a rational interpretation. And this is an appearance that Apollo holds in place.

It is, however, only an appearance. The world is, in some sense, not really like that, and to live in it as if it were is to range over a merely artificial surface. It is, moreover, to lose touch with something deeper and more primordial about life, and from which life itself draws its most fundamental energies – above all, as it turns out, the energy to *go on living*. The Apollonian world is orderly and beautiful, but ultimately quite pointless: individual success is transient, happiness rare and fragile, suffering and death unavoidable. The 'wisdom of Silenus' – that 'What is best of all is . . . not to be born, not to *be*, to be *nothing*. But the second best . . . is – to die soon'[5] – exerts a powerfully seductive influence. And to offset this influence, life must touch base with an energy that is blind to such thoughts, that is oblivious to the final futility of human living and that glories, simply (and, as it might be, irrationally), in itself. This is the energy of Dionysus. It lies at a level that is somehow beneath that at which we exist as distinct selves, and so undercuts the kinds of pessimistic reflection about individual lives that lend Silenus's wisdom its seductive force. Borne neat, this energy would destroy us. But (just) touching base with it refreshes our appetite for life, and returns us reinvigorated to the world of Apollo.

So life itself, on this picture, requires both the Apollonian principle (if we are to be able to act or function at all) and the Dionysian (if we are to bother to do either). And Greek tragedy, or so Nietzsche tells us, sustained the culture that produced it precisely because it answered to this requirement in a peculiarly adequate way.

The mechanics by which it is supposed to have done this, however, are complicated, and Nietzsche doesn't always offer a lot of help in sorting them out. But the following, at least, can be hazarded without too much violence to the text. The outer layers of the onion, to pick up on that image, consist of character and plot. The spectator recognizes the protagonist of the drama as an 'individual' like himself, and understands the unfolding of his or her story as an intelligible account of what might happen to someone like this under circumstances like these. Here, we are firmly in the realm of Apollo. Another layer down, however, and we encounter the chorus, which chants in unison. The chorus sets up a sort of hyper-reality – equivalent in kind to the world of the Olympian gods – which has the effect of nullifying the ordinary world of everyday experience ('as lamplight is nullified by the light of day' [BT 7]), and hence of undermining the spectator's easy identification with the events and characters portrayed on stage.[6] And then we meet the music. Music – or so Nietzsche follows Schopenhauer in insisting – is *the* primordial art. It operates beneath the level of 'individual' human selves, and articulates directly the irrational energy that is (in some sense) at the heart of things. It therefore brings the spectator not merely to see himself as an epiphenomenon of what humanity collectively *is*, but to recognize that collective as itself no more than an epiphenomenon of the energy of Dionysus. And the dénouement – the destruction (the dismemberment) of the tragic hero – is as close to the middle of the onion as one can intelligibly get. Here, the hero is simply ripped apart – or is finally revealed as having always been no more than ripped apart, as no more than the froth on a wave that has everything to do with life, but nothing – in the end – to do with *him*. And this is the news – the paradoxically energizing news – that the spectator intuits through the workings of music, chorus and plot, and – ultimately – the central character, in whom, illusory (i.e. dismembered) though he may have turned out to be, the spectator finds himself reflected.

This, then, for better or for worse, is Nietzsche's account of Greek tragedy; and the historical coming together of the various elements it comprises constitutes its birth, as he originally had it, 'from the spirit of music'.[7] But tragedy was soon to meet its death, also at Greek hands. And what killed it, in effect, was the hypertrophy of one aspect of the Apollonian, the aspect that gives the world the appearance of being rationally ordered. In the person of Socrates, the Greeks came to understand and value life solely in terms of reason and order, to the exclusion not only of the darker, irrational side of things symbolized by the dismembered god, but also of every other (i.e. every non-rational) aspect of the Apollonian.[8] And life in this newly 'real' Socratic world was made liveable – was inoculated against the seduction of Silenus – by a new equation of reason with goodness, so that the rational life could be held to be valuable in itself, without recourse to intoxicating supplements. And tragedy, which had been the expression of and an antidote to a fundamentally pessimistic take on existence, was thereby displaced by what Nietzsche terms 'Socratic optimism', a tendency that is neither Dionysian nor (properly) Apollonian, and which – in its rejection of some fundamental (i.e. Dionysian) truths about life – eventually produced Christianity.

For two thousand-and-something years this tendency held sway. But in modernity, Nietzsche suggests, it has begun to lose its grip, and the conditions are once again present for Dionysus to take the stage, and for the irrational, primordial forces associated with him to make their potency felt. The rebirth of tragedy is now possible. And in Wagner's work it has been achieved – in the re-entwining of the Apollonian and Dionysian principles through music, character and plot. The greatness of the Greeks had been sustained by such a synthesis: they turned their underlying pessimism to paradoxical account. And now the kind of vibrancy and creativity that they exemplified beckons again. We stand on the threshold of a new golden age.

2. Dionysus

Everything in this story swings on Dionysus. Nietzsche takes himself, together with Wagner and the pre-Socratic Greeks, to be serious about what Dionysus stands for, and to be serious, too, in rejecting the rationalistic optimism that supplanted him. But what, exactly, *does* Dionysus stand for?

Two rather different answers immediately suggest themselves. The first, which is metaphysically humdrum, one might term the 'psychological' thesis. This is the thought that our felt separateness from one another is ultimately quite superficial, and that certain experiences reveal that the apparent barriers between us are easily broken down. So, for example, immersing oneself in a crowd – at a football match, a political rally, a pageant – and finding oneself swept up in the common enthusiasm, as it might be, or the common anger, can lead to the sense that one's individuality, together with everyone else's, has been merged with (or swallowed up by) the collective, perhaps to the point of mass hysteria. One's inhibitions, which ordinarily function as a sort of bulwark between oneself and the wider social world, are overcome; one's habitual judgements about others, which operate as another sort of bulwark, are forgotten; one's identification with projects that are essentially one's own is suspended; rationality loosens its grip. And in losing oneself in this way there can be a tremendous – if also rather terrifying – feeling of liberation, of liberation from the self, a feeling that might quite aptly be described in terms of ecstatic intoxication. And there can be the sense that, in this state, one has somehow penetrated to a level that underlies one's individuality, and that makes it seem trivial or irrelevant by contrast. Everyday cares, hopes, plans, habits, tastes – all of them seem suddenly local and unimportant; and one feels as if one has, as it were, tapped into an energy much vaster than one's own.

Or, still more obviously, take sexual love. Inhibitions, judgements, projects, rationality go by the wayside; ordinary cares, hopes, plans, habits and tastes seem transcendently piffling, and the loss of the sense of self is or can be more or less total. One can feel oneself, moreover, the agent of forces wholly unpeculiar to oneself – in the grip, as one might be tempted to put it, not of this or that surge of personal energy, but of the energy of life itself, caught up in a current far more fundamental and primordial than any to which one could confidently attach the label 'me'. And 'ecstatic intoxication', surely, is just right here, pre-eminently so. Utterly absorbed in the other person, the ordinary limits of feeling seem swiftly transgressed, and something larger, more intense, more extreme moves centre-stage. Nietzsche's favourite work of Wagner's was *Tristan und Isolde*, its central characters exemplary of the power of sexual love. And Wagner, to music of incomparable potency, has them eventually – as the climax nears – addressing one another by one another's names: Tristan calls Isolde 'Tristan'; she calls him 'Isolde'.[9] The two have overcome, or feel themselves to have overcome, their numerical distinctness, and have merged and been sublimated into a force greater than either of them. And in doing so, according to the psychological thesis, they have grasped a fundamental truth: that the barriers that make us who we take ourselves to be, and that everyday life fosters and presupposes, are thin, superficial and – ultimately – trivial.[10]

On this reading of Dionysus, then, there is a level of experience – attainable, perhaps, in several ways – that undercuts our ordinary self-understandings, so that our sense of separate self-hood is undermined and shown up as altogether less deep and less foundational than we are accustomed to think. On this reading, therefore, Attic tragedy exploits and expresses a potentially extremely disruptive fact about us – a fact which, if acknowledgement of it were allowed to have the field to itself, would render ordinary life impossible – while softening its impact by presenting it through the Apollonian appurtenances of (individual) character and (intelligible) plot. We are invigorated by contact with a force that we recognize as raw, irrational, large, and also – crucially – as fundamental to what, at a deep level, we are really all about; and, enlivened by the contact, we return to everyday living with our appetite for it refreshed.

The other obvious answer to the question 'What does Dionysus stand for?' is the more traditional one, and it might be termed the 'metaphysical' thesis. It holds that Dionysus stands for the noumenal will of Schopenhauerian philosophy. Schopenhauer, about whom the young Nietzsche, like Wagner, was tremendously enthusiastic, held that the world, in its innermost nature, consisted of a blind, endless, meaningless turmoil and striving that he called the will, a reality whose refracted appearances make up the world of human experience. The world of experience is constituted by the forms of the 'principle of sufficient reason' – by space, time and causation – and as such it is populated by individual things, including people. All of this, however, is mere appearance. The principle of sufficient reason – or, as Schopenhauer also calls it, the *'principium individu-ationis'* (the principle of individuation) – does not operate at the level of the will, so that neither causes nor spatio-temporal things – such as people – are ultimately real. From our perspective within the world of experience, this is of course very difficult to accept. But we can gain an intimation of the truth of it, according to Schopenhauer, through music, which is somehow supposed to be (capable of being) a 'copy' of the will itself (1969: Vol. 1: 256–263).

Making sense of Schopenhauer on music is a task that thankfully lies beyond the scope of this book, and I will do no more here than note that the metaphysically glamorous role that he assigned to music did much to recommend his thought to Wagner, and that Nietzsche, similarly impressed, certainly took over from him the idea that music goes peculiarly deep. Whether, however, he also took over the idea that it goes *metaphysically* deep – as opposed to psychologically deep, say – it is too early to determine.

Schopenhauer's general philosophical position is thus, in effect, a metaphysical radicalization of elements of the psychological thesis. Where the psychological thesis holds that our felt (psycho-logical) separateness from one another is ultimately superficial, and that at a deeper (but still psychological) level we are all shot to the core with an energy that is larger than any of us, Schopenhauer holds that our separate individual existences are (metaphysically) wholly illusory, and that the only reality is the endless striving of the metaphysical will that underlies everything. But the psychological thesis also holds that touching base with the deeper energies that are fundamental to us restores our appetite for ordinary individual living. And this, in its metaphysically radicalized version, Schopenhauer flatly denies. Instead, he holds that recognition of the innermost nature of the world reveals the whole show – both appearance and reality – to be irremediably vile and ghastly: for him, the wisdom of Silenus is not to be gainsaid. So the 'metaphysical' thesis, as it might plausibly be attributed to Nietzsche, must be unSchopenhauerian in at least this respect. If Dionysus stands for the will in Schopenhauer's sense, then in Nietzsche, touching base with Dionysus is not the crowning confirmation of pessimism, as it is in Schopenhauer, but rather its revitalizing antidote. And in Greek tragedy, on this reading, that antidote is not only made available; it is also made just about safe to take by the Apollonian appearances – construed metaphysically – with which it is hedged about.

So there would seem to be two main ways of interpreting Dionysus – as standing for something psychologically fundamental, or as standing for something metaphysically fundamental. And with the distinctions between these that I have tried to sketch out in mind, we can now offer a more perspicuous characterization of what the 'bipartite' reading of *The Birth of Tragedy* might amount to – namely, that the account of the birth and death of Attic tragedy (sections 1–15) presupposes the psychological thesis, while the allegations about the rebirth of tragedy in the work of Wagner (sections 16–25) presuppose the metaphysical thesis. And this, in turn, suggests that, if we wish to assess the adequacy of the bipartite reading, we should now start to look properly at the text and see whether these shifting presuppositions are indeed in play. But this, unfortunately, would be to get ahead of ourselves. For there are reasons to doubt that Nietzsche could possibly have accepted or defended the metaphysical thesis, at least in the form described so far. And this, if true, would clearly scupper the bipartite reading (certainly as I characterized it a moment ago) from the start.

3. The metaphysical position

Nietzsche published *The Birth of Tragedy* in 1872. Four years earlier, however, and despite his general enthusiasm for Schopenhauer, his notebooks show that he already harboured doubts about the details of his predecessor's system. In particular, an unpublished essay, 'On Schopenhauer', constitutes a critique of some of the central elements of that system; and it would be odd, to put it no higher, if Nietzsche had simply put aside or forgotten his reservations when he came to write *The Birth of Tragedy*. So we need, first, to investigate how far his early critique of Schopenhauer went – where what is at issue is not the *quality* of that critique (it doesn't very much matter, that is, whether Nietzsche's criticisms of Schopenhauer are fair or well-directed) but, rather, how much of Schopenhauer's system Nietzsche *took himself* to have reason for rejecting. And viewed in that light, the answer is: quite a lot.

Schopenhauer's main mistake, according to Nietzsche, was to have remained too much of a Kantian. Kant had argued that there is an absolute metaphysical distinction between the world as it is 'in itself' (the noumenal world) and the world as it features in human experience (the phenomenal world). The phenomenal world presents itself through categories – space, time, causation – that we ourselves bring to it, so that our experience is of a world whose character reflects the structures of human thought. And of the world as it is or might be independently of those structures – the noumenal world, the world as it is 'in itself' – we can know nothing whatever: it is a mere 'X', forever and in principle inaccessible to us (OS 2). Schopenhauer takes over from Kant the distinction between noumenal and phenomenal worlds: the title of his main work, *The World as Will and Representation*, precisely shadows that distinction, and his claim that the world of representation is governed by the principle of sufficient reason recapitulates Kant's thought that the phenomenal world is structured by the categories of space, time and causation. But Schopenhauer, or so Nietzsche objects, turns out to know rather more about the noumenal world than he should. He turns out to know, for instance, that it consists of a blind, endless, meaningless striving and turmoil – of will – when all that anyone is really entitled to say is that it consists of . . . X, of we know not what. It is of course *possible*, Nietzsche concedes, that the noumenal world should be as Schopenhauer says it is. But, if so, that would be the merest lucky (and uncheckable) guess, and not the product of '[a]ny decent way of thinking' (OS 2).

In fact, Nietzsche seems sceptical whether there even *is* a noumenal world – Schopenhauer followed Kant on a 'dangerous path' in this respect, he says. And even if the possibility of such a world cannot be decisively ruled out, it survives, he suggests, 'only in the sense that in the region of transcendence everything is *possible* that ever was hatched in a philosopher's brain' (OS 2). A little later, however, he says this: 'it is completely correct of [Schopenhauer] to say, in *WWR* I: "that we can never get at the essence of things from outside. However much we may investigate, we obtain nothing but images and names"' (OS 3) – which, at any rate on the face of it, would seem to concede the existence of a noumenal world to Schopenhauer after all, even while underlining the objection that we can know or say nothing whatever about it.

Perhaps Nietzsche is simply confused here, or doesn't know what to think. But whether or not that is so, it is clear that he is convinced of at least one thing: that the noumenal world, if there is one, is wholly beyond our epistemic reach, and so cannot pointfully be said to consist of Schopenhauer's metaphysical will. And this is enough to make it extremely unlikely that the metaphysical thesis, as characterized in the previous section, can possibly be attributed to Nietzsche. If there neither is nor could be any reason to believe in a noumenal will, there can be no reason, either, to diagnose the power of (nascent or renascent) tragedy as residing in its capacity to put us in touch with such a thing. So the metaphysical thesis should not, I think, be taken to be Nietzsche's.[11] And this means, of course, that the bipartite reading of *The Birth of Tragedy*, at least as I set it up at the end of section 2, must be pretty much a non-starter.

So are we left only with a unipartite reading, as it were, that construes the whole of *The Birth of Tragedy* as presupposing just the psychological thesis? Perhaps not. I have argued against attributing the metaphysical thesis to Nietzsche by appealing to an essay that he wrote a little before *The Birth of Tragedy*. I now want to enlist an essay that he wrote very shortly after *The Birth of Tragedy* to suggest that, although the metaphysical thesis cannot be attributed to him in the strong, explicitly Schopenhauerian form considered so far, it is nevertheless plausible to think that he might have subscribed to a weaker thesis – still just about worth calling 'metaphysical' – that is quite different from the psychological thesis, and that might yet warrant a suitably adjusted bipartite reading of Nietzsche's first book. The essay in question is 'On Truth and Lies in a Nonmoral Sense' (1873), also unpublished by Nietzsche, but – like 'On Schopenhauer' – showing every sign of having been thought about quite hard.

'Truth and Lies' is entirely continuous with the Schopenhauer essay in one important respect: in it, Nietzsche repeatedly insists that, of the 'in-itself' of things (the noumenal world), we can know nothing at all (TL: 82–83) – a fact that would make it still more surprising had he identified the noumenal world with Schopenhauer's will in *The Birth of Tragedy*. But the later essay also does something more: it opens up, albeit in a fitful, inconclusive way, the prospect that there might be a half-way house, as it were, between the noumenal and the phenomenal – that there might be a metaphysical level which, while largely opaque to experience, is nevertheless not *merely* an unknowable X. And this, if so, would encourage the thought that the Nietzsche of *The Birth of Tragedy* might indeed have subscribed to a 'weak' version of the metaphysical thesis, of the sort alluded to a moment ago.

I won't pretend that the interpretation of the relevant aspects of 'Truth and Lies' that I am about to offer is definitive or water-tight. The essay is horribly confused, both internally and (or since or hence) philosophically, and it is very difficult to get anything out of it that is either stable or minimally believable. But we can make a start, at least, with the following passage, which needs to be quoted at length:

> Only by means of the petrification and coagulation of a mass of images that originally streamed from the primal faculty of the human

imagination like a fiery liquid, only in the invincible faith that *this* sun, *this* window, *this* table is a truth in itself, in short, only by forgetting that he himself is an *artistically creating* subject, does man live with any repose, security, and consistency. If but for an instant he could escape from the prison walls of this faith, his 'self-consciousness' would immediately be destroyed. It is even a difficult thing for him to admit to himself that the insect or the bird perceives an entirely different world from the one that man does, and that the question of which of these perceptions of the world is the more correct one is quite meaningless, for this would have to be decided previously in accordance with the criterion of the *correct perception*, which means, in accordance with a criterion which is *not available*. But in any case it seems to me that 'the correct perception' – which would mean 'the adequate expression of an object in the subject' – is a contradictory impossibility. For between two absolutely different spheres, as between subject and object, there is no causality, no correctness, and no expression; there is, at most, an *aesthetic* relation: I mean, a suggestive transference, a stammering translation into a completely foreign tongue – for which there is required, in any case, a freely inventive intermediate sphere and mediating force. 'Appearance' is a word that contains many temptations, which is I why I avoid it as much as possible. For it is not true that the essence of things 'appears' in the empirical [i.e. the phenomenal] world. A painter without hands who wished to express in song the picture before his mind would, by means of this substitution of spheres, still reveal more about the essence of things than does the empirical world.

(Nietzsche, TL 86–87)

We might distinguish three main sorts of thought in this passage: first, a thought about the ordinary perception of objects as somehow to be understood *'artistically'*; second, a thought about the unavailability of a 'criterion of correct perception'; and third, a thought about an 'intermediate sphere' that makes it possible for perception to get at the world at all. I will try to say something about each of these thoughts in turn.

Nietzsche's expression of the first thought is very difficult to read without being put in mind of *The Birth of Tragedy*. The world of individual objects (the sun, windows, chairs), which man requires if he is to live 'with any repose, security, and consistency', is in fact the illusory product of his own artistry. Man is, as it were, his own unwitting Apollo; and if he were to see through this illusion, and become aware of the 'mass of images' streaming from his most 'primal faculty' like 'a fiery liquid', 'his "self-consciousness" would be immediately destroyed'. So we have in place much of the basic pattern familiar from the outline given in section 1, above. But here Nietzsche is talking about perception; and his claim would appear to be that, from the raw stuff of sensation, we artistically create (through the 'petrification and coagulation' of the original 'mass of images') a world of stable objects, a world whose construction is constrained, in the interests of self-preservation, by the need 'to exist socially and with the herd' (TL: 81). So although each individual is in some sense the creator of the world that he perceives, that world is at the same time common to man as such, in virtue of shared needs, predicaments and dangers.[12]

Nevertheless, and this is the second thought, the human world is, in a sense, arbitrary – 'the insect or the bird' perceive 'an entirely different world from the one that man does', in virtue, presumably, of facing different pressures and encountering different threats to their survival. Other species, we must assume, petrify and coagulate the original 'fiery liquid' of images into different configurations, according to their needs. And a 'criterion of correct perception' for adjudicating between these configurations is simply *not available*', Nietzsche says: the primal 'mass of images' doesn't come complete with instructions for how to read it, and so it can in principle be coagulated in an indefinitely wide variety of ways.

Up to this point, nothing that Nietzsche claims requires us to understand him as making a distinction between noumenal and phenomenal worlds. Everything that he refers to seems quite clearly to belong to the world of experience – including, importantly, the original 'fiery liquid' of images: if these were noumenal, after all, Nietzsche could not, on his own insistence, know anything (i.e. even this much) about them. But then there is a slide: 'it seems to me', Nietzsche says, 'that "the correct perception" . . . is a contradictory impossibility' – a remark that only makes sense if Nietzsche has suddenly, and seemingly without noticing, started to talk about things 'in-themselves', about the noumenal world. For only of that world, which is by definition and of necessity inaccessible to us, would the thought that there might be a criterion of correct perception be not merely false (because no such criterion is in fact available), but a 'contradictory impossibility'. And with this slide, Nietzsche finds himself in danger of denying that perception is possible at all – 'for between two absolutely different spheres', as he puts it, 'there is no causality, no correctness, and no expression'.

The third thought offers to rectify this difficulty, by positing an 'intermediate sphere' between the noumenal and phenomenal worlds. What Nietzsche means by this, exactly, is rather hard to say. But we may note, first, that he introduces a new metaphysical category – the 'essence of things' – in his efforts to explain himself. This category is not straightforwardly phenomenal: 'it is not true', he says, 'that the essence of things "appears" in the empirical world' (i.e. in the world of stable objects, of windows and chairs). Yet nor is it noumenal: the handless painter (somehow) manages to 'reveal' at least something 'about the essence of things', which if that essence were noumenal would be a 'contradictory impossibility'. So we do seem to have a new metaphysical level here.[13] And the sorts of things that go on there, said to be 'freely inventive' and to be the site of an *'aesthetic* relation' between the noumena and the phenomena, strongly suggest that Nietzsche has returned (or takes himself to have returned) to the first thought, about perception having to be understood *'artistically'*. The best guess, then, is that the 'essence of things' must refer to Nietzsche's original 'fiery liquid' of images, or perhaps to what these are images *of* (although it is far from clear what sense might be attached to this latter thought).[14]

The passage we've been considering, like the essay as a whole, is undeniably a vexed one, as I've remarked.[15] But it does at least seem reasonably clear that, with whatever warrant, Nietzsche commits himself in it to a metaphysical level intermediate between the noumenal and phenomenal worlds, and that this level – comprising the 'essence of things' – is logically *prior* to any sort of world of stable, coagulated objects (chairs, windows, and whatever might be perceived by insects or birds). So it is a level that undercuts individuality as we would normally understand it (even if it may not, strictly speaking, undercut Schopenhauer's *principium individuationis*: the *principium individuationis* goes together with the principle of sufficient reason, and if *that* principle were undercut we would be in the realm of the noumena). It is, in other words, a level that Nietzsche might quite plausibly have thought of as 'Dionysian', and have had in mind, given the strong continuities between 'On Schopenhauer' and 'Truth and Lies', when writing *The Birth of Tragedy*. And, if so, this makes a weak version of the metaphysical thesis a genuine interpretative possibility – a thesis that is more ambitious, if altogether less credible, than the psychological thesis, but which still stops short of the full-blown Schopenhauerianism of the strong version of the metaphysical thesis, a thesis that Nietzsche can safely be assumed to have rejected. And with this possibility on the table, the prospects for a bipartite reading of *The Birth of Tragedy* look suddenly brighter.

4. Between psychology and metaphysics

The question for us now, then, is whether there is any reason to think that the Wagner sections of *The Birth of Tragedy* do, and that the first fifteen sections do not, presuppose the weak metaphysical thesis – the thesis that tragedy, by putting us (guardedly) in touch with the Dionysian 'essence of things', returns us to ordinary individual living with our appetite for it refreshed, the wisdom of Silenus notwithstanding.

The most powerful discussion of the bipartite reading is Henry Staten's.[16] 'Nietzsche apparently tried', Staten says, 'to write the metaphysical will out of *The Birth of Tragedy* but found, on arriving at section 16, that he could not do it'; and as evidence for this, he remarks that prior to that section

> Nietzsche avoids using the term 'will' in its metaphysical sense, preferring instead terms such as 'primal unity' and 'ground of being'. I notice only one use of 'will' in what looks like its universal, metaphysical sense (in section 3), and it comes with quotation marks, so that it looks like a metaphorical usage. Furthermore, in at least three places

in the early sections Nietzsche has removed the word 'will' which he
had used in the corresponding passages of an early draft called *The
Dionysian Worldview*.

(Staten 1990: 192)

The point is then reinforced when Staten notes that Nietzsche,
having found that he couldn't do without the will, follows
Schopenhauer in claiming that music is 'an immediate copy of the
will itself' and so represents 'what is *metaphysical*, the thing in
itself' (BT 16) – which would seem to put us squarely back into the
territory of the strong metaphysical thesis (ibid.: 193).

But does it? Staten doesn't believe so, and nor, I think, should
we. I have already registered Nietzsche's tendency to slide between
the 'essence of things' and things 'in-themselves'; and Staten, too,
is fully alive to Nietzsche's slipperiness in this vicinity, as also to
his (unpublished) denials that anything whatever could be known
about the noumenal 'thing-in-itself'. So what Staten goes on to
argue, in effect, is that from section 16 onwards, and despite his slip
there into something stronger, Nietzsche should be understood as
defending the weak version of the metaphysical thesis. Staten's
reasons for attributing this position to Nietzsche are complex, and
refer not to the 'essence of things' but to what he calls the 'universal form' of appearance (ibid.: 208). But I think that his reasons are
at least consistent with those adduced in the previous section, and
my position and his seem to me to be very close to one another.
Staten's summation of what this version of the metaphysical thesis
amounts to would be difficult to better:

The will is the name of the receptiveness to the world of an embodied
being, the name of the way in general in which the world registers on
a being capable of sensation . . . Transcendent being . . . is so to speak
off the scale; it does not register on our sensorium. But even if it is
not directly knowable, there is one thing we can know about it: it is
the limit of individuation, the totality or nothingness out of which
individuals come and which swallows them up again.

This *limit of individuation*, which is the only irreducible kernel of
Nietzsche's allegory in *The Birth of Tragedy*, is not itself capable of
being represented, yet there is, phenomenologically or aesthesiologi-

cally, something that corresponds to it as its effect or affect: it is the passage to the limit of sensation, its extreme, ultimate intensification along both dimensions to the point that pleasure and displeasure cease to be distinguishable and a rupture of the scale occurs. This is the *excess* of nature (BT 4), the Dionysian *Rausch* [ecstasy] . . .

(Staten 1990: 208)

– it is, in the terms that we have been using, the (as Nietzsche insists ecstatic) experience of the original 'fiery liquid' of images, the primal stuff out of which individuals are formed by 'petrification and coagulation'. So Staten's view is that the Wagner sections of *The Birth of Tragedy* presuppose the weak metaphysical thesis in this sense, while the earlier ones don't, or at least don't necessarily.

Let's have a quick look at the Wagner sections first. These are undeniably metaphysically charged: in Dionysian art, Nietzsche says, we 'are really for a brief moment primordial being itself . . . ; the struggle, the pain, the destruction of phenomena, now appear necessary to us, in view . . . of the exuberant fertility of the universal will' (BT 17); 'Dionysian art', moreover, 'gives expression to the will in its omnipotence, as it were, behind the *principium individuationis*, the eternal life behind all phenomena' (BT 16); while 'truly Dionysian music presents itself as . . . a general mirror of the universal will' (BT 17). This is all heady stuff, and it is impossible to read it as presupposing anything less than the weak metaphysical thesis (indeed, quite hard not to read it as presupposing something stronger than that). So the later stages of the book are very much as the bipartite reading would lead one to expect.

But what about the first fifteen sections? As Staten notes, the word 'will' is less conspicuous in these – even if we do get quite a good deal about 'primal unity' and the 'ground of being' (in, e.g., BT 1, 5, 6). But the relative absence of the word 'will' doesn't by itself tell us all that much. For what is at issue here is whether, in these sections, Nietzsche is committed to the possibility of a metaphysical level (rather than a psychological one, say) that, first, underlies the ordinary existence of individual objects, and, second, amounts to something more than an unknowable 'X'. And looked at in this way, the answer must be yes, Nietzsche is certainly committed to the possibility of such a level, whatever label he might attach to it. In 'the Dionysian orgies of the Greeks', he tells us, ' . . . nature for the first time attains her artistic jubilee; it is with them that the destruction of the *principium individuationis* for the first time becomes an artistic phenomenon' (BT 2) (the *principium individuationis* is also said to be susceptible to 'collapse' [BT 1]). And in perhaps the most striking of the many passages that might be appealed to in this context, Nietzsche claims that music *'appears as will'*, that it 'stands in symbolic relation to the primordial contradiction and primordial pain in the heart of the primal unity, and therefore symbolizes a sphere which is beyond and prior to all phenomena' (BT 6), a claim that makes no sense whatever except on the assumption that there is a level – perhaps even a noumenal one, although I don't think that Nietzsche can have meant that – which underlies the ordinary world of experience. And this is precisely what the metaphysical thesis, in either of its versions, asserts.

My own view, then, is that there is no reason to accept a bipartite reading of *The Birth of Tragedy*. The Wagner sections clearly presuppose (at least) the weak version of the metaphysical thesis, and there are no obvious grounds to think that the first fifteen sections are any different.[17] This is not to deny, of course, that Nietzsche may have held the psychological thesis too – indeed, there is every sign that he did (in, e.g., BT 1). But the relation between that thesis and the weak metaphysical one is not, it seems to me, one of succession, with the former giving way to the latter. Rather, in some admittedly hazy manner, I suspect that Nietzsche regarded the truth of many of the considerations informing the psychological thesis as *evidence* for the truth of the corresponding elements of the weak metaphysical thesis: our capacity, in certain intense and important-seeming experiences, to lose our sense of individuality, of self, gives us reason to think that individuality and self-hood must, at some sort of metaphysical level, be illusory. This may not be a very compelling line of thought. But it does lend a certain degree of intelligibility to what Nietzsche appears to be up to in *The Birth of Tragedy*; and it lends a lot more intelligibility to it than the bipartite reading does – the main motivation for which, it seems to me, must be to rescue the book from its avowed Wagnerianism. For if – with the later Nietzsche's blessing – the

Wagner sections can be seen as radically discontinuous with the earlier discussion of classical culture, the way is clear, for non- or anti-Wagnerians, to take that discussion seriously without having to take Wagner seriously too. But that, for the reasons I have given, is just a dodge. The truth is that *The Birth of Tragedy* is a piece of propaganda throughout, and that there is no wishing the Wagner sections away. However much he may later have come to regret it, in other words, Nietzsche's first book is not merely metaphysically compromised (as he admits in the 'Attempt at a Self-Criticism'); it is also, from beginning to end, by far the most ambitious defence of an individual artist ever mounted by a philosopher.

5. Child's play

It is tempting to think that the best way to read *The Birth of Tragedy* might be simply to bracket its questionable metaphysical commitments, and to treat it (all of it) as if it traded only on the psychological thesis, which would at least leave one with an internally consistent, and perhaps an insightful, discussion of the topics that Nietzsche set out to address. And in many ways I think that this temptation is probably worth giving in to. The book has some intriguing things to say, and this sort of reading would certainly allow them to come out with a minimum of distraction. But it would be a mistake, even so, to underestimate the amount that would need to be bracketed.

In a notorious passage towards the end of the book, Nietzsche remarks, first, that the 'Dionysian, with its primordial joy experienced even in pain, is the common source of music and tragic myth', and then goes on:

> we desire to hear and at the same time long to get beyond all hearing. That striving for the infinite, the wing-beat of longing that accompanies the highest delight in clearly perceived reality, reminds us that in both states we must recognize a Dionysian phenomenon: again and again it reveals to us the playful construction and destruction of the individual world as the overflow of a primordial delight. Thus the dark

> Heraclitus compares the world-building force to a playing child that
> places stones here and there and builds sand hills only to overthrow
> them again.
>
> (Nietzsche, BT 24)

And this image – the image of a playing child – is offered by him
as a gloss on the claim, first made in section 5 but now repeated,
'that existence and the world seem justified only as an aesthetic
phenomenon' – in which 'even the ugly and disharmonic are part
of an artistic game that the will in the eternal amplitude of its pleasure plays with itself' (ibid.).

Justification – indeed redemption – of existence and the world is
thus to be had *only* if one can somehow adopt a perspective that is
external to either – namely, the perspective of the 'world-building
force' itself. And this force must be logically prior to the world of
'individual' experience that it makes possible; which means that
the justification that the adoption of its perspective offers must
presuppose the weak metaphysical thesis at the very least, that is, a
thesis that posits a level of being which is orthogonal to ordinary
human experience, but which is nonetheless something more than
a merely unknowable 'X'.

It is very difficult, as I have repeatedly said, to attach a great
deal of sense to a thesis of this sort. But for our present purposes
what is more significant is the fact that Nietzsche commits himself
to the possibility of the perspective that it licenses from the very
beginning of *The Birth of Tragedy* (i.e. not just in the Wagner sections):

> The entire comedy of art is neither performed for our betterment or
> education nor are we the true authors of this art world. On the con-
> trary, we may assume that we are merely images and artistic projec-
> tions for the true author, and that we have our highest dignity in our
> significance as works of art – for it is only as an *aesthetic phe-
> nomenon* that existence and the world are eternally *justified* – while of
> course our consciousness of our own significance hardly differs from
> that which the soldiers painted on canvas have of the battle repre-
> sented on it. Thus all our knowledge of art is basically quite illusory,
> because as knowing beings we are not one and identical with that

being which, as the sole author and spectator of this comedy of art, prepares a perpetual entertainment for itself. Only insofar as the genius in the act of artistic creation coalesces with this primordial artist of the world, does he know anything of the eternal essence of art; for in this state . . . he is at once subject and object, at once poet, actor and spectator.

(Nietzsche, BT 5)

This, clearly enough, is exactly the thought that Nietzsche expresses at the end of the book in his talk of a 'world-building force' that is like a 'playing child'; and here, just as there, the justification of existence and the world is to be secured by identifying with a perspective – this time the perspective of the 'primordial artist' – that transcends ordinary human experience altogether, and that presupposes a metaphysical level which will accommodate that possibility. It is also, of course, Nietzsche's ultimate rebuff to the wisdom of Silenus – his ultimate paean to the redemptive possibilities of art – and the fact that it requires a version of the metaphysical thesis to be true is surely the final nail in the coffin of the bipartite reading of *The Birth of Tragedy*.

This is not the only place in Nietzsche's published writings where he resorts to metaphysically suspect perspectives.[18] His discussion of eternal recurrence, for instance, relies on such a move (see Chapter Four), as does his late treatment of the tragic artist (see Chapter Five). It is, then, a recourse by which he was tempted throughout his life. But here, in *The Birth of Tragedy*, we see it at its most innocent. For while Nietzsche may already have harboured doubts about some of the details of full-blown Schopenhauerianism, he did not yet have any reasons to repudiate transcendentalizing moves *as such*. And the fact that, once he'd acquired some (by 1882, say), he continued – on occasion – to make such moves speaks eloquently of the grip on him that his early Romanticism continued to exert. *The Birth of Tragedy* may be an infuriating and often indigestible book. But it really is – as Nietzsche himself insisted, albeit for slightly different reasons – a fully authentic first instalment of his corpus as a whole.

2

REDEMPTION THROUGH SCIENCE: *HUMAN, ALL TOO HUMAN*

Human, All Too Human is the monument of a crisis. It is subtitled 'A Book for *Free* Spirits': almost every sentence marks some victory – here I liberated myself from what in my nature did not belong to me . . . The term 'free spirit' here is not to be understood in any other sense; it means a spirit that has *become free*, that has taken possession of itself.

(Nietzsche, *Ecce Homo*, 'Human, All Too Human')

Introduction

In the later 1870s, Nietzsche's thought as a whole underwent some seismic changes. He became altogether more sceptical than he had been about the value of Schopenhauer's philosophy, and – a profounder shift, although not an unrelated one – he fell out with Wagner. The ardour of his attachment to Wagner, which had been white-hot in *The Birth of Tragedy*, had already cooled somewhat by the time he came to write the fourth of his *Untimely Meditations*, 'Richard Wagner in Bayreuth' (1876) – an essay which, while still officially running a Wagnerian line, has something of a going-through-the-motions feel about it, and never really rings true (the *Festspielhaus* at Bayreuth[1] was opened in that year, an event which Nietzsche found distasteful[2]). One has the sense that the hero-worshipper of *The Birth of Tragedy* has begun to find his hero, or at any rate his worship of his hero, oppressive, and that he is preparing to spread his wings as an independent spirit in his own right. The final break with Wagner came two years later, in 1878. It was precipitated, ostensibly, by Wagner's sending him a copy of what would turn out to be his last music drama, *Parsifal*, a work that struck Nietzsche as an outright capitulation to Christianity[3] (Wagner 'suddenly sank down helpless and shattered before the Christian cross' [HH II:P3]), and so as a betrayal of the hopes for cultural regeneration that Nietzsche had celebrated so uninhibitedly in his first book, six years earlier. It doesn't matter for present purposes that Nietzsche was hopelessly wrong about *Parsifal*.[4] The important point here is, rather, that his alienation from Wagner, together with his obsessive raking over of the ashes, prompted him to develop new and radically more sceptical accounts of art and artistry than he had espoused hitherto – accounts from which the spectre of Wagner, even when Wagner isn't mentioned by name, is never far away.

These accounts were developed in the books that Nietzsche published between 1878 and 1881: *Human, All Too Human, Assorted Opinions and Maxims* and *The Wanderer and his Shadow*[5] – the works in which Nietzsche first began to discover his mature voice. In them, we find him beginning to experiment with the aphoristic style, setting out his thoughts in numbered sections ranging in length from a single sentence to a substantial paragraph;[6] and, just as strikingly, we find a new coolness and detachment of tone. In place of the unashamed and passionate advocacy of *The Birth of Tragedy*, here we have a writer who is determined to be disinterested, critical, ironical, aloof. In one sense, however, Nietzsche's preoccupations have not changed. Just as much as in *The Birth of Tragedy*, his driving concern remains the possibility of a post-Christian regeneration of culture, of new ways of living now that God is dead. The difference – and it's a big difference – is simply that Nietzsche no longer has a Wagnerian blue-print to offer. Instead he pins his hopes to science (and his new tone is partly a reflection of that).[7] Science is now the bedrock upon which the post-Christian world is to be built, and Nietzsche's task, essentially, is to help it along by showing that every human phenomenon previously or traditionally thought to require supernatural or metaphysical explanation – such as religion, morality or art – is in fact explicable in purely naturalistic terms – that is, as Christopher Janaway has put it, in terms that are 'falsified by nothing from [our best] archaeology, history, philology, psychology, biology or physics' (2006: 340).[8] At the root of these allegedly transcendent phenomena, Nietzsche now wants to show, lie nothing more than the entirely this-worldly needs and impulses of the human (the all-too-human) animal.

Richard Schacht describes Nietzsche's approach at this period in exactly the right way, I think:

> For the Nietzsche of *Human, All Too Human* nothing is beyond criticism – and there is a strong suspicion that (as he would later put it) all 'idols' of our reverence will turn out to be hollow and all-too-human when subjected to critical scrutiny ... Yet the spirit of the investigation is profoundly and pervasively affirmative; for the passion that drives it is not only that of an honesty that will tolerate no nonsense or groundless wishful thinking, but also of a desperate search for enough to work with and ways of doing so to sustain ourselves despite all ... [I]f we are to make something worthwhile of ourselves, we have to take a good hard look at ourselves. And this, for Nietzsche, means many things. It means looking at ourselves in the light of everything we can learn about the world and ourselves from the natural sciences ... It also means looking at ourselves in the light of everything we can learn about human life from history, from the social sciences, from the study of arts, religions, languages, literatures, mores and other features of various cultures.
>
> (Schacht 1996: xv–xvi)

At work, then, in the writings of Nietzsche's so-called 'positivist' phase is a spirit that is simultaneously debunking and optimistic – 'a kind of tough-minded and yet doggedly affirmative naturalism, the upshot of which is that our all-too-human humanity leaves a good deal to be desired, and yet gives us something to work with that is not to be despised' (ibid.). And one of the things that it gives us to work with is art, the human impulse to beauty. We can expect, then, that art will be subjected to ruthless criticism – especially to the extent that it is tied up with pretensions to the transcendent. But we can also expect that Nietzsche will be alert to any regenerative opportunities that art might nevertheless present. And both expectations, as we will see, are borne out.

1. The metaphysical position

There is some disagreement about the metaphysical position underpinning the works from this period of Nietzsche's life. Julian Young, for example, makes the following 'hypothetical' claims: first, that Nietzsche continues to cleave to the metaphysical position presupposed in *The Birth of Tragedy*, namely, according to Young, that there is a firm distinction between the 'apparent' world of everyday experience and the 'real' world as it is in itself; second, that Nietzsche now holds that the 'real' world is the world described by science; and so, third, that the 'real' world, contrary to Nietzsche's earlier position, can be known about, quite directly, by human beings (1992: 62–64). Maudemarie Clark, by contrast, accepts a very weak version of the first claim, namely, that Nietzsche continues to believe, as he had believed in *The Birth of Tragedy*, that the distinction between appearance and (noumenal) reality is in principle an intelligible one; but she rejects the second claim, and with it the third – that is, she denies that Nietzsche thinks that science or anything else can show us the 'real' world, the world as it is in itself, either directly or indirectly (1990: 95–99). In the present context, this is a disagreement that matters: if Young is right, after all, art can only ever be second-rate, a metaphysical and epistemological loser to the power of science. If Clark is right, on the other hand, the playing field is level: neither art nor science can hope to do more, on Nietzsche's view, than tell us about the appearances (although of course one of them might do this more satisfactorily or more comprehensively than the other).

Young's case is perplexingly constructed. He offers no supporting textual evidence from *Human, All Too Human* (which is why, presumably, he describes his case as 'hypothetical'), and contents himself, in the event, with just one quotation – from *Beyond Good and Evil* (1886). In this, Nietzsche claims that the physicist Roger Boscovich[9] (whose work Nietzsche had first encountered in 1872) 'taught us to abjure belief in . . . "substance", in "matter", in the earth-residuum and particle-atom: it was the greatest triumph over the senses hitherto achieved on earth' (BGE 12). The relevance of this remark, from Young's point of view, is that it shows that Nietzsche came to believe that the world of individual *things*, of discrete material objects, had been revealed as an illusion *by science*; and this, in effect, brought science into line, as it were, with what Young takes to be the metaphysics of *The Birth of Tragedy*, and its claim that the *principium individuationis* belongs only to the apparent world, and not to the world as it is in itself. Thus, suggests Young, by the time of writing *Human, All Too Human* Nietzsche may well have come 'to the view that far from there being, as he had originally supposed, an opposition between his metaphysical [position] and the scientific world-picture, there is, in fact, a perfect congruence' (1992: 63). On this construction, then, the world described by science is not the apparent world, but the 'real' world – the world of ceaseless flux (of Schopenhauerian will) which had formerly, on Young's reading, been the purview of tragedy.

How plausible is this as a reconstruction of Nietzsche's position in *Human, All Too Human*? At first sight, or at one level, it is very plausible indeed, since – in a passage from Book I that Young oddly fails to cite[10] – Nietzsche has this to say:

> The invention of the laws of numbers was made on the basis of the error . . . that there are identical things (but in fact nothing is identical with anything else); at least that there are things (but there is no 'thing'). The assumption of plurality always presupposes the existence of *something* that occurs more than once: but precisely here error holds sway, here already we are fabricating beings, unities which do not exist . . . The establishment of conclusions in science always unavoidably involves us in calculating with certain false magnitudes: but because these magnitudes are at least *constant* . . . the conclusions of science acquire a complete rigorousness and certainty in their coherence with one another; one can build them up – up to that

REDEMPTION THROUGH SCIENCE

final stage at which our erroneous basic assumptions, those constant errors, come to be incompatible with our conclusions, for example in the theory of atoms. Here we continue to feel ourselves compelled to assume the existence of a 'thing' or material 'substratum' which is moved, while the whole procedure of science has pursued the task of resolving everything thing-like (material) into motions: here too our sensations divide that which moves from that which is moved, and we cannot get out of this circle because our belief in the existence of things has been tied up with our being from time immemorial.

(Nietzsche, HH I.19)

Nietzsche's argument in this passage is hardly pellucid, but we can at least see from it that he is committed, first, to the claim that material 'things' do not really exist, and, second, to the claim that modern science, in seeking to resolve 'everything thing-like' into 'motions', agrees with this. To this extent, then, Young is warranted in the thought that Nietzsche now regards the scientific world-picture as consistent with his beliefs about the unreality of 'things',[11] and so perhaps as consistent with the view that the *principium individuationis* belongs only to the world of appearance.

The question, though, is whether Young is right to connect this agreement about 'things' – between Nietzsche and science as Nietzsche understands it – to the claim that the world described by science is the 'real' world as it is in itself. Alternatively: the question is whether it is true, as Young assumes, that the reality side of the appearance/reality distinction is occupied in this period, as Young thinks it was in *The Birth of Tragedy*, by a world of ceaseless flux. If it is, then Young's case is as good as made.

Here, however, the evidence in his favour dries up. There are no passages in *Human, All Too Human* that lend unambiguous support to his position, and quite a few that count unambiguously against it. Perhaps the most striking of these is the following:

It is true, there could be a metaphysical world; the absolute possibility of it is hardly to be disputed. We behold all things through the human head and cannot cut off this head; while the question nonetheless remains what of the world would still be there if one had cut it off . . . [O]ne could assert nothing at all of the metaphysical world except that it was a being-other, an inaccessible, incomprehensible being-other; it would be a thing with negative qualities. – Even if the existence of such a world were never so well demonstrated, it is certain that knowledge of it would be the most useless of all knowledge: more useless even than knowledge of the chemical composition of water must be to the sailor in danger of shipwreck.

(Nietzsche, HH I.9)

Here and elsewhere[12] – the passage is entirely consistent with the general tenor of his early work – Nietzsche makes it clear, first, that if there *is* a 'metaphysical' world – that is, a noumenal world, a world as it is in itself – then we could neither say nor know anything about it (for instance, that it has the character of ceaseless flux); and, second, that even if we *were* able to say or know anything about it what we could say or know wouldn't be worth saying or knowing (and so could scarcely be the content of the modern science to which Nietzsche, at this point, pins his hopes for cultural regeneration). His position, in other words, seems to be exactly what it had been in *The Birth of Tragedy* – at any rate on the reading offered, *contra* Young, in Chapter One of this book: that of the noumenal world, if there is such a thing, there is nothing whatever to be said.

These considerations, I suggest, are easily sufficient to undermine Young's case. It may be true, as he says, that 'things' are illusory according to both Nietzsche and Nietzsche's version of science. But it doesn't follow from this – and certainly Nietzsche didn't think that it followed – that science *therefore* describes the world as it is in itself, the world as it would be if the 'human head' had been 'cut off'.

In my view, then, Clark must be closer to the truth. In *Human, All Too Human* Nietzsche apparently continues to subscribe to a strong distinction between appearance and reality, or at least to the intelligibility of such a distinction; and in this much his metaphysical position seems to be continuous with the position of *The Birth of Tragedy*. And, in denying that we can say or know anything, or anything pointful, about the reality side of that distinction, the continuity is underlined: no informative characterization of the 'real' world is possible. Therefore Nietzsche cannot think either that science describes the world as it is in itself or that the world as it is in itself is accessible – or pointfully accessible – to human beings in any way at all. (At most, if his position here really is continuous with that of *The Birth of Tragedy*, science might be said to describe the world at an intermediate level, at the level of the 'essence of things'[13] – although nowhere in *Human, All Too Human* does Nietzsche say anything that indicates that this is his view.) So the playing field would seem to be level. Science and art are both confined to the world of appearances.

2. Art and science

Metaphysically, then, art and science are on a par. But that, for the vast majority of Nietzsche's writings at this period, is about as close to science as art is able to get. In the epistemological domain, for instance, art limps in a distant second, utterly out-paced – although this sounds paradoxical – by the capacity of science to amass piece-meal those 'little unpretentious truths . . . discovered by means of rigorous method', which it is 'the mark of a higher culture to value . . . more highly than the errors handed down by metaphysical and artistic ages and men' (HH I.3). The estimation of 'little unpretentious truths', and of the patient, methodical accumulation of them, is integral, at this stage, to Nietzsche's naturalising turn. First, it underlines his rejection of those more glamorous or comprehensive-seeming sources of 'knowledge' that have been revered hitherto – for instance, revelation, metaphysical speculation, inspiration. And, second, it affirms that knowledge *is* possible for human beings, provided only that they will restrict themselves to their all-too-human, essentially small-scale and local, means of acquiring it. In this respect, science is paradigmatic for Nietzsche, and he spends a good deal of time contrasting it favourably with, for example, religion (HH I, Part 3) and philosophy as it has been practised so far (HH I, Part 1).[14]

Our concern, though, is with art; and it is worth understanding exactly why and in what sense Nietzsche holds that art, specifically, is a poorer source than science of 'little unpretentious truths'. One can see easily enough why art is no longer a candidate for the delivery of big pretentious truths (as it might in some sense have been in *The Birth of Tragedy*): Nietzsche's new metaphysics rules that out for art and science alike. But why, for instance, can't art tell us at least a few of the humdrum little things that a self-acknowledged all-too-human investigator might want to know? A portrait – one of Ingres', say – might tell us what Napoleon looked like; or *Othello* might tell us something about jealousy; or Homer and Sophocles might tell us something about the way in which life and the world seemed to the pre-Socratic Greeks. These, in their different ways, are little and unpretentious enough pieces of information – and it isn't at all clear that science could offer or encapsulate them better. So what's wrong with art?

It turns out that Nietzsche doesn't actually have an answer to this question, certainly not as so posed. He does think, it emerges, that art can tell us quite a lot about artists, and also that our responses to art can tell us quite a lot about ourselves. But he appears to be more or less indifferent, officially at least, to the thought that art might tell us something about the world. The explanation of this indifference, I think, has three main dimensions. First, he has misgivings about the *usefulness* of such truths as art might be able to convey in promoting the kind of human future that, at this stage in his thinking, he regards as possible (and indeed as desirable). For Nietzsche is quite clear about at least one aspect of that future. 'Modern science has as its goal,' he says, 'as little pain as possible, as long life as possible – thus a kind of eternal bliss, though a very modest kind in comparison with the promises of the religions' (HH I.128). The arts, by contrast, merely 'soothe and heal', and this 'only provisionally, only for a moment; they even hinder men from working for a real improvement in their conditions by suspending and discharging in a palliative way the very passion which impels the discontented to action' (HH I.148). And Nietzsche makes the comparison explicit in the following passage:

> When we are assailed by an ill we can dispose of it either by getting rid of its cause or by changing the effect it produces on our sensibilities: that is to say by reinterpreting the ill into a good ... Religion and art (and metaphysical philosophy too) endeavour to bring about a

change of sensibility . . . The more a man inclines towards reinterpretation, the less attention he will give to the cause of the ill and to
doing away with it . . . The more the domination of the religions and
all the arts of narcosis declines, the stricter attention men pay to the
actual abolition of the ill: which is, to be sure, a bad lookout for the
writers of tragedies – for there is less and less material for tragedy,
because the realm of inexorable, implacable destiny is growing narrower and narrower.

(Nietzsche, HH I.108)[15]

This thought – that science can get at the underlying causes of suffering, while art can only ameliorate the effects, and so that science, which promises a future that is progressively free from
suffering, is to be preferred to art – is perhaps the least
Nietzschean thought that Nietzsche ever had. In *The Birth of
Tragedy* he had been committed to the claim that suffering is
intrinsic to human existence; and by the time he wrote *The Gay
Science* he had re-committed himself to that claim, and never again
retracted it.[16] But here, quite unambiguously, Nietzsche envisages –
and welcomes – the possibility of a future without suffering, a
future that is to be delivered by the painstaking accumulation of
the 'little unpretentious truths' of science. And from this point of
view, one can see why the humdrum truths (putatively) on offer
from the arts would seem irrelevant.

   The second part of the reason for Nietzsche's lack of interest in
the capacity of art to tell us unpretentious truths has a strongly
Platonic feel about it.[17] As we have already seen, Nietzsche esteems
the capacity of science to take us, as it were, beyond the *immediate*
appearances (although not, of course, beyond the appearances altogether): the finding, which he attributes to science, that there are
no such things as 'things' is a good example of this. And he anticipates that science 'will one day celebrate its greatest triumph in a
history of the genesis of thought',[18] a history whose conclusion
'may well be' that 'That which we now call the world is the outcome of a host of errors and fantasies which have gradually arisen
and grown entwined with one another in the course of the overall
evolution of the organic being, and are now inherited by us as the
accumulated treasure of the entire past'. Nietzsche sees science,

then, as having the capacity to penetrate beneath our ordinary, everyday beliefs and practices, 'and, for brief periods at any rate', to 'lift us up out of the entire proceeding' (HH I.16), so that we can see ourselves for the all-too-human creatures that we are. Art, by contrast, or so Nietzsche seems to suggest, cannot do this. We are inclined to suppose, he says, that artists have 'a direct view of the nature of the world, as it were a hole in the cloak of appearance, and' to believe 'that, by virtue of this miraculous seer's vision, they are able to communicate something conclusive and decisive about man and the world without the toil and rigorousness required by science' (HH I.164). But this is an illusion: instead, art serves only 'to blind us and make us happy' (HH I.3); it 'lays a veil over reality' and 'makes the sight of life bearable by laying over it the veil of unclear thinking' (HH I.151). The contrast with the position in *The Birth of Tragedy* could hardly be clearer.

The final – and equally Platonic – dimension of the explanation of Nietzsche's indifference lies in his thought that art is, as one might put it, incurably anthropocentric.[19] Part of what it is, in his view, to appreciate the all-too-human character of the human condition is to appreciate that man is just one *more* piece of nature, with no necessarily privileged position within it, and that the nature of which he is a part is not necessarily organised with human purposes in mind. As Nietzsche puts it at one point: '*Fundamental insight.* – There is no pre-established harmony between the furtherance of truth and the well-being of mankind' (HH I.517). Science, although it can undoubtedly be turned to human *ends* – for instance, the end of abolishing suffering – gets its power from the fact that it is, methodologically, *not* committed to the centrality of the human. Art, by contrast, is so committed, and is so not least through its capacity (and aim) to engage us *emotionally*. Nietzsche's line here is predictably austere: people believe, he says,

> that profound feelings take one deep into the interior, close to the heart of nature. But such feelings are profound only . . . because we regard the thoughts that accompany [them] as profound. But a profound thought can nonetheless be very distant from the truth, as, for example, every metaphysical thought is; if one deducts from the profound feeling the element of thought mixed in with it, what remains is

the *strong* feeling, and this has nothing to do with knowledge as such, just as strong belief demonstrates only its strength, not the truth of that which is believed.

(Nietzsche, HH I.15)[20]

And art, in Nietzsche's view, is peculiarly able to exploit this sort of slippage, sometimes, as he himself attests, to memorable effect:

even when the free spirit has divested himself of everything metaphysical the highest effects of art can easily set the metaphysical strings, which have long been silent ... , vibrating in sympathy; so it can happen, for example, that a passage in Beethoven's Ninth Symphony will make him feel he is hovering above the earth in a dome of stars with the dream of *immortality* in his heart: all the stars seem to glitter around him and the earth seems to sink farther and farther away. – If he becomes aware of being in this condition he feels a profound stab in the heart and sighs ... It is in such moments that his intellectual probity is put to the test

(Nietzsche, HH I.153)

In this much, then, Nietzsche's claim is that, in moving us, art can distort, exaggerate or simply fabricate the significance of what it has to say, and so that – even in those cases (assuming that there are such cases) where its 'truths' are indeed true – their import is liable to be misrepresented. Science doesn't labour under this disadvantage. Therefore *its* 'little unpretentious truths' are to be preferred, and those of art – again – can be discounted.[21]

The cumulative thrust of Nietzsche's critique of the epistemological pretensions of art is, in effect, twofold. Most obviously, it is to insist – against Romanticism – that art is not a viable alternative, let alone a higher alternative, to the sciences as a source of knowledge. Instead, and for much of *Human, All Too Human*, Nietzsche regards art as the proper domain, chiefly, of pre-scientific cultures, and, indeed, as perhaps being on its last legs today: 'Just as in old age one remembers one's youth and celebrates festivals of remembrance,' he suggests, 'so will mankind soon stand in relation to art: it will be a moving recollection of the joys of youth' (HH I.223).[22] The degeneration of art is a constant theme of

Nietzsche's at this period[23] – partly, no doubt, as a result of his disenchantment with Wagner (whom Nietzsche took, entirely reasonably, to be emblematic of later nineteenth century German culture in general), and partly out of a sense that art was stifling itself through a kind of hypertrophy of sophistication.[24] But even in its alleged dotage, art may have its uses: 'To effect a transition' from the needs characteristic of Christianity, for instance, 'it is much more useful to employ *art*' than (metaphysical) philosophy, for those needs 'will be nourished far less by art ... From art it will then be easier to go over to a truly liberating philosophical science' (HH I.27). Moreover, art 'has taught us for thousands of years to look upon life in any of its forms with interest and pleasure', a lesson that will survive its demise: 'if art disappeared the intensity and multifariousness of the joy in life it has implanted would still continue to demand satisfaction. The scientific man is the further evolution of the artistic' (HH I.222).[25] So art is still accorded a modest (if non-epistemic) utility.

The other noteworthy upshot of Nietzsche's critique is to present a picture of the man of knowledge – the 'scientific man' – as one who is so far lifted 'up out of the entire proceeding' that he sees more deeply, more benevolently (in a broadly utilitarian sense), more disinterestedly and dispassionately than other people do, and indeed becomes a 'man from whom the ordinary fetters of life have fallen to such an extent that he continues to live only so as to know better' (HH I.34). This is a picture that Nietzsche would devote a considerable portion of the following decade to ridiculing;[26] but – for the moment – he is committed to it; and the power and value of art are down-graded accordingly.

3. Genius and inspiration

Perhaps the most conspicuous and sustained critique in *Human, All Too Human* of traditional, or Romantic, conceptions of artistry concerns the nature of genius and inspiration. Artists – and their audiences – have an interest, Nietzsche thinks, in encouraging and endorsing the impression that works of art appear ready-made out of the blue. 'The artist', he says, 'knows that his work produces its full effect when it excites a belief in improvisation, a belief that it came into being with a miraculous suddenness; and so he may assist this illusion . . . as a means of deceiving the soul of the spectator . . . into a mood in which he believes that the complete and perfect has suddenly emerged instantaneously'. And Nietzsche ties this observation to a larger theme: *'What is perfect is supposed not to have become.* – In the case of everything perfect we are accustomed to abstain from asking how it became: we rejoice in the present fact as if it came out of the ground by magic' (HH I.145). Our tendency, in fact, is to regard any case of perfection as if it had a higher, mysterious, other-worldly origin,[27] and so to presuppose what Nietzsche's new naturalism denies, namely, that there are phenomena which require supernatural or metaphysical explanation. Nietzsche's critique of traditional notions of genius and inspiration, then, isn't merely an expression of his scepticism at this period about the powers of art; it is, rather, an integral part of his attempt to show that all things human – including the things that human beings revere the most – are, indeed, all-too-human in origin, and so explicable in naturalistic terms.

So why do artists have an interest in perpetuating the impression of spontaneity, as Nietzsche repeatedly insists that they do?[28] Partly, as he says, it is to secure for their work its 'full effect': an audience that can be encouraged to regard a work of art as a sudden, miraculous gift is an audience predisposed to think well of what it has been given, and to respond accordingly. Also, an audience that is inclined to think of a work of art as something that has sprung fully-formed from the inspiration of genius is that much more likely to believe that the artist has been vouchsafed 'a direct view of the nature of the world, as it were a hole in the cloak of appearance,' by virtue of which he is 'able to communicate something conclusive and decisive about man and the world' – a belief in which the artist might well take some satisfaction. Moreover, says Nietzsche, because the artist 'refuses to give up the presuppositions which are *most efficacious* for his art, that is to say the fantastic, mythical, uncertain, extreme, the sense for the symbolical', he is reluctant 'to be deprived of the glittering, profound interpretations of life' that his art appears to convey (HH I.146), a deprivation that is made less likely if he can disarm his audience's critical capacities (by, for instance, encouraging the impression that his works, and their 'profound interpretations of life', have appeared ready-made, spontaneously).

Artists have an interest in giving the impression of spontaneity, then, for the sake of the reception of their work, of the reception of themselves and for the sake of those 'presuppositions which are *most efficacious*' for the practice of their art. Audiences, on the other hand, have two main sorts of motivation for taking the impression of spontaneity at face value. The first is that, in playing along with the thought that art has a more-than-human origin, they are able to satisfy something of their appetite for the meta-physical ('How strong the metaphysical need is', Nietzsche remarks, 'and how hard nature makes it to bid it a final farewell' [HH I.153]) – and, indeed, for the religious: 'Art raises its head where the religions relax their hold. It takes over a host of moods and feelings engendered by religion, ... so that the feelings expelled from the sphere of religion ... throw themselves into art' (HH I.150).[29] By treating art as a substitute for religion, then, and the artist as a kind of surrogate god, the audience is able to gratify impulses that an increasingly secular and sceptical culture other-wise threatens to leave unsatisfied. The audience's other main motivation is rather different: it springs, as Nietzsche makes clear in a brilliant passage, from a paradoxical sort of self-regard:

> *Cult of genius out of vanity.* – Because we think well of ourselves, but nonetheless never suppose ourselves capable of producing a painting like one of Raphael's or a dramatic scene like one of Shakespeare's, we convince ourselves that the capacity to do so is quite extraordinar-ily marvellous, a wholly uncommon accident, or, if we are still reli-giously inclined, a mercy from on high. Thus our vanity, our self-love, promotes the cult of genius: for only if we think of him as being very remote from us, as a *miraculum*, does he not aggrieve us ... To call something 'divine' means: 'here there is no need to compete'. Then, everything finished and complete is regarded with admiration.
>
> (Nietzsche, HH I.162)

Only, that is, if we can persuade ourselves – for instance, by treating the products of genius as if they had appeared from nowhere – that the activity of genius is of an altogether different order from other sorts of activity can we avoid the conclusion that we ourselves are not different in kind from the genius, but are, simply, very very inferior to him. And so our regard for ourselves requires us to make a deity of him.

These observations – about artists and audiences alike – are acute, I think, and, while they certainly don't show that there *is* no such thing as inspiration, or genius as Romantically conceived, they do sow enough suspicions to pave the way for Nietzsche's alternative account of artistic creativity.

This, as one might anticipate, is thoroughly down-to-earth: it amounts, in effect, to a version of the remark that genius consists in 'an infinite capacity for taking pains'.[30] There is, Nietzsche insists, no fundamental difference between the genius's activity and that of

> the inventor of machines, the scholar of astronomy or history, the master of tactics . . . Genius too does nothing except learn first how to lay bricks then how to build . . . Every activity of man is amazingly complicated, not only that of genius: but none is a 'miracle'.
>
> (Nietzsche, HH I.162)

And he elaborates in the following section:

> *The serious workman.* – Do not talk about giftedness, inborn talents! One can name great men of all kinds who were very little gifted. They *acquired* greatness, became 'geniuses' (as we put it), through qualities the lack of which no one who knew what they were would boast of: they all possessed that seriousness of the efficient workman which first learns to construct the parts properly before it ventures to fashion a great whole; they allowed themselves time for it, because they took more pleasure in making the little, secondary things well than in the effect of a dazzling whole.
>
> (Nietzsche, HH I.163)

It is necessary to grasp, Nietzsche continues, 'what purely human qualities have come together in' the genius 'and what fortunate circumstances attended' him: 'undiminishing energy, resolute application . . . , then the good fortune to receive an upbringing which offered in the early years the finest teachers, models and methods' (HH I.164), and the opportunity for *'practice'* (HH I.203). Throughout, the picture is of the genius as one who is utterly single-minded, hugely energetic, immensely disciplined, so practised in the fundamentals of his art that they have become second nature to him, a little lucky, perhaps – and human, entirely human, all the way down.

It would be very difficult, I think, to read this as a *hostile* characterisation of the artistic genius. To be sure, it trims the artist's metaphysical wings, and deprives him of his claim to enjoy 'a direct view of the nature of the world'. It also refuses 'to abstain from asking how' something 'perfect' has 'become': 'the imagination of a good artist', Nietzsche says, 'is productive continually, of good, mediocre and bad things, but his *power of judgement*, sharpened and practiced to the highest degree, rejects, selects, knots together; as we can now see from Beethoven's notebooks how the most glorious melodies were put together gradually and as it were culled out of many beginnings' (HH I.155). But the figure who emerges is none the less exceptional for that; and, in one sense at least, he is more impressive: the credit – the responsibility – for the perfections that he achieves is now unambiguously *his*. Only someone with an extremely strong investment in the Romantic conception of genius could feel that the artist is being belittled here.

This last fact raises some interesting points. Nietzsche himself is obviously *praising* the artist in these passages – for what he *is*, of course, rather than for what he might want to be taken to be – and, in this much, his otherwise predominantly negative tone about art and artists appears to have been suspended. This encourages the thought that, even at this period, when he seems at his most dismissive, Nietzsche might still have room for *some* kind of positive conception of art. It is also noteworthy that the features of artistry that Nietzsche draws attention to are, above all, hard work, method, discipline, rigour – precisely the virtues, in other words, said to be exemplified by the activity of science. This may, of course, simply bolster his claim that the 'scientific man is the further evolution of the artistic'. But it surely, at the same time, also diminishes the gulf between them, and makes one wonder whether, or to what extent, Nietzsche – who was, after all, always far more engaged and taken up with works of art than with actual pieces of science[31] – hasn't in fact modelled science after art. I am not suggesting, of course, that his campaign against art and artists is any sort of charade. Nietzsche clearly does want to prick their metaphysical pretensions; and he clearly is committed to the view that, compared with science, art is a nugatory source of those 'little unpretentious truths' upon which the future is to be built. But it does seem, here, that when Nietzsche has, as it were, flushed the all-too-human artist out from his other-worldly cover, he likes what he sees, and discerns in him the very traits of character that the building work he anticipates will require.

In *Human, All Too Human*, however, Nietzsche makes nothing of this (although he will make something of it later); and we can do no more at the moment than note, merely, that his discussion of genius and inspiration does at least strike a few more positive notes about art and artistry than we have heard so far.

4. 'Monumental' art

Even if not very prominently, Nietzsche does in fact have a few explicitly nice things to say, not only about artists, but also about three kinds of art. These can be classified according to the schema he had introduced in 1874, in 'On the Uses and Disadvantages of History for Life', the second of his *Untimely Meditations*. There, he claims that 'History pertains to the living man in three respects: it pertains to him as a being who acts and strives, as a being who preserves and reveres, and as a being who suffers and seeks deliverance.' To the first category, 'monumental' history is fitting – history that holds up exemplary figures and models from the past as inspiration; to the second category, 'antiquarian' history answers – history that tends to what has been valuable in the past, and ensures a continuity between past and present; and to the third category, 'critical' history is appropriate – history which confronts the past, and condemns it (UM II.2).

Artistic analogues of each of these kinds of history are mentioned in *Human, All Too Human*, and Nietzsche clearly approves of them, by and large. So, for instance, he describes 'today's great artists' as 'unchainers of the will and for that reason under certain circumstances liberators of life'; their value 'may lie in unharness-ing, unfettering, destroying' (HH II.172) – a fact that is connected to their position in history:

> *The seditious in the history of art.* – If we follow the history of an art, . . . as we proceed from master to master and behold the ever increasing care expended on obedience to all the ancient rules and self-limitations and to those added subsequently, we are aware of a painful tension . . . : we grasp that the bow *has* to break and that the so-called inorganic composition bedecked and masked with the most marvellous means of expression . . . was sooner or later a necessity and almost an *act of charity.*
>
> (Nietzsche, HH II.131)

'Seditious' art such as this, and the artists who produce it, may safely be described as 'critical'. 'Antiquarian' artists, by contrast, perform one of the 'subsidiary duties of art', namely,

> that of conserving, and no doubt of taking extinguished, faded ideas and restoring to them a little colour: when it performs this task it winds a band around different ages and makes the spirits that inform them return . . . [T]he old emotions are again aroused, if only for a few moments, and the heart beats to a rhythm it had forgotten . . . Without his knowing it, [the artist's] task becomes that of making mankind childlike; this is his glory and his limitation.
>
> (Nietzsche, HH I.147)[32]

Nietzsche's praise may be qualified here, but it *is* praise, and is noteworthy enough for that.[33] The kind of art that principally attracts his attention, however, is the kind that we might term 'monumental'.[34]

In *Untimely Meditations* Nietzsche's idea had been that the 'man of deeds and power' may need 'models, teachers, comforters', and that 'monumental' history serves to supply these, by showing, for instance, that 'in earlier times someone passed through this existence infused with pride and strength, someone else sunk in profound thoughtfulness, a third exhibiting mercy and helpfulness'. From these exemplars, the 'man of the present' learns 'that the greatness that once existed was in any event once *possible* and may thus be possible again', a lesson that is not best imparted, Nietzsche says, by means of 'absolute veracity'. Rather, 'monumental' history must 'deal in approximations and generalities, in making what is dissimilar look similar; it will always have to diminish the differences of motives and instigations so as to exhibit the *effectus* monumentally, that is to say as something exemplary and worthy of imitation'. And in this tendency to approximation, such history 'incurs the danger of becoming somewhat distorted, beautified and coming close to free poetic invention', so that there may, in the end, be little discernible difference between 'a monumentalised past and a mythical fiction' (UM II.2). In *Human, All Too Human*, Nietzsche exploits this last point, and explicitly assigns the monumentalising role to art.[35] The pivotal passage is this:

> *The poet as signpost to the future.* – . . . [P]oetic power . . . ought to be dedicated, not so much to the representation of the contemporary world or to the reanimation . . . of the past, but to signposting the future . . . [W]hat [the poet] will do . . . is emulate the artists of earlier times who imaginatively developed the existing images of the gods and *imaginatively develop* a fair image of man; he will scent out those cases in which, in the *midst* of our modern world and reality . . . the great and beautiful soul is still possible, still able to embody itself in the harmonious and well-proportioned and thus acquire visibility, duration and the status of a model, and in doing so through the excitation of envy and emulation help to create the future . . . Strength, goodness, mildness, purity and an involuntary inborn moderation in the characters and their actions . . . : – all this would make up the general and all-embracing golden ground upon which alone the tender *distinctions* between the different embodied ideals would then constitute the actual *painting* – that of the ever increasing elevation of man.
>
> (Nietzsche, HH II.99)

Artists such as this, therefore, are to become (as 'earlier artists' were) 'transformers of animals, creators of men, and in general sculptors and remodellers of life' (HH II.172).

Julian Young reconstructs Nietzsche's line of thought here as an argument for the claim that good art must necessarily be (neo-) classical art or (neo-)Hellenic art, a conclusion derived, on Young's reconstruction, from three premises. The first premise is that good art, according to Nietzsche, 'is art which offers vivid and seductive models of desirable personality types'. The second premise is that the *ideal* personality type is one that exhibits 'Strength, goodness, mildness, purity and an involuntary inborn moderation', qualities that are very close, or so Young remarks, to those of Plato's ideally just soul: 'we may', he says, therefore 'refer to Nietzsche's ideal personality type as "Platonic man".' The third premise is that 'only those forms which are . . . limited, balanced, symmetrical, and harmonious are capable of expressing . . . the beautiful soul. Models of Platonic man can only be expressed by classical forms.' Therefore 'good art can only be (neo-)classical art' (1992: 78).

Young accepts – and I agree with him – that the third premise is true, but he objects to the other two (and hence to the conclusion). His worry about the first premise is that there is no reason to think that there is just *one* way in which art can be good. But, as we have seen, Nietzsche also acknowledges the value of what I have called 'critical' and 'antiquarian' art,[36] so this worry need not detain us: Nietzsche's argument here is about what makes for good *'monumental'* art (and Young's premise should be amended accordingly). To the second premise, Young objects 'that there is *no* single personality type to which it is desirable that everybody should conform' – and describes Nietzsche's view here as having 'the face of Stalinism' (1992: 79). But this is surely an overstatement. First, Nietzsche speaks expressly about 'the tender *distinctions* between the different embodied ideals' – and even if, as Young objects, these distinctions may be unlikely to be very wide, it simply isn't true that Nietzsche has some single, one-size-fits-all, personality in mind. We may recall that in the 'Uses and Disadvantages' essay he distinguishes between exemplars whose characters are 'infused with pride and strength', those who are 'sunk in profound thoughtfulness' and those who exhibit 'mercy and helpfulness' – and any of these personality types might be painted against the 'golden ground' of 'goodness, mildness, purity and an involuntary inborn moderation'. He also, in that essay, identifies the beneficiary of monumental history as the man 'who acts and strives' – that is, he sees history of this sort as suited, not to everyone, but only to certain sorts of people. And it is reasonable, surely, to suppose that Nietzsche would have thought the same about 'monumental' art (it would be most unlike him, after all, to think that the task of building the future would be spread evenly across the population as a whole: in 'Uses and Disadvantages', for instance, he proposes that German culture could be transformed by as few as 'a hundred men educated and actively working in a new spirit' [UM II.2]). So, again, it doesn't seem to me that Young's objection is compelling: rather than proposing a one-size-fits-all model, I suggest, Nietzsche is more naturally to be read as proposing a model in which several sizes are intended to fit a few. So the second premise, too, needs to be re-written.

Given his understanding of Nietzsche's premises, however, it is almost inevitable that Young should also hold that the first two sit uneasily with one another. The first premise, Young rightly notes, attributes to the artist a special ability to 'scent out those cases in which, in the *midst* of our modern world and reality . . . the great and beautiful soul is still possible', from which cases he will go on to *'imaginatively develop* a fair image of man'. The second premise, however, on Young's reconstruction,

> undercuts this special valuing of the artist. For here the petty party bureaucrat (Nietzsche is, of course, a great artist, but on occasions such as the present one speaks as a bureaucrat) *tells* the artist what she must see, announces, in the manner of Stalin, the program to which the artist must adhere. And this produces a contradiction: in the first premise the artist is someone we, the ordinary, need on account of her unique powers of mediocrity-transcending vision; but in the second the mediocre tells the artist what she is to see, thereby ensuring precisely the mediocrity of vision one sought to avoid.
>
> (Young 1992: 82)

This seems wholly mistaken to me, and not only because I am anyway inclined, for the reasons already given, to doubt that Young's reading of Nietzsche's second premise is correct. For the fact is that Nietzsche is very well aware of the danger of precisely

the kind of aesthetic 'Stalinism' with which Young here charges
him. In 'Uses and Disadvantages' he warns of the mis-use of monumental history, saying that it can encourage 'the inspired to
fanaticism', even among men of 'power and achievement'. Given
which, he exclaims, what 'is it likely to do when the impotent and
indolent take possession of it and employ it!':

> Let us take the simplest and most frequent example. Imagine the
> inartistic natures, and those only weakly endowed, armoured and
> armed by a monumentalist history of the artists: against whom will
> they now turn their weapons? Against their arch-enemies, the strong
> artistic spirits, that is to say against those who alone are capable of
> learning from that history in a true, that is to say life-enhancing sense,
> and of transforming what they have learned into a more elevated prac-
> tice. Their path will be barred, their air darkened, if a half-understood
> monument to some great era of the past is erected as an idol and
> zealously danced around, as though to say: 'Behold, this is true art:
> pay no heed to those who are evolving and want something new!' . . .
> [Those who] have solemnly proclaimed the canon of monumental
> art . . . are connoisseurs of art because they would like to do away
> with art altogether . . . For they do not desire to see new greatness
> emerge: their means of preventing it is to say 'Behold, greatness
> already exists!' In reality, they are as little concerned about the great-
> ness that already exists as they are about that which is emerging . . .
> Monumental history is the masquerade costume in which their hatred
> of the great and powerful is disguised . . . , and . . . in which they
> invert the real meaning of that mode of regarding history into its
> opposite.
>
> (Nietzsche, UM II.2)

It would be very surprising, it seems to me, if having written this
(superb) passage Nietzsche were to have gone on in his next book
to write precisely as one of those 'connoisseurs' – or petty bureau-
crats – whom he here denounces. Indeed, in making clear exactly
the sense in which 'monumentalism', as he understands it, has
nothing whatever to do with bureaucratic prescriptivism – but is,
rather, a matter of offering a spur to those capable of 'transforming
what has been learned into a more elevated practice', of imagina-

tively developing 'a fair image of man' – Nietzsche clearly under-scores the distance separating his sort of advice to artists from, for example, Stalin's. And these considerations confirm me in the view that Nietzsche cannot possibly have subscribed to Young's version of the second premise.

So how does Nietzsche's 'argument' for '(neo-)classicism' look now? Like this: premise 1 – good 'monumental' art offers 'vivid and seductive models of desirable personality types'; premise 2 – there is a *range* of desirable personality types, having in common 'Strength, goodness, mildness, purity and an involuntary inborn moderation'; premise 3 – these personality types can be expressed only through forms of art that are 'harmonious and well-propor-tioned'; therefore good 'monumental' art must be 'harmonious and well-proportioned' – and so, to the extent that art having those properties is to be called '(neo-)classical', good 'monumental' art must be '(neo-)classical'. I think that Nietzsche is indeed commit-ted to this line of thought, and I can't see any reason, particularly, why he shouldn't be – especially if one bears in mind, first, that harmoniousness and proportion are presumably characteristic of any kind of integrated personality, whether exemplary or not, and, second, that the equation of harmony and proportion in art with '(neo-)classicism' is a stipulation of Young's – a harmless one, I think, but still a stipulation.[37] Just as – or so Nietzsche tells us – 'the ugly side of the world, the side originally hostile to the senses, has now been conquered for' art, so that we can take pleasure in what was formerly considered ugly (HH I.217), so, presumably, we might come to detect and appreciate harmony and proportion in places where earlier ages would have said there was none. Indeed, even since Nietzsche's time, we clearly *have* done that. So I don't think that we need be too bothered by the term '(neo-)classicism'.

None of this, however, brings into good focus what is – or will turn out to be – of real importance in Nietzsche invocation of 'monumental' art. For that, simply, is the role – the ethical role – of the exemplar. James Conant has shown, in a compelling essay on the third of the *Untimely Meditations* ('Schopenhauer as Educator'), how Nietzsche regards the exemplar as integral to the process of ethical education (Conant 2001); and this is a view that Nietzsche never subsequently deviated from. What is really significant, then, in the 'monumentalism' of *Human, All Too Human*, is that for the first time it connects *art* to ethical exemplarity, and does so in something like a systematic way.[38] Nietzsche's understanding of that connection evolved over the next decade, and became considerably more interesting. But in *Human, All Too Human* we see it at its inception; and that is a fact worth noting.

5. Art and the self

I have saved the most prophetic-seeming theme in *Human, All Too Human* until last. In Book I, Nietzsche makes a couple of remarks about the connections between art, the self and beauty and ugliness. With what may be 'critical' art in mind, he claims that it is a mistake to demand 'that only well-ordered, morally balanced souls may express themselves in' art. For 'there is an art of the ugly soul beside the art of the beautiful soul; and the mightiest effects of art, that which tames souls, moves stones and humanizes the beast, have perhaps been mostly achieved by precisely that art' (HH I.152). And, a little earlier, he asks: 'What is it we long for at the sight of beauty? To be beautiful ourselves: we imagine we would be very happy if we were beautiful. – But that is an error' (HH I.149).

These remarks are rather inconclusive, but they appear to gesture at the thought that there is no firm connection between personal beauty (of soul?) and either happiness or the ability to produce the 'mightiest' art; and so at the thought that the aesthetic state of *oneself* is of little real consequence. If so, Nietzsche changed his mind. In the *Genealogy* he commends Stendhal for linking the sight of beauty, precisely, to 'the promise of happiness' (GM III.6). And in *Twilight of the Idols* he describes the (genuine) artist as one whose works 'are reflections of his [own] perfection': 'in art, man takes delight in himself as perfection' (TI IX.9). But he begins to change his mind, quite explicitly, as early as Book II of *Human, All Too Human*.[39] The most striking passage is this:

> *Against the art of works of art.* – Art is above and before all supposed to *beautify* life, thus make *us* ourselves endurable, if possible pleasing

to others ... Then, art is supposed to *conceal* or *reinterpret* everything ugly, those painful, dreadful, disgusting things which, all efforts notwithstanding, in accord with the origin of human nature again and again insist on breaking forth ... After this great, indeed immense task of art, what is usually termed art, *that of the work of art*, is merely an *appendage*. A man who feels within himself an excess of such beautifying, concealing and reinterpreting powers will in the end seek to discharge this excess in works of art as well; so, under the right circumstances, will an entire people. – Now, however, we usually start with art where we should end with it, cling hold of it by its tail and believe that the art of the work of art is true art out of which life is to be improved and transformed – fools that we are!

(Nietzsche, HH II.174)

Here, Nietzsche sounds themes that will later become prominent: that the *real* task of 'art' is to make oneself tolerable to oneself (and perhaps to others); that art in this sense is largely a matter of beautifying, concealing or reinterpreting one's own raw materials (i.e. one's character); and that actual works of art ought to be epiphenomenal with respect to this activity, a kind of happy side-effect of the process of self-beautification. Nietzsche doesn't do a lot with these thoughts here. He insists (again) that the art of the self must come first, noting with disapproval that the 'ceaseless desire to create on the part of the artist, together with his ceaseless observation of the world outside him, prevent him from becoming better and more beautiful as a person, that is to say from creating *himself*' (HH II.102). And – not obviously consistently with that – he attributes the persistence of 'the art of works of art' to the boredom of the leisured classes who consume them, and suggests that, deprived of such works, these consumers might, in effect, themselves become artists of the self, and 'learn how to *reflect* ... upon their work, for example, their relationships, upon pleasures they might bestow' – in which case, 'all the world, the artists alone excepted, would derive advantage from it' (HH II.175).

Nietzsche describes the 'monumental' artist as a 'signpost to the future'. And in his remarks about an art of the self, protean as they are, we have a further signpost – to add to those offered by his emphasis on the discipline and rigorousness of artistic production and by his connection of art to ethical exemplarity – to the future direction of Nietzsche's own thoughts about art. *Human, All Too Human* can take us no further than this. But in *The Gay Science* we will begin to see how some of these themes are played out.

3

ART TO THE RESCUE: *THE GAY SCIENCE*

Daybreak is a Yes-saying book, deep but bright and gracious. The same
is true also and in the highest degree of the *gaya scienza*: in almost
every sentence profundity and high spirits go tenderly hand in hand.
(Nietzsche, *Ecce Homo*, 'The Gay Science')

Introduction

The Gay Science was originally conceived by Nietzsche as a con-
tinuation of his previous book, *Daybreak* (1881),[1] in much the way
that *Assorted Opinions and Maxims* and *The Wanderer and his
Shadow* were continuations of – and indeed became the second
volume of – *Human, All Too Human*. And it may be that the relative absence of art and artists from *Daybreak* is to be explained by
this fact. *The Gay Science* has a good deal to say about both, and it
is possible that Nietzsche deferred discussion of these topics in
Daybreak to this putative second volume – which, because of the
way that (what became) *The Gay Science* developed, never materi-
alised. However this might be, though, *Daybreak* remained largely
art-free,[2] and we can sensibly pass it over in favour of the first four
Books of *The Gay Science* (Book V was added in 1887).

The original version of *The Gay Science* was published in 1882, and was intended, in some sense, to be a latter-day exercise in the *'gaya scienza'* of the mediaeval troubadours of Provence. In the section of *Ecce Homo* devoted to *The Gay Science*, Nietzsche describes the 'appendix' of songs at the end of it as 'quite emphatically reminiscent of the Provençal concept of *gaya scienza* – that unity of *singer, knight,* and *free spirit'* (EH, 'The Gay Science'), and this gives a hint of the sort of thing that he had in mind in giving the book its title.

It is probably safe to say that the gaiety at issue is occasioned, and perhaps made necessary, by an event to which Nietzsche for the first time accords real prominence, namely, the death of God. In *The Birth of Tragedy* and *Human, All Too Human,* God's death was taken more or less as a given, as an uncontentious fact about the condition of modern culture; and so, in both books, Nietzsche assumes, in effect, that the task of building the future can *begin,* if not exactly with a blank slate, then at least with a slate from which God has been fairly thoroughly erased. In *The Gay Science,* however, Nietzsche arrives at a much more penetrating understanding of the kind of event that the death of God constitutes, and so at a far richer conception not only of its likely consequences, but also of the factors that might, whether we like it or not, inhibit our appreciation of those consequences.[3]

In the opening section of Book V of *The Gay Science,* Nietzsche summarises the understanding of the death of God developed in Books I–IV as follows: 'The event itself is far too great', he says, 'too distant, too remote from the multitude's capacity for comprehension even for the tidings of it to be thought of as having *arrived* as yet ... [H]ow much must collapse' when those tidings *do* arrive (GS 343). The non-arrival of these tidings is dramatised by Nietzsche in two chief ways. In the first instance he puts it like this: 'God is dead; but given the way of men, there may still be caves for thousands of years in which his shadow will be shown. – And we – we have still to vanquish his shadow, too' (GS 108). Here, the *event* has clearly taken place; but the 'shadow' of the dead God prevents the import of that event from being realised – much as, for instance, the persistence of certain symptoms of an illness may mask the fact that the virus responsible for their original

appearance has been knocked out. And then, in one of the most celebrated passages in the entire book, Nietzsche has a 'madman'
announce the death of God before an audience of self-proclaimed
atheists, who greet the news with laughter and derision. As far as
they can see, the madman has nothing new to tell them – and, in
one sense, he hasn't: he, like his audience, thinks that God is dead.
Unlike them, however, the madman also thinks that this event has
the most momentous consequences. '"Who gave us the sponge to
wipe away the entire horizon?"' he asks. '"What were we doing
when we unchained this earth from its sun? Whither are we
moving? . . . Backward, sideways, forward, in all directions? Is
there still any up or down? Are we not straying as through an infinite nothing?"' The madman's point, in other words, is that the
death of God takes away from us the fixed frame of reference with
respect to which we have been accustomed to understand ourselves
and our world, and so leaves us, or *ought* to leave us, utterly disori-
entated. To the madman's frustration, however, his audience cannot
see this; and he is driven to conclude that he has 'come too early':

> 'my time is not yet. This tremendous event is still on its way, still wan-
> dering; it has not yet reached the ears of men. Lightning and thunder
> require time; the light of the stars requires time; deeds, though done,
> still require time to be seen and heard. This deed is still more distant
> from them than the most distant stars – *and yet they have done it*
> *themselves.*'

> (Nietzsche, GS 125)

The madman's problem, in effect, is that his audience, although
they believe that God is dead, and indeed believe that they themselves have killed God, do not recognise that the frame of reference
by which they continue to orientate themselves is, in fact, the dead
God's 'shadow', and therefore something which they are no longer
entitled to take for granted.

A large part of Nietzsche's project in *The Gay Science* is precisely to 'vanquish' God's shadow in this sense, to show that once
we relinquish belief in God the whole landscape is not only transformed, but is transformed in ways that may be unobvious, unset-
tling and even unbearable – but also, at least potentially, liberating.

The gaiety of *The Gay Science* is thus of a rather ambivalent kind: on the one hand it is, as one might put it, an exhilarated laugh at our newly found freedom; on the other, it is a kind of nervously light-hearted laugh in the face of the unknown. Nietzsche's naturalism is also affected. He remains dedicated to the task of understanding man in determinedly non-supernatural terms (God is, after all, dead); but the sheer *resistance* to this form of understanding is no longer, as it perhaps had been in *Human, All Too Human*, underestimated (the shadow of God lingers on). So, for example, we have, as a culture, internalised a whole style of moral thinking that depends, Nietzsche claims, on the presuppositions of an essentially supernatural conception of life and the world. And so the naturalising project finds itself confronted by what, in the subtitle to *Daybreak*, Nietzsche calls 'the prejudices of morality': to try to understand ourselves naturalistically is, given the shape of the shadow that God has left behind, necessarily to engage in a form of immoralism; and the depth (and difficulty) of the problem of imagining a post-Christian regeneration of culture increases accordingly.

The Nietzsche of *The Gay Science* is therefore faced with an altogether richer and trickier undertaking than he had previously thought, and some of the more problematic suggestions that he offers are a symptom of that. The thought of 'eternal recurrence', for example, finds its first, and arguably best, expression in this book; as indeed does the injunction to 'love fate'. Not all of these suggestions, however, are equally relevant to what Nietzsche has to say about *art* in *The Gay Science*,[4] and the focus of discussion will now narrow accordingly. But the background provided by – and the ambivalent kind of gaiety necessitated or occasioned by – Nietzsche's new understanding of what the death of God amounts to must be presupposed throughout. This is a much edgier affair than it was before.

1. The metaphysical position

As with his earlier books, there is disagreement about the character of Nietzsche's metaphysical commitments in *The Gay Science*.

Julian Young claims that Nietzsche here reverts to the position of *The Birth of Tragedy*. In *Human, All Too Human*, on Young's reading, Nietzsche had moved away from that position by claiming that the reality side of the distinction between appearance and reality is accessible to science. In *The Gay Science*, by contrast, Nietzsche retracts that claim, according to Young, and concludes, as he had concluded in *The Birth of Tragedy*, that '[r]eality as such is ineffable, in principle incongruent with *any* structure proposed by human thought or language . . . and hence unknowable by science' (Young 1992: 96–97). Reality has, in other words, gone back to being a world that altogether defies the resources of human conceptualisation. Maudemarie Clark – again – disagrees, seeing instead a small and hesitant step *away* from the metaphysics of *The Birth of Tragedy* (1990: 100–103). In my view, Clark's position is once more closer to the truth; but in order to see why, and to see what the step that Nietzsche took was, it will be helpful to understand where, and exactly how, Young goes wrong.

In Chapter Two – with respect to *Human, All Too Human* – I argued that Young was mistaken to claim that Nietzsche's belief in the unreality of 'things' (i.e. of discrete material entities), together with his belief that the unreality of 'things' had now been demonstrated by modern science, entailed that science must have access to the 'thingless' character of the world as it is in itself. In place of Young's view, I tried to show that Nietzsche's position was that even a 'thingless' science must be confined to the world of appearances, and that of the world as it is in itself nothing at all – or certainly nothing of any consequence – can possibly be said (by science or by anything else). And it is this latter position, of course, that Young now attributes to *The Gay Science*.

His reasons for doing so are again couched as a 'hypothesis'. Drawing exclusively on writings from the later 1880s, he speculates that Nietzsche came to think that, just as the apparent world of common sense is in some way the product of human projection,[5] so too must be the world described by, e.g., physics – even 'thingless' physics (Young 1992: 95). So, for example, Young notes that, having praised Boscovich[6] for teaching 'us to abjure belief in . . . substance, in . . . the particle atom', Nietzsche continues: 'One must, however, go still further and also declare war on the "atomistic need"' (BGE

12) – a claim that Young reads as a criticism of Boscovich. '[T]hough abolishing the *extended* atom', Young says, 'his *puncta* [or centres of force] . . . mimic the extended atom in being spatially mobile, temporally persistent entities. Boscovichian physics, therefore, still . . . caters to the "atomistic need". Boscovich's *puncta* are really just immaterial atoms' (1992: 96). And he connects this, not unreasonably, to Nietzsche's claim, two sections later, that 'physics too . . . is only an interpretation and arrangement of the world' (BGE 14). Young's 'hypothesis', then, is that on the basis of considerations such as these, together with the (uncontroversial) fact of Nietzsche's uninterrupted disbelief in the reality of 'things' (see, e.g., GS 111), it is reasonable to conclude that the position of *The Gay Science* is not only different from that of *Human, All Too Human*, but is different, specifically, in holding that not even science can get beyond the world produced by human projection – that is, beyond the world of appearances. The world as it is in itself is altogether inaccessible to us.

This 'hypothesis' has the merit, on Young's view, of explaining some things that Nietzsche actually does say, not merely in *Beyond Good and Evil*, but in the 1882 edition of *The Gay Science* as well. The remarks that he concentrates on are these (I quote them as Young does): 'delusion and error are conditions of human knowledge' (GS 107); and 'The total character of the world . . . is in all eternity chaos – in the sense not of a lack of necessity but of a lack or order, arrangement, form' (GS 109). He takes the latter remark to refer to the world as it *really* is, as it is in itself, and the former to be what follows from that – namely, that *because* the world as it is in itself is chaotic, all 'human knowledge', science included, must consist in 'delusion and error'.

Young is right about two things. He is right that, in *The Gay Science*, Nietzsche does not regard science as able to describe the world as it is in itself. He is also right that Nietzsche sometimes seems to speak as if this meant that all human 'knowledge' must be erroneous. But about everything else, as far as I can see, he is quite wrong. We can bring out why if we look a little more closely – or less selectively – at the remarks that he takes to be explained by, and so to support, his 'hypothesis'. Here is what Nietzsche actually says in the first of them:

Our ultimate gratitude to art. – If we had not welcomed the arts and invented this kind of cult of the untrue, then the realisation of general untruth and mendaciousness that now comes to us through science – the realisation that delusion and error are conditions of human knowledge and sensation – would be utterly unbearable. *Honesty* would lead to nausea and suicide. But now there is a counterforce against our honesty that helps us to avoid such consequences: art as the *good* will to appearance. We do not always keep our eyes from rounding off something and, as it were, finishing the poem.

(Nietzsche, GS 107)

It is perfectly plain from this that the 'realisation that delusion and error are conditions of human knowledge' is one that comes to us *through science* – that is, through one modality of, precisely, human knowledge. Nietzsche's point here, then, is not that *all* human knowledge is incurably erroneous, but, rather, that our scientific knowledge shows that our *non*-scientific knowledge is erroneous. And this is precisely the view, *contra* Young, that Nietzsche held in *Human, All Too Human*. If we note, further, that what the 'cult of the untrue' amounts to in the case of art is that we do not always keep ourselves 'from rounding off something and, as it were, finishing the poem', we won't be much troubled by (a longer version of) Young's second piece of evidence, either:

Let us beware of thinking that the world is a living being . . . Let us even beware of believing that the universe is a machine . . . Let us beware of positing generally and everywhere anything as elegant as the cyclical movements of our neighbouring stars . . . The astral order in which we live is an exception; this order and the relative duration that depends on it have again made possible an exception of exceptions: the formation of the organic. The total character of the world, however, is in all eternity chaos – in the sense not of a lack of necessity but of a lack or order, arrangement, form, beauty, wisdom, and whatever other names there are for our aesthetic anthropomorphisms.

(Nietzsche, GS 109)

The passage is, in fact, nothing more than a statement of Nietzsche's naturalism, as he makes clear at the end of it: 'When will we complete our de-deification of nature?' he asks. 'When may we begin to *"naturalise"* humanity in term of a pure, newly discovered, newly redeemed nature?' (GS 109). The focus, then, is on the need to 'translate man back into nature' (BGE 230), rather than, as our 'aesthetic anthropomorphisms' try to do, translating nature into man. The chaotic, formless, disorderly character of the world is thus *not* the character of the world as it is in itself: it is the character of the world, as revealed by science, that we are given, through art, to 'rounding off' in order 'as it were' to finish 'the poem'. As far as I can see, then, Young's 'hypothesis' is falsified by precisely the passages that he takes to support it. Nietzsche has nothing to say in them about the world as it is in itself, and has nothing to say, either, about the necessarily erroneous nature of (all) human knowledge.

It may seem from this as if Nietzsche's position in *The Gay Science* is identical to his position (on my interpretation, not Young's) in *Human, All Too Human* – namely, that there is an intelligible distinction to be drawn between the world as it is in itself and the world of appearances; that science is restricted to the world of appearances; and that nothing – or nothing pointful – can be said or known about the world as it is in itself. But that isn't quite right. I said that Young was correct about two things, and the first was that, in *The Gay Science*, Nietzsche does not regard science as able to describe the world as it is in itself. Young, of course, takes that to mean that science *falsifies* the world as it is in itself. But, as Maudemarie Clark has shown, there is at least one passage in *The Gay Science* that points in a different direction: 'What is "appearance" for me now?' Nietzsche asks. 'Certainly not the opposite of some essence: what could I say about any essence except to name the attributes of its appearance! Certainly not a dead mask that one could place on an unknown x or remove from it!' (GS 54). The implication of this passage, as Clark says, is that Nietzsche now rejects the view that he had held in *Human, All Too Human* – that there is, or could be, a world as it is in itself that is radically different from any of the ways in which it might appear to human beings (1990: 100–101). He rejects, that is, not only the claim that we can know about the world as it is in itself, but also the claim that there *is* such a world (as it is in itself) to be known about. There is, in this much, nothing any longer that could in the relevant way be said to underlie, and so to contrast metaphysically with, the world of appearances. Therefore the reason why science cannot describe the world as it is in itself is not – as Young alleges – that '[r]eality as such is ineffable, in principle incongruent with *any* structure proposed by human thought or language ... and hence unknowable by science'; it is, rather, that there is no such thing as 'reality', in this sense, to describe. In which case, it must be a mistake to think (at least on these grounds) that science *falsifies* the real character of the world.

This seems right to me; and it is consistent with a great deal of what Nietzsche says elsewhere in *The Gay Science*. We have already seen that it is science, quite explicitly, that allows us to realise (what Nietzsche clearly holds to be true) that our non-scientific knowledge is shot to the core with delusion and error. And, in another passage, he makes it plain that, even if against the odds, science *is* reliable:

> *Our amazement.* – It is a profound and fundamental good fortune that scientific discoveries stand up under examination and furnish the basis, again and again, for further discoveries. After all, this could be otherwise. Indeed, we are so convinced of the uncertainty and fantasies of our judgements ... that we are really amazed how *well* the results of science stand up ... [O]ur bliss is like that of a man who has suffered shipwreck, climbed ashore, and now stands with both feet on the firm old earth – amazed that it does not waver
>
> (Nietzsche, GS 46)

In passages such as this, then, it seems clear that Nietzsche regards science as the source of those truths upon which his naturalising project depends – as the source of truths that are, moreover, in a perfectly straightforward sense, *true* (and not merely true of an apparent world that contrasts unfavourably, from a metaphysical point of view, with a world as it is in itself). Certainly this is the position that Nietzsche went on to develop, explicitly, in *Twilight of the Idols*.[7]

And yet ... The second thing that I said that Young was right about (and here Clark agrees with him) was that in *The Gay*

Science Nietzsche sometimes seems to speak as if all human 'knowledge' must be erroneous, all human beliefs false. The operative word here, though, really is 'seems'. Young's sole examples are the two passages that we have already looked at – GS 107 and GS 109.[8] And these, as we have seen, expressly treat *scientific* knowledge, at any rate, as true. And Walter Kaufmann (1974: 147, n.37), who shares Young's view, cites GS '108ff.' as evidence, by which he must mean, apart from section 109 (section 108 is not to the point), sections 110–12, after which Nietzsche moves on to other themes. Section 110 is not helpful to Kaufmann's case: it begins by noting that 'Over immense periods of time the intellect produced nothing but errors', some of them 'useful' and species-preserving. Eventually, though, and it 'was only very late', Nietzsche says, 'truth emerged . . . A thinker is now that being in whom the impulse for truth and those life-preserving errors clash' (GS 110). This would therefore suggest that at least some human knowledge claims are true, even if only a few of the rather recent ones. Section 111 rehearses Nietzsche's disbelief in the reality of 'things', and so is irrelevant unless Young's Boscovichian speculations are correct – and, as we have seen, sections 107 and 109 suggest that they are not. Which leaves section 112.

This is the passage that offers the strongest evidence for the claim that Nietzsche thought that *scientific* 'knowledge', at any rate, is systematically erroneous (and so, perhaps, that all of our beliefs are false):

> *Cause and effect.* – 'Explanation' is what we call it, but it is 'description' that distinguishes us from older stages of knowledge and science. Our descriptions are better – we do not explain any more than our predecessors. We have uncovered a manifold one-after-another where the naïve man and inquirer of older cultures saw only two separate things. 'Cause' and 'effect' is what one says: but we have merely perfected the image of becoming without reaching beyond the image or behind it . . . But how could we possibly explain anything? We operate only with things that do not exist: lines, planes, bodies, atoms, divisible time spans, divisible spaces. How should explanation be at all possible when we first turn everything into an *image*, our image! It will do to consider science as an attempt to humanise things as faithfully as

possible; as we describe things and their one-after-another, we learn how to describe ourselves more and more precisely. Cause and effect: such a duality probably never exists ... An intellect that could see cause and effect as a continuum and a flux and not, as we do, in terms of an arbitrary division and dismemberment, would repudiate the concept of cause and effect and deny all conditionality

(Nietzsche, GS 112)

On Kaufmann's reading, I take it, Nietzsche's argument must be this: that modern science marks an advance over its predecessors, and does so in virtue of its employment of causal reasoning; that causal reasoning nevertheless misrepresents the true character of the world, by imposing human categories upon it; and so that science – however much of an advance it might mark – is still in the business of humanising, and so of falsifying, the world as it really is, the world that would be described by an intellect capable of perceiving continuum and flux; and therefore, finally, that scientific knowledge is systematically erroneous (and so, in principle, that all of our beliefs – scientific and otherwise – might be false).

Perhaps such a reading is not, on the face of it, implausible. But three things are surely worth noting. First, Nietzsche calls our descriptions 'better' than those of 'older cultures' – and it is natural to think that one description's being better than another must be a matter of its being more accurate or informative, of its being closer to the truth.[9] And that is obviously what Nietzsche thinks, too: our causal reasoning may not tell us, as we believe that it does, about the (non-human) world; but it does allow us 'to describe ourselves more and more precisely' – it allows us, that is, to arrive at increasingly accurate (i.e. true) beliefs about our own epistemic capacities and propensities.[10] Second, it is far from clear that Nietzsche believes that all (worthwhile) human reasoning is causal: a mere two sections previously, after all, he has insisted that it is only now – 'very late' – that 'truth' has finally 'emerged'; and it is natural to read the sections that follow immediately afterwards as an indication of what truths, according to Nietzsche, *have* 'emerged'. So: section 111 tells us that there are no such things as 'things'; and the present section (112) tells us that there are, or might be, no such things as causes and effects. These, then, are (two of) the truths that Nietzsche holds now to be known to us. Third, Nietzsche *himself* seems to have a pretty good idea of what a different and perhaps more penetrating sort of intellect would perceive – he seems to have, that is, what he holds to be true (and indeed scientific) beliefs about the world, beliefs based on precisely those truths that have lately 'emerged', namely, that there are, or might be, no such things as 'things' or as causes and effects.

It is surely very unlikely, in light of these considerations, that Nietzsche could think that our scientific 'knowledge' is uniformly erroneous (the 'results of science' – of *Wissenschaft* – do, after all, 'stand up'), even if he might think that our best science does not depend on causal reasoning.[11] And it is surely even more unlikely that he could think that *all* human beliefs might be false, since, in this passage, he explicitly tells us about some beliefs that he holds to be true. There is no denying that Nietzsche is committed to the claim that the *majority* of our beliefs are false: he repeatedly describes our most widespread convictions as errors – perhaps as useful, or as species-preserving, or even as indispensable, but as errors none the less for that. But it must surely be a mistake to allow this aspect of Nietzsche's thought to occlude his equally clear commitment to the possibility of our knowing at any rate *some* things to be true – not least since his naturalising project would be unintelligible in the absence of that commitment. So the conclusion to draw, I suggest, is this: Nietzsche holds that (our best) science is a source of truths; that one of those truths is that most or all of our non-scientific beliefs are false; and that the world of which scientific truths are true is not an apparent world (in contradistinction to a 'real' world, a world as it is in itself) but, simply, the world – the world that is directly accessible to human beings, but about which, all too often, human beings go wrong, and form false beliefs.[12]

2. Suffering and the intellectual conscience

We have already seen, from the brief discussion of section 107, that Nietzsche envisages a new role for art in *The Gay Science*. We must be grateful to art, he says, for telling us those untruths without which life 'would be utterly unbearable. *Honesty* would lead to nausea and suicide'. This is quite different from the position of *Human, All Too Human*: there, the (alleged) epistemic inadequacy of art constituted a criticism of it, and Nietzsche had no room for the thought that *untruth* might have any sort of positive value. So what has changed?

Young – quite rightly – regards this as a central question that any adequate reading of *The Gay Science* must answer. His own response to it, however, cannot be accepted as it stands, largely because it depends upon his misconstruction of Nietzsche's metaphysics. According to him, the principal thing that has changed is that Nietzsche no longer has available to him the kind of scientific optimism that had sustained him (and his argument) in *Human, All Too Human* – which is true enough (1992: 97). But the reason for that is not, as Young would have it, that Nietzsche came to believe in *The Gay Science* that science could not, after all, describe the world as it is in itself, since he hadn't believed that it could do so in *Human, All Too Human* either. It is not the case, that is, that Nietzsche came to doubt the epistemic power of science. What he did come to doubt, however, was the power of science to underwrite his earlier optimism about the possibility of a post-Christian regeneration of culture. And this doubt has two closely connected sources.

It is '*[h]onesty*', recall, that threatens to 'lead to nausea and suicide'; and the theme of honesty, or truthfulness, and its possible costs, is one that begins to loom increasingly large in Nietzsche's writings at this period. In one sense, the theme had already been sounded in *Human, All Too Human*: I have already quoted his remark that 'There is no pre-established harmony between the furtherance of truth and the well-being of mankind' (HH I.517); and this shows that, even then, Nietzsche's optimism about the redemptive possibilities of science wasn't without its shades. But in *The Gay Science* the impulse to 'the furtherance of truth' is subjected to a kind of scrutiny that it had not received before, and indeed is given a sort of pedigree. At first, Nietzsche tells us, 'the intellect produced nothing but errors', some of them useful and species-preserving, but all 'erroneous articles of faith'. Then, a later and 'subtler honesty and scepticism came into being', and did so

wherever two contradictory sentences appeared to be *applicable* to life because *both* were compatible with the basic errors, and it was therefore possible to argue about the higher or lower degree of *utility* for life; also wherever new propositions, though not useful for life, were also evidently not harmful to life: in such cases there was room for the expression of an impulse to intellectual play, and honesty and scepticism were innocent and happy like all play. Gradually, the human brain became full of such judgements and convictions, and a ferment, struggle, and lust for power developed in this tangle ... The intellectual fight became an occupation, an attraction ... – and eventually knowledge and the striving for the true found their place as a need among other needs ... Thus knowledge became a piece of life itself, and hence a continually growing power – until eventually knowledge collided with those primeval basic errors ... A thinker is now that being in whom the impulse for truth and those life-preserving errors clash for their first fight ... [T]he ultimate question about the conditions of life has been posed here ... [:] To what extent can truth endure incorporation?
(Nietzsche, GS 110)

Nietzsche's passage is intended to give a naturalistic account of the origin of what he would later call the 'will to truth', an account that locates that origin in disputes about which of two beliefs (both, as it happens, false) is, as a matter of fact, of greater utility, where what settles such a dispute is one or the other of the competing claims (about relative utility) being true. In this way, he suggests, truth becomes 'a need among other needs' (such as, for instance, utility) and so comes to be valued in its own right, an outcome reinforced by the occasional opportunity to engage in what he calls 'intellectual play'.[13] And when the 'furtherance of truth' is established, at least among thinkers, as an independent need – as an intrinsic value – it comes into potential conflict with other needs and values that are already in play, for instance those connected to 'the well-being of mankind'. For such thinkers, therefore, the extent to which the pursuit of truth can be accommodated within life as a whole becomes an issue – and perhaps, indeed, poses the 'ultimate question'.

This, at any rate, is what Nietzsche appears to be saying. And he himself is clearly committed to the value of truth: the 'de-deification of nature' depends upon it, and, in the second section of *The Gay Science*, headed '*The intellectual conscience*', he insists on the need not to tolerate 'slack feelings' in 'faith and judgements': 'to stand in the midst of . . . this whole marvellous uncertainty and rich ambiguity of existence *without questioning*, without trembling with the craving and the rapture of such questioning . . . – that', he says, 'is what I feel to be *contemptible*' (GS 2).[14] So we can take it that for Nietzsche himself the question 'To what extent can truth endure incorporation?' is a live and pressing one. But what, exactly, is it about the truths that might emerge through the exercise of the intellectual conscience that would make them unincorporable, that would make them 'lead to nausea and suicide' if honestly acknowledged? The truths that Nietzsche has in mind are, as one should expect, the truths of (his version of) science, which include the denials of the following claims: 'that there are enduring things; that there are equal things; that there are things, substances, bodies; that a thing is what it appears to be; that our will is free; that what is good for me is also good in itself' (GS 110) – and, one might as well add, that there are such things as causes and effects. It is these truths that reveal all non-scientific human 'knowledge' to be rooted in 'delusion and error', and so which threaten, according to Nietzsche, to result in 'nausea and suicide'. But why should that be their effect? These are, after all, much the same truths that, in *Human, All Too Human*, were going to be the building blocks of a bright new future. So what has become 'unbearable' about them?

In *Human, All Too Human*, the truths of science were supposed in some fairly routine way to supplant the false beliefs engendered by religion, metaphysical philosophy and art, while also (somehow) catering to the needs that those sources of error had, until now, met.[15] In *Daybreak*, however, Nietzsche recognises more explicitly[16] that the mere removal of false beliefs may not be sufficient to remove, or even very much to alter, the patterns of need and feeling that those beliefs had satisfied and supported. 'We still draw the conclusions of judgements we consider false,' he says, 'of teachings in which we no longer believe – our feelings make us do it' (D 99) – a point made again, from the other side, four sections later: 'We have to *learn to think differently* – in order at last, perhaps very late on, to attain even more: *to feel differently*' (D 103). By the time he came to write *The Gay Science*, therefore, Nietzsche no longer regarded the replacement of false by true beliefs as a simple matter, either historically or psychologically: entrenched falsehoods almost certainly answer to some need (or utility), and they pattern our affective constitution in return, endowing us with a 'second nature' (D 38) that may well survive their demise.[17] It is in light of this that he opens *The Gay Science* by underlining just how difficult the truths of science – for instance, the truth that the 'total character of the world . . . is in all eternity chaos' – may be to incorporate; for these truths fly in the face of our deepest needs and feelings. For example, Nietzsche says, man needs 'teachers and teachings of a "purpose"' in life: 'man *has* to believe, to know, from time to time *why* he exists; his race cannot flourish without a periodic trust in life – without faith in *reason in life*'. But these, of course, are *precisely* the kinds of need that the truths of science threaten to leave not merely unsatisfied, but – if honestly acknowledged – unsatisfiable; and this prospect is unbearable, so much so that no one has yet been able 'To laugh at [him]self as one would have to laugh in order to laugh *out of the whole truth*' (GS 1).

One source, then, of Nietzsche's doubt that science can any longer (single-handedly) underwrite optimism about a post-Christian regeneration of culture is not simply that its truths may fail to meet the needs that the errors of its predecessors had met, but that it might, in effect, in declaring those needs unmeetable, leave the (all too human) architects of any potentially regenerated culture without the motivation required for the work of building it – and might, indeed, leave them suicidal.

The other main source of Nietzsche's doubt is connected to this. In *Human, All Too Human*, scientific progress had held out the prospect that the causes of human suffering would eventually be identified and eliminated,[18] a prospect that Nietzsche welcomed (and presumably therefore thought motivating). But the mere *absence* of suffering is not equivalent to a *justification* of life, and to the question, 'What is the 'purpose' of life?', the answer 'To eliminate suffering from it' is no kind of answer at all. If one of man's fundamental needs is to have 'faith in *reason in life*', in other words, that need is no more to be satisfied by the (mere) abolition of suffering than it would be by seeking to bring about as much suffering as possible. Nietzsche only makes this point explicitly later, in the *Genealogy* – where he remarks that 'What really arouses indignation against suffering is not suffering as such but the senselessness of suffering' (GM II.7); sufferers thirst 'for reasons – reasons relieve' (GM III.20) – but it is clear that the same thought underlies several passages in *The Gay Science*. So, for example, Nietzsche is repeatedly concerned to emphasise, from a variety of directions, that suffering *as such* is not necessarily an evil, and that it is a mistake to turn 'it into a reproach against the whole of existence' (GS 48).[19] Partly, it's true, he simply wishes to insist that people are prone to '*exaggerate* when they speak of pain and misfortune' (GS 326), and so to exaggerate the 'reproach' against existence that suffering might constitute. But also, and more interestingly, he suggests that suffering is in fact internally related to pleasure – that 'the path to one's own heaven always leads through the voluptuousness of one's own hell'. He exclaims: 'How little you know of human *happiness*, you comfortable and benevolent people, for happiness and unhappiness are sisters and even twins that either grow up together or, as in your case, *remain small* together' (GS 338).[20] And the same point is made elsewhere, this time linked explicitly to science:

> *On the aim of science.* – What? The aim of science should be to give men as much pleasure and as little displeasure as possible? But what if pleasure and displeasure were so tied together that whoever *wanted* to have as much as possible of one *must* also have as much as possible of the other . . . To this day you have the choice: either *as little displeasure as possible*, painlessness in brief – . . . or *as much displeasure as possible* as the price for the growth of an abundance of subtle pleasures and joys that have rarely been relished yet. If you decide for the former and desire to diminish and lower the level of human pain, you also have to diminish and lower the level of their *capacity for joy* . . . Actually, *science* can promote either goal [and] might yet be found to be the *great dispenser of pain*. And then its counterforce might be found at the same time: its immense capacity for making new galaxies of joy flare up.
>
> (Nietzsche, GS 12)[21]

And, as if this weren't clear enough, he goes on expressly to repudiate the position of *Human, All Too Human*, describing it as an *'error'* to have promoted science 'because one believed in the absolute utility of knowledge, and especially in the most intimate association of morality, knowledge, and happiness – this was the main motive of the great Frenchmen (like Voltaire)' (GS 37).[22]

Nietzsche's point, then, is two-fold. First, he denies that the abolition of suffering – *simpliciter* – could possibly satisfy our need for 'faith in *reason in life'*, for faith in a 'purpose' in life. And, second, he denies that it would even be *desirable* to abolish suffering, since, to the extent that 'joy', 'happiness' and 'heaven' constitute worthwhile human goals, suffering is necessary to their realisation. Taken together, therefore, Nietzsche's grounds for doubting the fitness of his optimism about science in *Human, All Too Human* come to this: that some of the truths of science may be unbearable for creatures with needs such as ours; and that the ideal that he had attributed to science – the ideal of abolishing suffering – is not only not an ideal (it wouldn't satisfy our deepest needs), it isn't even something whose realisation we should want. So the future cannot be built on science alone.

3. The need for art

The discussion of the previous two sections should have given us a good idea of the shape of the gap, as it were, that art is supposed to plug in *The Gay Science*. And it *is* only a gap. Nietzsche's worries about science (*Wissenschaft*) do not indicate that he now denies to science any role in building the future: on the contrary, he envisages a kind of cooperative endeavour, in which the whole is greater than the sum of its parts:

> artistic energies and the practical wisdom of life will join with scientific thinking to form a higher organic system in relation to which scholars, physicians, artists, and legislators – as we know them at present – would have to look like paltry relics of ancient times.
>
> (Nietzsche, GS 113)

In the event, though, Nietzsche tends to concentrate chiefly on the contribution that artists – rather than 'the practical wisdom of life', say – might make to supplying the needs that cannot be met by science.

So what is art supposed to be able to do? It obviously can't be meant to give us an insight into the world as it is in itself, since either nothing can (if Young is right) or else there is no such world into which any insight might be had (if I am right). But it must be able to do at least two things: it must be able to take the edge off the more unbearable truths of science, and so steer off 'nausea and suicide'; and it must be able to satisfy our need for 'faith in *reason in life*', or else, again, bad things beckon. And since these requirements are precisely the ones that the truths of science (the only truths we have) not only leave unfulfilled, but declare to be unfulfillable, art cannot meet them except through 'untruth'. Nietzsche's position, in other words, is the paradoxical-sounding one that the 'intellectual conscience', which insists on honesty, drives us – once we honestly recognise the character of our most fundamental needs (as Nietzsche, in *Human, All Too Human*, had not) – to cultivate and value the false.

Nietzsche is aware of this seeming paradox, and seeks to disarm it by distinguishing between 'the *good* will to appearance' – that is, to untruth – and the acceptance or promotion of untruth out of a 'bad intellectual conscience' (GS 2). This is a difficult distinction to pin down; but we will perhaps do best to approach it by trying, first, to get clear what is meant by the '*good* will to appearance' – not least since it is from this, according to Nietzsche, that art of the sort that we need arises.

Let's remind ourselves of two key passages. In GS 109 we are told of those 'aesthetic anthropomorphisms' – 'order, arrangement, form, beauty, wisdom' – which the de-deified nature revealed by science neither exhibits nor supports; and, in GS 107, the '*good* will to appearance' is said, in effect, to supply the lack of these, by 'rounding off something' and 'finishing the poem'. What is striking about these passages, I think, is just how *modest* the falsifying role that Nietzsche reserves for art is. There is no hint here of outright invention, or of art's being supposed to conjure up *ex nihilo* an alternative, more bearable version of reality. Rather, the role of art would appear to be more like joining up the dots, or drawing a 'best curve' through a set of plotted coordinates, or, perhaps, like bringing out the shape of a camel in a cloud. And it is in doing *this* – in imposing form, order – that art caters to our need for 'faith in *reason in life*', that it takes the edge off the more unpalatable truths of science, and so renders life tolerable. In *The Birth of Tragedy* it was 'only as an *aesthetic phenomenon* that existence and the world are eternally *justified*' (BT 5); in *The Gay Science*, by contrast, it is only 'As an aesthetic phenomenon' that 'existence is still *bearable* for us' (GS 107). Eternal justification requires, at the very least, that what does the justifying be true, and in *The Birth of Tragedy* Nietzsche thought that he had a candidate for that. But in *The Gay Science* it is precisely the truth that is the problem, and so art, which is enlisted in order to falsify, in order to *evade* the truth, can no longer, even potentially, offer justifications of existence (eternal or otherwise). It can, at most, offer to make life liveable.

The modesty of the falsifying role that Nietzsche assigns to art is no accident, and he emphasises it. So, for example, he is stern about the art of intoxication – 'Does he that *is* enthusiastic need wine?' he asks: 'The strongest ideas and passions brought before those who are not capable of ideas and passions but only of intoxication!' (GS 86); and he criticises artists for often being 'too vain' and for fixing 'their minds on something prouder than those small plants seem to be that really can grow on their soil to perfection' (GS 87). And the reason for this insistence on modesty is that it is crucial to his claim that art represents 'the *good* will to appearance'. It is, indeed, only in falsifying things that art can hope to render life bearable; but it is only in falsifying them *as little as possible* that art can *also* discharge its responsibility to the demands of the 'intellectual conscience'. Nietzsche's point, in other words, is that 'the *good* will to appearance' requires the maximum amount of honesty, of courageousness in the face of the truth, that is consistent with steering off 'nausea and suicide'; that the falsifications of art must, if they are to be the expressions of a good intellectual conscience, be maximally modest. And this tells us what the acceptance or promotion of untruth out of a 'bad intellectual conscience' must amount to – namely, to falsification *without regard* for the demands of honesty.

That this is what Nietzsche means emerges clearly through the first two sections of *The Gay Science*. Having noted that *'the great majority of people lacks an intellectual conscience'*, that the majority 'does not consider it contemptible to believe this or that … without first having given themselves an account of the final and most certain reasons pro and con, and without even troubling themselves about such reasons', he back-handedly compliments 'some pious people' among whom he found an explicit 'hatred of reason and was well disposed to them for that: for this at least *betrayed* their bad intellectual conscience' (GS 2). And in the previous section, he links this kind of failing to the inventors of ethical systems. Their 'inventions and valuations may be utterly foolish and overenthusiastic'; they 'may badly misjudge the course of nature and deny its conditions – and all ethical systems hitherto have been so foolish and anti-natural that humanity would have perished of every one of them if it had gained power'. But, he asks,

> What is the meaning of the ever new appearance of these founders of moralities and religions, these instigators of fights over moral valuations, these teachers of remorse and religious wars? … It is obvious that these [people], too, promote the interests of the *species*, even if they should believe that they promote the interest of God or work as God's emissaries. They, too, promote the life of the species, *by promoting the faith in life* … From time to time this instinct … erupts as reason and as passion of the spirit. Then it is surrounded by a resplendent retinue of reasons and tries with all the force at its command to make us forget that at bottom it is instinct, drive, folly, lack of reasons … In order that what happens necessarily and always, spontaneously and without any purpose, may henceforth appear to be done for some purpose and strike man as rational and an ultimate commandment, the ethical teacher comes on stage, as the teacher of the purpose of existence; and to this end he invents a second, different existence and unhinges by means of his new mechanics the old, ordinary existence.
>
> (Nietzsche, GS 1)

'Ethical teachers', then, are engaged in a project of falsification: they falsify the predominance of 'instinct, folly, lack of reasons', of spontaneity and purposelessness, and indeed so far misrepresent 'the course of nature and deny its conditions' that they are obliged to invent an alternative existence, one whose effect is to unhinge 'the old, ordinary existence' – that is to say, existence as it really is. Like the artist, then, the ethical teacher promotes untruths that make existence bearable. Unlike the artist, however, the ethical teacher does this wholesale – he does not merely join up a few dots so as to create a pattern, he jettisons all truth in favour of a different, invented, 'reality'. And it is this *immodesty* in his falsifications that marks him out as a man of 'bad intellectual conscience', as one to whom the demands of honesty are simply inaudible or irrelevant. The artist's 'intellectual conscience', which insists on honesty, drives him – once he has honestly recognised the character of his and our most fundamental needs – to cultivate and value the false, but to do so to the minimum extent necessary to ward off 'nausea and suicide'. The ethical teacher, by contrast, is a wanton: he will falsify anything (and, indeed, everything).

It is worth getting clear why, exactly, this constitutes a criticism of the ethical teacher; or, to put the question another way, it is worth getting clear what, exactly, is *wrong* with the 'bad intellectual conscience'. To be sure, honesty is sacrificed: but the *effect* of that sacrifice, after all, is to make life not merely bearable, but, at least potentially, to make it a good deal better than bearable. And what would be the matter with that? We have already seen a part of Nietzsche's answer to this question in the previous section: the indiscriminate amelioration of existence may, he claims, come at the price of *reducing* the possibility of human happiness ('happiness and unhappiness are sisters and even twins that either grow up together or, as in your case, *remain small* together'). But he has a further reason, too – and one that goes to the heart of his project. This is, quite simply, that his naturalism, taken seriously, requires not only that we come to understand ourselves as parts of nature, but that we *live* in the light of the best understanding of ourselves that we can have, namely, as creatures who are, indeed, parts of nature. And this makes the (good) intellectual conscience integral to Nietzsche's conception of our situation in the wake of the death of God (an event brought about, at least in part, *by* the intellectual conscience), and hence integral to his hopes for a post-Christian regeneration of culture (since the intellectual conscience, or honesty, may well be the primary virtue of our age [GS 159], and so offer our most powerful resource for the work of building the future).[23]

Art, then – or 'the *good* will to appearance' – represents that minimum level of falsification without which we cannot hope to proceed. And, taking up a theme from *Human, All Too Human*, Nietzsche includes under this head, for example, the provision of inspiring exemplars: artists praise and '*glorify*' (GS 85),[24] he says, and in doing so 'have taught us to esteem the hero that is concealed in everyday characters' and so 'have taught us the art of viewing ourselves as heroes – from a distance and, as it were, simplified and transfigured' (GS 78). But perhaps his chief emphasis is on the need to do what the ethical teacher does not, namely, to judge correctly 'the course of nature' and 'its conditions':

> we must become the best learners and discoverers of everything that is lawful and necessary in the world: we must become *physicists* in order to be *creators* in this sense – while hitherto all valuations and ideals have been based on *ignorance* of physics or were constructed so as to *contradict* it. Therefore: long live physics! And even more so that which *compels* us to turn to physics – our honesty!
>
> (Nietzsche, GS 335)

As we might by now expect, then, it is a condition of the kind of creativity that Nietzsche is interested in that one *first* face the truth, and only then embark upon one's (modest) falsifications and roundings off of it. And, indeed, it is possible that, having faced the truth, one may not have to falsify anything – or at least this is a prospect that Nietzsche finds inspiring (and to which he gives inspiring expression):

> *For the new year.* – . . . I want to learn more and more to see as beautiful what is necessary in things; then I shall be one of those who make things beautiful. *Amor fati*: let that be my love henceforth! I do not want to wage war against what is ugly. I do not want to accuse; I do not even want to accuse those who accuse. *Looking away* shall be my only negation. And all in all and on the whole: some day I wish to be only a Yes-sayer.
>
> (Nietzsche, GS 276)

The creative spirit envisaged in *The Gay Science* is thus one who, first, faces the truth as honestly as possible; second, tries to see as beautiful as much as possible of 'what is necessary in things', of the 'course of nature' and 'its conditions'; and then, finally, falsifies those conditions that defeat this attempt – that is, turns 'existence' into an 'aesthetic phenomenon' – to the least possible degree consistent with making life 'bearable'.

4. Art and the self

In *Human, All Too Human* Nietzsche had floated the idea that the *real* task of 'art' is to make oneself tolerable to oneself (and perhaps to others) by beautifying, concealing or reinterpreting one's own raw materials (i.e. one's character).[25] He revisits the theme in *Daybreak*, suggesting, first, that one should 'reflect on one's circumstances and spare no effort in observing them', since 'our circumstances do not only conceal and reveal' our power 'to us – no! they magnify and diminish it' (D 326) – an injunction clearly related to Nietzsche's insistence, discussed above, that one should attempt to judge correctly the 'course of nature' and 'its conditions'. And then he remarks that, having reflected on one's 'circumstances',

> One can dispose of one's drives like a gardener and . . . cultivate the shoots of anger, pity, curiosity, vanity as productively and profitably as a beautiful fruit tree on a trellis . . . All this we are at liberty to do: but how many know we are at liberty to do it?
>
> (Nietzsche, D 560)

– an idea that is clearly continuous with the one expressed in *Human, All Too Human*.

It is only in *The Gay Science*, however, that Nietzsche's thoughts about an art of the self acquire substance and focus (not surprisingly, since it is only there that art re-acquires real significance in his efforts to grapple with life after the death of God). And his thoughts on the topic are, in many ways, an extension of his thoughts about art in general, as set out in the previous section. Indeed, one of the passages that I have already quoted – namely,

'As an aesthetic phenomenon existence is still *bearable* for us' –
continues: 'and art furnishes us with eyes and hands and above all
the good conscience to be *able* to turn ourselves into such a phenomenon . . . How then could we possibly dispense with art . . . ?'
(GS 107). So Nietzsche suggests that art – in the ordinary sense of
works of art, or of the production of works of art – furnishes us
with the resources we need in order to turn ourselves into an 'aesthetic phenomenon', and so make us 'bearable' to ourselves. This
suggestion is expanded upon a little later. 'How', he asks, 'can we
make things beautiful, attractive, and desirable for us when they
are not?' And he answers: by

> moving away from things until there is a good deal that one no longer
> sees and there is much that our eye has to add if we are still to see
> them at all; or seeing things round a corner and as cut out and
> framed; or placing them so that they partially conceal each other and
> grant us only glimpses of architectural perspectives . . . – all this we
> should learn from artists while being wiser than they are in other mat-
> ters. For with them this subtle power usually comes to an end where
> art ends and life begins; but we want to be the poets of our life – first
> of all in the smallest, most everyday matters.
>
> (Nietzsche, GS 299)

But the most complete and well-known expression of this thought
is given in the following passage, which needs to be quoted at some
length:

> *One thing is needful.–* To 'give style' to one's character – a great and
> rare art! It is practised by those who survey all the strengths and weak-
> nesses of their nature and then fit them into an artistic plan until
> every one of them appears as art and reason and even weaknesses
> delight the eye. Here a large mass of second nature has been added;
> there a piece of original nature has been removed – both times
> through long practice and daily work at it. Here the ugly that could not
> be removed is concealed; there it has been reinterpreted and made
> sublime. Much that is vague and resisted shaping has been saved and
> exploited for distant views . . . It will be the strong and domineering
> natures that enjoy their finest gaiety in such constraint . . . Conversely,

> it is the weak characters without power over themselves that *hate* the constraint of style. They feel that if this bitterly evil constraint were to be imposed on them, they would be demeaned – they become slaves as soon as they serve; they hate to serve . . . [But] one thing is needful: that a human being should *attain* satisfaction with himself, whether it be by means of this or that poetry and art . . . For the sight of what is ugly makes one bad and gloomy.
>
> (Nietzsche, GS 290)[26]

Before attempting to unpack this important passage, however, we should get clear about what problem, exactly, Nietzsche's art of the self, or art of self-stylisation, is here supposed to address.

The context, as always, is provided by the death of God. Before that event, we could understand ourselves as, essentially, immortal souls, as beings for whom two things are placed 'high above' all other considerations: '"revealed truth" and the "eternal salvation of the soul". Compared to that, what are ornaments, pride, entertainment and the security of life . . . ?' (GS 123). Under these circumstances, in which we thought 'that there was nothing of which men suffered more than their sins' (GS 138), and believed that '"Only if you *repent* will God show you grace"', every deed was 'to be considered *solely with respect to its supernatural consequences*, without regard for its natural consequences' (GS 135). Our concern for ourselves, in other words, was played out in a world in which the final *upshot* of that concern, its reason and vindication, lay somehow *beyond* the world, in the kind of 'second, different existence' invented (out of a bad intellectual conscience) by 'the ethical teacher'.

Once the death of God is acknowledged, however, we have to understand ourselves, and so our concern for ourselves, differently. We must understand ourselves naturalistically (as all too mortal pieces of nature) and must therefore consider our deeds solely with regard for their 'natural consequences'. We must repudiate 'revealed truth' and the 'eternal salvation of the soul' as the site and vindication of our concern for ourselves. We must, in short, find a way of living that satisfies, within the constraints of naturalism, not only our need for 'faith in *reason in life*' – a need met, at least potentially, by works of art in the ordinary sense – but for faith in reason in *our lives*, mine and yours. And it is this need that Nietzsche's art of self-stylisation is intended to address.

The discussion of the previous section should tell us to expect, first, that this art is to be done out of a good intellectual conscience and therefore, second, that its falsifications will be as modest as is consistent with making life – my life, your life – bearable. And these expectations give us a way into GS 290, the passage that chiefly concerns us here. We may note, to begin with, that the first thing that self-stylists do is to 'survey all the strengths and weaknesses of their nature', that is (as Nietzsche would later put it), to 'open their eyes to themselves' (GM III.19), to be honest with themselves about themselves. So this builds in the intellectual conscience from the outset. The second point to note is that is that it is 'strong' characters who revel in self-stylisation, while the 'weak' resent the constraints that it represents or requires. This indicates two things. First, that since those constraints include the constraint of being honest with oneself about oneself, the exercise of the intellectual conscience requires strength of character. This is perhaps hardly surprising; but it is an important point, and is one that Nietzsche went on to make explicitly: 'the strength of a spirit', he suggests, 'should be measured according to how much of the "truth" one could still barely endure – or to put it more clearly, to what degree one would *require* it to be thinned down, shrouded, sweetened, blunted, falsified' (BGE 39). The other thing indicated by the strength and intellectual conscience of the self-stylist is that he honestly acknowledges the self-imposed constraints *of* his style, an acknowledgement construed by the 'weak' as self-abasement, as submission to servitude. The self-stylist must be able to see as beautiful, that is, not only 'what is necessary in things', but also those self-imposed necessities that constitute his 'style' – an undertaking which, because those necessities are imposed out of a good intellectual conscience, requires a kind of honesty of which the 'weak' are incapable. (A final thing to note: here, in Nietzsche's insistence on the self-stylist's need for 'long practice and daily work' at his task, is the re-emergence of another theme from *Human, All Too Human*, namely, the indissoluble connection between the best sort of art and the humble-sounding virtues of the *'serious workman'* [HH I.163].) But these are all points that

Nietzsche will take up again, and take further, in the writings considered in Chapter Five.

The expectation that a 'good' intellectual conscience is involved in self-stylisation is thus borne out, I think. The second, correlative expectation is borne out too: Nietzsche clearly signals that the self-stylist's self-falsifications are very modest – as modest, presumably, as is consistent with the attainment of 'satisfaction with himself',[27] with making *his* life bearable. From this point of view, Nietzsche's horticultural metaphors are well-chosen. To 'cultivate the shoots of anger, pity, curiosity, vanity as productively and profitably as a beautiful fruit tree on a trellis' is only possible, after all, given a willingness to work *with* the grain of the materials that one has available; one must judge correctly the 'course of nature' and 'its conditions'. And the landscape-gardening images that populate the *'One thing is needful'* passage point in the same direction. The self-stylist has learned exactly 'what we should learn from artists', in other words, and is engaged in rounding things off, in joining up his materials, so as to finish the poem. He is *not* engaged in a self-regarding analogue of the ethical teacher's 'invention' of a 'second, different existence'. The character to which he is to give style is, emphatically, *his*.

The foregoing is clear enough, I think, in showing that Nietzsche's version of an art of the self is continuous with what he says about art, ordinarily so-called, elsewhere in *The Gay Science*. It is much less clear, however, in suggesting what such an art of the self might amount to in practice. We can say what it doesn't amount to – for instance, that it hasn't got anything to do with the more obviously self-serving kinds of self-deception: the intellectual conscience is fundamental to it, after all. And we can perhaps indicate what sort of thing a person's 'style' must be, namely, whatever structure of (modest) self-falsifications is sufficient to render his or her life bearable.[28] But beyond that? It is hard to say. Here, though, are two thoughts. The first is that Nietzsche himself wasn't all that clear what he had in mind, and that that fact became unignorable to him by the time he had finished his next work, *Thus Spoke Zarathustra*. The second thought is that, in his final writings, he did succeed in working out what, in *The Gay Science*, he might perhaps have meant by an art of the self. These thoughts are among those to be explored, or tried out, in the final two chapters of this book.

4

PHILOSOPHY AS ART: *THUS SPOKE ZARATHUSTRA*

> Perhaps the whole of *Zarathustra* may be reckoned as music; certainly a rebirth of the art of *hearing* was among its preconditions . . . This work stands altogether apart. Leaving aside the poets: perhaps nothing has ever been done from an equal excess of strength.
>
> (Nietzsche, *Ecce Homo*, 'Thus Spoke Zarathustra')

Introduction

Having completed the first four books of *The Gay Science*, Nietzsche embarked on what, in many ways, is the most ambitious of all his works, *Thus Spoke Zarathustra*.[1] The first two books of it were published in 1883, the third in 1884 and the final book in 1885. In one sense, *Zarathustra* can be read as an odd sort of novel. It tells the story of a prophet, Zarathustra,[2] who descends from his mountain top, announces that God is dead, and proceeds to promulgate a number of doctrines, to the general indifference of his audience. He does succeed in attracting a small band of disciples, however, and discourses at them before dismissing them (twice). In his second period of solitude, he is at first depressed; but then, in the climax to the whole work (the latter part of Book III), he rouses himself to a state of supreme intellectual exaltation, and gives boundless thanks for himself, life and the world. Book IV (something of an after-thought on Nietzsche's part), which sees Zarathustra again engaged with other people (the so-called 'higher men'), ends with another paean to existence.[3]

It *is* an odd sort of novel. The plot, as just indicated, is pretty thin; and in manner, it most closely resembles an over-heated parody of parts of the Old Testament: in its portentousness and tiringly hieratic style it can be something of a chore to read, and hard to like. Certainly it is the least readable of any of Nietzsche's mature works; and Nietzsche's unwavering conviction that it is a work of high art seems likely to remain a minority view. But for all its oddness and (frankly) awfulness, *Zarathustra* retains a certain fascination, and it contains themes that are among Nietzsche's best-known. So, for example, Zarathustra, having announced the death of God, proclaims a new sort of human being – a naturalised successor to God – whom he calls the '*Übermensch*' (a term – sometimes translated as the 'overman', sometimes as the 'superman' – that is probably best left in the original German). 'The *Übermensch* is the meaning of the earth', Zarathustra asserts. 'Let your will say: the *Übermensch* shall be the meaning of the earth! I beseech you, my brothers, *remain faithful to the earth,* and do not believe those who speak to you of otherworldly hopes!' (Z, Prologue, 3). We are not, in the event, told a great deal about the *Übermensch*,[4] except that his distinguishing feature is that he can joyfully affirm the thought of 'eternal recurrence' – another theme that enjoys a good deal of prominence in this work. It is in *Zarathustra*, too, that we first encounter any sort of extended treatment of 'will to power': 'Only where life is', Zarathustra says, 'there is also will: not will to life, but – so I teach you – will to power!' (Z II, 'Of Self-Overcoming'), as well as Nietzsche's most gripping evocation – in the person of the 'Last Man' (Z, Prologue, 5) – of the mediocrity of human living with which modernity threatens us.

What *Zarathustra* does not contain, however, is anything very much about art. There are some remarks on authorship (Z I, 'Of Reading and Writing') and a short critique of poets (Z II, 'Of Poets'), but really none of the extended discussion that most of Nietzsche's other writings contain. This fact may make the inclusion of

Zarathustra in the present book seem rather puzzling, so I should explain why this chapter is here. The reason, very briefly, is that since *Zarathustra* is *intended* to be a work of art (and may indeed be one, even if it's not as good as Nietzsche himself maintained) we might expect that it would show us what kind of thing Nietzsche thought that works of art were capable of doing, and so tell us, in an especially direct way, something about Nietzsche's conception of art. In this sense, *Zarathustra* offers a case study of a sort that is arguably unparalleled in the history of aesthetics; and that, I think, makes it more or less unignorable for our purposes here. I won't, in this chapter, begin with a discussion of the metaphysical position: first, I don't think that there is any reason to suppose that it is substantially different from the position underpinning *The Gay Science*, and, second, the type of interest that *Zarathustra* has for us simply doesn't require that sort of approach. Instead, I will start by trying to indicate some important aspects of Nietzsche's overall project to which *Zarathustra* can be seen as a response.

1. The teaching of ideals

It has been widely noted that Zarathustra's relationship to his public – to those to whom he attempts to get his message through – is a fraught one. Michael Tanner expresses one aspect of this issue nicely when he remarks that Zarathustra

> is a prophet who is intent on not having disciples, a desire which he is keen to stress, since it singles him out from all other prophets. But one might ask whether someone who speaks the truth should not want disciples, as many as possible. The answer would seem to be that Zarathustra is not at all sure of the truth which impels him to leave his mountain ... [He is] a self-doubting prophet, one who advises caution as to anything he says ... : we are in the presence of an incarnate oxymoron.
>
> (Tanner 1994: 46–47)

But this, while to some extent apt, is only part of the story. For although it is true that Zarathustra is, at most, ambivalent about having disciples, he *does*, at the beginning anyway, want to be heard. And his early experience of trying to reach an audience (in a market place) is strikingly like the madman's experience in section 125 of *The Gay Science*: 'all the people laughed at Zarathustra' (Z, Prologue, 3) – 'There they stand (he said to his heart), there they laugh: they do not understand me, I am not the mouth for these ears' (Z, Prologue, 5). And *this* experience – the experience, in effect, of being inaudible to those whom one is trying to reach – was, of course, precisely Nietzsche's experience of the (non-)reception of his own works to date, all of which had been greeted either with hostility and derision (*The Birth of Tragedy*) or else with a deafening silence (everything else).[5]

This point is not only of biographical interest. Nietzsche had, by the time of writing *Zarathustra*, come to realise that he faced a particular sort of problem in making himself heard – a problem, indeed, to whose diagnosis his previous two books had been largely devoted. In *Daybreak* and, decisively, *The Gay Science*, he came to see how very deeply Christian interpretations and understandings of life and the world had penetrated into the contemporary psyche – so deeply, in fact, that those interpretations and under-standings had survived, and threatened to survive for a long time to come, the event that should, in some sense, have undermined them, namely, the death of God. It is for this reason that Nietzsche's primary target-audience, like the madman's, is not Christian believers, but self-proclaimed atheists, those who do not need to be convinced that God is dead, but who *do* need to be convinced that the consequences of that fact are, or should be, momentous. Like the madman, Nietzsche wants to persuade his audience that God's death changes everything: that we are no longer entitled to our accustomed frame of reference and points of orientation; that a fully naturalised humanity must find a way of re-orientating itself in a world that has been thoroughly de-deified, that has no super-natural dimension to it at all; that 'morality' – even contemporary, so-called 'secular' morality – is the product, a hang-over, of Christianity, and so that we may no longer, after the death of God, be entitled to our familiar habits of moral thought; that we must, in short, be prepared to give our lives a completely new *kind* of meaning and value, and to give them that meaning and value precisely *as* the human, all too human creatures that we (should) now acknowledge ourselves to be. This is not only a big package to get across. It is a package whose every item runs more or less directly against the grain of precisely the style of thinking that it seeks to displace, namely, a style of thinking across which the shadow of the dead God still looms large. And so, Nietzsche came to recognise, it is in the *very nature* of the thoughts that he wishes to impart that they should, almost inevitably, fall upon deaf ears: he is, from the perspective of the vast majority of his audience, quite literally thinking the unthinkable.

Having diagnosed the problem, Nietzsche's first solution is to turn to fictionalized representations of someone (else) trying to communicate his (Nietzsche's) thoughts to a fictionalized audience in such a way that Nietzsche's real audience, his readers, not only recognise themselves and their reactions in the fictional audience – and so are enabled to adopt a certain reflective distance on themselves – but also, perhaps, through implicit identification with the fictional protagonist, are enabled to understand how those responses must seem from the standpoint of the person trying to do the communicating (e.g. from the madman's standpoint, or from Zarathustra's standpoint, or, above all, from Nietzsche's standpoint).[6] In this way, he hopes, a new kind of relationship to his reader can be established, within which, even if only through a sort of ventriloquism, what he has to say might actually stand a chance of getting heard. Certainly this appears to be the tactic that he adopts in the madman passage from *The Gay Science*; and it is also, on a much larger scale, a tactic that underpins *Zarathustra*.[7]

With this in mind, it is obviously essential that Nietzsche's fictional audiences should (at least to begin with) greet his protagonists' announcements with ridicule, contempt or a blank silence, as indeed they do, since this is the response that Nietzsche has learned to expect from his own audience. But this is not the only sort of relationship between protagonist and audience to be exploited; and, in *Zarathustra* especially, Nietzsche explores a whole range of such relationships. So, for example, Zarathustra, after failing to make any impact in the market place, determines henceforth to speak to individuals rather than crowds:

'A light has dawned for me: Zarathustra shall not speak to the people but to companions! Zarathustra shall not be herdsman and dog to the herd!' (Z, Prologue, 9); and, by speaking to 'companions', while Zarathustra does indeed gain disciples, Nietzsche invites *his* audience to take up a different stance towards themselves (and so to him). And similar shifts – when Zarathustra dismisses his disciples, for example, or when he retires into solitude, or when he re-engages with the world – can be traced throughout the work. The changing relationship between Zarathustra and his audience, in other words, is an integral part of Nietzsche's attempt to make himself heard, to make *his* thoughts audible to his readers.

But there is another dimension to Zarathustra's often troubled relationship with his audience; and this connects directly to Michael Tanner's observations, quoted above. For Zarathustra's (and Nietzsche's) problem is not *merely* one of audibility. Rather, it is also a matter of what, if the message can be got across, its recipients ought to make of it, or ought to be encouraged to make of it. In *Daybreak*, Nietzsche makes the following important points:

> *Insofar* as the individual is seeking happiness, one ought not to tender to him any prescriptions as to the path to happiness: for individual happiness springs from one's own unknown laws, and prescriptions from without can only obstruct and hinder it. – . . . Only if mankind possessed a universally recognised *goal* would it be possible to propose 'thus and thus is the *right* course of action': for the present there exists no such goal. It is thus irrational and trivial to impose the demands of morality upon mankind.– To *recommend* a goal to mankind is something quite different: the goal is then thought of as something which *lies in our own discretion*; supposing the recommendation appealed to mankind, it could in pursuit of it also *impose* upon itself a moral law, likewise at its own discretion. But up to now the moral law has been supposed to stand *above* our own likes and dislikes: one did not actually want to *impose* this law upon oneself, one wanted to *take* it from somewhere or *discover* it somewhere or *have it commanded to one* from somewhere.
>
> (Nietzsche, D 108)[8]

The relevance of this passage lies in the attention that it draws to one crucial aspect of life after the death of God. Before that event, mankind did possess 'a universally recognised *goal*', namely salvation, in pursuit of which it was not at all 'irrelevant and trivial' to follow and act upon (divinely sanctioned) prescriptions and commands, that is, an externally imposed 'moral law'. But prescriptions and commands require a prescriber or commander; and, with God's death, that is precisely what goes missing.[9] Now, therefore, mankind does *not* possess 'a universally recognised *goal*'; salvation is no longer a possibility; and, even if it is true, in some sense, that all human beings seek happiness, that is not a goal that can be realised by following 'prescriptions from without' – for 'happiness springs from one's' *own* 'unknown laws'.

What this means is that, henceforth, there is no room or role for externally imposed prescriptions of any sort. Or, to put the point another way: it means that a naturalised humanity must impose its own laws upon itself, laws which, because humanity as such has no goal in common, cannot necessarily be understood as universally binding; rather, as human beings – as individuals – we must impose laws upon *ourselves*, a matter that *'lies in our own discretion'*. With respect to each other, then, we can only *'recommend a goal'*, recommend a law: it would be 'irrational and trivial' to try to do anything more (indeed it would be the expression of a *'bad intellectual conscience'* [GS 2]).

This, clearly enough, has consequences for the business of being a prophet. To the extent that Nietzsche and Zarathustra are engaged in promulgating ideals by which a post-Christian future might be lived, they immediately risk slipping into prescribing and commanding, rather than recommending. And it is this fact that accounts for much of the 'self-doubt' that Tanner detects in Zarathustra's prophesying, and, indeed, for his (relative) reluctance to have disciples. There is an excellent scene in the Monty Python film, *The Life of Brian*. A (reluctant) Brian, the Christ-figure, is besieged by followers demanding that he tell them what to do, tell them how to live; and finally – exasperated – he tells them: 'Think for yourselves!' And this command or prescription is, in effect, the only one that Nietzsche or Zarathustra can, in good conscience, permit themselves: 'Think for yourselves; take responsibility for yourselves; stop passing the buck for yourselves on to an other-worldly commander – He is dead, and the authority of His laws has died with Him; be a law unto yourselves'. Indeed, it is precisely because he fears that his disciples show signs of being too much like Brian's that Zarathustra first leaves or dismisses them:

> I now go away alone, my disciples! You too now go away and be alone! So I will have it.
>
> Truly, I advise you: go away from me and guard yourselves against Zarathustra! And better still: be ashamed of him! Perhaps he has deceived you . . .
>
> One repays a teacher badly if one remains only a pupil. And why, then, should you not pluck at my laurels . . .
>
> You say you believe in Zarathustra? But of what importance is Zarathustra? You are my believers: but of what importance are all believers?
>
> You had not yet sought yourselves when you found me. Thus do all believers; therefore all belief is of so little account.
>
> Now I bid you to lose me and find yourselves; and only when you have all denied me will I return to you.
>
> (Nietzsche, Z I, 'Of the Bestowing Virtue', 3)

Even through the sub-Biblical rhetoric the message is plain: in the wake of the death of God, Zarathustra can only tell his disciples to think for themselves, to find themselves. To the extent that they expect him to command them, they have misunderstood what he has to say.

This should make it clear just *how* fraught Zarathustra's (and implicitly Nietzsche's) relationship to his audience really is. Not only does what he has to say to them require that they break free of some very entrenched habits of thought (if his message is to be audible at all); he also has to say it to them in a way that, if they can be brought to hear it, will not lead them to misunderstand it (in accordance with the same habits of thought) as an externally imposed set of commands. In the next two sections I attempt to spell out Nietzsche's tactics for addressing these problems.

2. The power of art

I have already said a certain amount about Nietzsche's approach, in *Zarathustra,* to the problem of making what he has to say audible: one of his main techniques is to establish and exploit some carefully calculated relationships between his own audience and Zarathustra's, and so between his own audience and himself. But this move is made within a wider context. In *The Birth of Tragedy*, Nietzsche had spoken warmly of the possibility of a *'Socrates who practices music'* (BT 15), by whom he might have meant either a further development of Wagner, or else himself. And this was a thought about which he remained serious. He appeared to think, that is, that philosophy might in some way benefit if it could harness, or express itself through, music – if it could, as it were, sing itself.

To get some sort of idea what Nietzsche might have had in mind here, the following short dialogue from *The Gay Science* is helpful, I think (I quote the passage in full):

> *Music as an advocate.* – 'I am thirsting for a composer,' said an innovator to his disciple, 'who would learn my ideas from me and transpose them into his language; that way I should reach men's ears and hearts far better. With music one can seduce men to every error and every truth: who could refute a tone?' – 'Then you would like to be considered irrefutable?' said his disciple. The innovator replied: 'I wish for the seedling to become a tree. For a doctrine to become a tree, it has to be believed for a good while; for it to be believed it has to be considered irrefutable. The tree needs storms, doubts, worms, and nastiness to reveal the nature and strength of the seedling; let it break if it is not strong enough. But a seedling can only be destroyed – not refuted'. When he had said that, his disciple cried impetuously: 'But I believe in your cause and consider it so strong that I shall say everything, everything that I still have in my mind against it'. The innovator laughed in his heart and wagged a finger at him. 'This kind of discipleship', he said then, 'is the best; but it is also the most dangerous, and not every kind of doctrine can endure it'.
>
> (Nietzsche, GS 106)

Nietzsche's thought here is essentially threefold. First, he suggests that a certain kind of doctrine needs 'to be believed for a good while' before it can pointfully be subjected to rational criticism (to 'storms, doubts, worms, and nastiness'). Second, he suggests that if this condition is not met, the doctrine 'can only be destroyed – not refuted'. And third, he suggests that the condition might more easily be met if the doctrine were to be transposed into music.

We can make some sense of the first two of these points if we refer back to the madman's experience when he tries to persuade his audience that the death of God changes everything. The madman, we may suppose, has, like Nietzsche, mulled over the meaning of the death of God deeply, and for a good while; he has gradually come to realise just how *much* is tied up with belief in God, and so how much is cast adrift once God is dead – 'The illumination and the colour of all things have changed' (GS 152).[10] In the madman, as one might put it, the doctrine – that God is dead – has become a 'tree': it has spread its roots down and its branches up. For his audience, by contrast, the doctrine is merely a 'seedling': it has not been lived with or thought through. And their immediate response to the madman – namely, laughter and silly suggestions ('Has [God] got lost? asked one. Did he lose his way like a child? asked another. Or is he hiding? Is he afraid of us? Has he gone on a voyage? Emigrated? – Thus they yelled and laughed' [GS 125]) – is not a refutation of the madman's doctrine, but simply an attempt to destroy it, to make it go away. They are in no position to refute it, precisely because they are in no position to take it seriously *as* a doctrine; and in order for *that* to be possible, the doctrine would have to become a 'tree' for them; but they have destroyed the 'seedling'.

These first two points, then, are a recasting of what I have called the problem of audibility: the audience rejects the 'seedling' and so never even hears the 'tree'. The third point, however, proposes a measure that is supposed, as it were, to by-pass the seedling-stage altogether: the transposition of the doctrine into music. If this could be made to work, Nietzsche suggests, the doctrine 'should reach men's ears and hearts far better. With music one can seduce men to every error and every truth.' The *effect* that Nietzsche is envisaging here, I take it, is that of showing an audience how, once the roots of the doctrine have spread down and its branches have spread up, the 'illumination and the colour of all things' can be seen to 'have changed'; and I take it that the *means* to that end is, quite directly, to show the audience the world *in* its new colours and illumination. Thus it is through art – or, more precisely, music[11] – that the full weight and significance of the doctrine is to be imparted, and is to be imparted, moreover, without the audience's having had the chance to scupper the whole enterprise at the seedling-stage (although they may of course *then* subject the 'tree' to 'storms, doubts, worms, and nastiness').

Nietzsche's doctrine – that the death of God changes everything – is the same as the madman's; as indeed is Zarathustra's. It is, therefore, exactly the sort of doctrine that he regards as vulnerable to early destruction, rather than refutation. Part of Nietzsche's purpose, then, in writing *Zarathustra* (and he claims that 'the whole of *Zarathustra* may be reckoned as music' [EH Zarathustra 1]) is to try to exploit the power of art to 'reach men's ears and hearts' in a peculiarly direct way, to try to get his message past his audience's ingrained tendency to reject what he is saying before they have so much as begun to understand it.

A related theme is pursued in *Zarathustra* itself: 'Of all writings', the prophet says, 'I love only that which is written with blood. Write with blood: and you will discover that blood is spirit.' He remarks that 'It is not an easy thing to understand unfamiliar blood', before making it a little clearer, perhaps, what might be meant by 'blood' in this context:

> He who writes in blood and aphorisms does not want to be read, he wants to be learned by heart.
>
> In the mountains the shortest route is from peak to peak, but for that you must have long legs. Aphorisms should be peaks, and those to whom they are spoken should be big and tall of stature.
>
> (Nietzsche, Z I, 'Of Reading and Writing')

The connection of 'blood' to 'spirit', on the one hand, and to 'aphorisms' on the other, suggests that to 'write with blood' is to write out of what is most essential in oneself, but to concentrate and encapsulate what one writes into the most succinct (and pregnant) form possible. In this much, writing with 'blood' sounds rather like writing poetry. And this impression is strengthened by Zarathustra's claim that such a writer wants – as poets perhaps want – 'to be learned by heart' and not just 'to be read'.

This last point is crucial. Learning by heart is not a critical process, not an evaluative process. It is, rather, an activity through which something is allowed to take up residence in one's mind, as it were, and to bed-in there. Once it has been taken in, it can be mulled over, reflected upon, and its connections to other items in one's mental furniture – including items derived from the same source (other aphorisms, other 'peaks') – can be explored or can gradually emerge, often not at a fully conscious level. In this way, to all intents and purposes, something learned by heart has a chance of becoming one of Nietzsche's 'trees', something with well-developed roots and branches; and it has the chance to become that *without*, as a 'seedling' is, being vulnerable to peremptory destruction or rejection at the outset (once it has been learned it has, after all, been *learned*).[12] So here again we find Nietzsche (this time in the person of Zarathustra, and with a rather more hard-working audience in mind) imagining how the resources of art might be deployed to get a 'doctrine' across – an art that, like *Zarathustra* itself, consists of aphorisms, and perhaps of poetry. We can conclude, then, given the kind of para-cognitive power that Nietzsche attributes to art, that *Zarathustra*'s being, or being intended to be, a work of art is a central part of Nietzsche's strategy for making himself heard.[13] He wants to turn himself into an 'artistic Socrates' (BT 14).

3. Zarathustra as exemplar

The second problem that Nietzsche has come to recognise that he faces in reaching his audience is the problem of being understood to be recommending something, rather than commanding something. And indeed – as I have already said – he dramatises that difficulty in *Zarathustra*. But this dramatisation is, again, part of a wider overall strategy.

In each of the previous two chapters I have given some space to the connection that Nietzsche draws between art and exemplarity, and, specifically, to his claim – made in both *Human, All Too Human* and *The Gay Science* – that it is part of the value of art that it can present exemplary figures for our edification or improvement. It is therefore natural to suppose that Nietzsche intended the figure of Zarathustra to be, in some way, exemplary – indeed it would be strange to suppose anything else. And this links directly to the issue of recommending rather than commanding, of encouraging an audience to think for itself rather than telling it what to think. Recall Nietzsche's remark that artists 'have taught us to esteem the hero that is concealed in everyday characters' and so 'have taught us the art of viewing ourselves as heroes' (GS 78); recall, too, his (anti-Stalinist) insistence that those who learn from an exemplar 'in a true, that is to say life-enhancing sense' transform 'what they have learned into a more elevated practice' (UM II.2). The direction in which these observations point is clear: one learns from an exemplar not by becoming a slavish imitator, but by seeing the relevance of the example to one's *own* life, and by living a different (and ideally 'more elevated') life as a consequence. As Zarathustra himself puts it, 'One repays a teacher badly if one remains only a pupil'.

To offer or portray an exemplar, then – as those who make what I have called 'monumental' art do[14] – is to provide an *occasion* for an audience to reflect upon itself (by comparing itself to the exemplary figure with which it has been presented) and then, at least potentially, to live differently, or to think about itself differently, as a result. But whether or not an audience in fact does do this is a matter that lies wholly in its *'own discretion'*; it is not something that the exemplar, or the person offering the exemplar, can impose upon it 'from without'.[15] The offering of exemplars, therefore, lines up firmly on the recommending side of the distinction between recommending and commanding – and so, in consequence, falls naturally into just the sort of territory that Nietzsche needs to occupy if he is to pursue his project within the constraints that concern him. It is therefore wholly understandable and appropriate that, having recognised this, Nietzsche should have decided himself to produce a work of 'monumental' art – should have decided, that is, to write *Zarathustra*.[16]

So what kind of exemplar is Zarathustra? Or, to put the question slightly differently, what is it, exactly, that Zarathustra exemplifies?

At a rather general level, he might be taken to exemplify an increasingly sophisticated understanding of the sorts of relations that are proper between a prophet who can only recommend and his audience. But this, surely, is too general-purpose to be of any real interest, while also being, in one way, absurdly over-specific: how many non-commanding, non-prescribing prophets do we really need? Much more promising – as well as more obvious – is the thought that Zarathustra exemplifies a particular kind of triumph over himself, the kind of triumph that Nietzsche calls 'self-overcoming'. This, after all, is where the meat of what passes for the 'action' in *Zarathustra* is to be found, as well as most of the drama. So what does Zarathustra's achievement consist in? It consists – officially, at any rate – in his finally finding a way of celebrating life after the death of God, in his arriving at an exalted form of affirmation that is nevertheless rooted in an open-eyed acknowledgement of the profound, and perhaps horrifying, implications of living, not only without God, but without his 'shadow' either. And this, we are told, he achieves when he affirms the thought of 'eternal recurrence'.

4. Eternal recurrence

In *Zarathustra*, the doctrine of eternal recurrence is described as follows: 'The complex of causes in which I am entangled will recur – it will create me again! ... I shall return, with this sun, with this earth, with this eagle ... – *not* to a new life or a better life or a similar life' but 'to this identical and self-same life, in the greatest things and the smallest' (Z III, 'The Convalescent', 2). This description is reasonably clear, but it doesn't bring out the sense in which it is the *thought* of eternal recurrence (rather than the putative fact of it, say) that is the important thing. It doesn't bring out, in other words, the sense in which the thought of eternal recurrence constitutes a kind of test. This emerges much more clearly from Nietzsche's first statement of the doctrine, given in Book IV of *The Gay Science*.[17] The passage must be quoted in its entirety:

> *The greatest weight.* – What, if some day or night a demon were to steal after you into your loneliest loneliness and say to you: 'This life

as you now live it and have lived it, you will have to live once more and innumerable times more; and there will be nothing new in it, but every pain and every joy, and every thought and sigh and everything unutterably small or great in your life will have to return to you, all in the same succession and sequence – even this spider and this moonlight between the trees, and even this moment and I myself. The eternal hourglass of existence is turned upside down again and again, and you with it, a speck of dust!' Would you not throw yourself down and gnash your teeth and curse the demon who spoke thus? Or have you once experienced a tremendous moment when you would have answered him: 'You are a god and never have I heard anything more divine.' If this thought gained possession of you, it would change you as you are or perhaps crush you. The question in each and every thing, 'Do you desire this once more and innumerable times more?' would lie upon your actions as the greatest weight. Or how well disposed would you have to become to yourself and to life *to crave nothing more fervently* than this ultimate confirmation and seal?

(Nietzsche, GS 341)

It is clear from this that the thought of eternal recurrence is indeed being proposed as a test of some kind, as a thought experiment that will somehow distinguish between different sorts of people. It is *not* being offered as a cosmological hypothesis about the nature of the universe (Nietzsche did toy with eternal recurrence as a physical theory in his notebooks, but wisely chose not to enter it under that head in any of his published works). So the thought of eternal recurrence is a thought experiment designed to test something. And one passes the test, it seems, if one can experience the thought as maximally welcome; one fails if one falls to the floor and starts gnashing one's teeth.

The context of the test is provided, as I have already said, by the death of God. That event, once fully acknowledged, closes the door on the kinds of comforts and consolations that mankind has been accustomed to living with. It therefore also poses a challenge: can we find a way of celebrating life, of learning how to value a 'deified' world, without taking refuge in the dead God's 'shadow'? To be able to say 'Yes' to the demon, Nietzsche implies, is to have succeeded in this – it is to have become 'well disposed' to oneself and to life *as they really are*. If one answers the demon 'No', on the other hand, then one must either take refuge in the dead God's 'shadow', or else – presumably – destroy oneself.

Or so at least Nietzsche implies. There is no doubt that the rhetorical effect of the passage is sufficiently powerful to make one almost believe him: one can almost feel oneself being torn between the 'Yes' and the 'No' as one reads it. But then, when one sits back and reflects, things begin to look rather different. Indeed, on reflection, it seems clear that the test that Nietzsche proposes simply couldn't be worth taking: the only proper response to the demon, surely, is a shrug of the shoulders. If my life is to be repeated infinitely in all its details, then those details include my ignorance of the fact that my life is to be repeated infinitely – I can't, as it were, smuggle memories from one cycle to the next. And if the demon is coming to me *now*, he has presumably also been to me at precisely the same point of my life innumerable times before – and what difference has *that* made? If I passed the test I passed, if I failed I failed, and I'll go on doing whichever I did infinitely many more times, without it changing a thing. The thought of eternal recurrence, then, should be a matter of the deepest indifference.[18] Why *care*?

This difficulty with Nietzsche's thought experiment has been very widely noticed, and all sorts of attempts have been made to turn it into something that has bite (including, desperately enough, the suggestion that Nietzsche's test can only be understood properly when read carelessly, so that one construes it as meaning the eternal recurrence of the same-only-slightly-different). None of these attempts has been successful, in my view, and I won't be trying to add to their number here.[19] What I want to do instead is try to understand why, despite the obviousness of the deficiencies that his rhetoric at first conceals, Nietzsche thought the thought of eternal recurrence worth having in the first place. What sort of job was it meant to do? What sort of gap was it meant to fill? If we can answer those questions, I suggest, we may arrive at a better understanding of what Nietzsche's – and perhaps Zarathustra's – 'greatest weight' really was.

Eternal recurrence, as we have seen, is a thought that arises for Nietzsche in the context of the death of God; and for present purposes it is best approached in the context of the death of the specifically Christian God. Christianity, Nietzsche tells us in *Daybreak*, had provided mankind with 'a universally recognised *goal*', with something to aim for that would give life meaning – namely, salvation. In *that* context one had a reason for taking one's decisions exceedingly seriously: the fate of one's soul might depend upon it. But, with the death of God, that goes. Indeed, it becomes an open question whether it matters *at all* what you decide to do – and more than that: if, with the departure of God, the accustomed meaning and therefore the accustomed value of life depart too, it becomes an open question whether life is so much as worth living at all. So the death of God leaves an almost incalculable vacuum behind it. Why, now, does it matter what I decide to do, what I aim for?

Considered temporally, the death of God leaves three interrelated gaps unplugged: the meaning of the future, the meaning of the past, and the meaning – above all – of the present. For the Christian, the future is the site of infinite hope: after death, he can hope to enjoy eternal bliss – and this future is the object of all his strivings. The past, on the other hand, where the sins that he has committed currently languish, will, if he is saved, be wiped clean: God will forgive him, and his past will, in effect, have been erased. This attitude to the past, as erasable in a future of infinite hope, lends to the Christian's *present* the greatest possible significance. What he decides to do now may influence decisively his prospects of future salvation. Moreover, what he decides to do now is not only destined to become a part of his potentially erasable past but is also, if he decides well and so improves his chances of securing an infinitely desirable future, a contribution to the future erasure of whatever there is in his past to lament or regret. The Christian's present, then, because it works on *both* the past and the future, is a limitlessly meaningful site of potentially redemptive action.

The linchpin in all of this, plainly enough, is the Christian's infinitely meaningful future. Take that away, and the prospect of erasing the past disappears. And in the absence of an all-redeeming future to aim for, the present, too, is deprived of its redemptive significance. The death of God – of *that* kind of future promise – seems to rob existence of its meaning and point, most decisively in robbing the present (and we do after all live in the present) of its gravity. Why, now, does it matter what I decide to do? What is the meaning (to put it in suitably Nietzschean terms) of my *will*?

And this, it seems to me, is what Nietzsche takes to be his problem: he wants to invest time – the dimension within which the will has its being – with an *immanent* significance, with a non-transcendent meaning: he wants to make the present *matter* again. Indeed his problem is – quite literally – 'the unbearable lightness of being'[20] (in the present), of living without other-worldly guarantees. Remember what Nietzsche claims: that the thought of eternal recurrence should 'lie upon your actions as the greatest weight' – that the thought of eternal recurrence should, in other words, operate as a this-worldly replacement for Christianity which, in a non-transcendent way, will make the present heavy with significance now as the present *was* heavy with significance for the Christian. So how are the mechanics of eternal recurrence supposed to be able to do this?

The present, one imagines, is meant to acquire weight through pure repetition. What happens once only is unique, singular – its significance is exhausted in its happening, and it goes off to join the past. If the present can be made to happen infinitely often, by contrast, its character as pure happening is never over and done with, and so its significance is, in that sense, never exhausted: the significance of what I will *now*, that is, is never quite worked through. If things happen only once, they are over once and for all – they go and join the past. And the past, of course, is beyond the influence of my will entirely. That this is close to the heart of the matter is something that Zarathustra, when *he* is about to grapple with the test, makes very clear:

> [W]hen my eye flees from the present to the past, it always discovers the same thing: fragments and limbs and dreadful chances – but no men!
>
> The present and past upon the earth – alas! my friends – that is *my* most intolerable burden . . .
>
> To redeem the past and to transform every 'It was' into an 'I wanted it thus!' – that alone do I call redemption! . . .
>
> 'It was': that is what the will's teeth-gnashing and most lonely affliction is called. Powerless against that which has been done, the will is an angry spectator of all things past.

> The will cannot will backwards; that it cannot break time and time's desire – that is the will's most lonely affliction . . .
>
> It is sullenly wrathful that time does not run back; 'That which was' – that is what the stone which it cannot roll away is called.
>
> (Nietzsche, Z II, 'Of redemption')

The past, then, is a great weight – a stone – which, because it eludes the influence of the will, is incapable of lending the will significance (the will gets its point from what it can do). The Christian's past wasn't like this: its weight *could* be shifted by acting now in such a way as to secure the future erasure of all that has been. So how to make the past subject to the will again? Eternal recurrence, thinks Nietzsche: because the demon asks you to affirm *everything* – past as well as present – you are, as it were, being given a second bite at the cherry. The past was once present, and was fleetingly but meaninglessly available to the will then. But in suggesting that the past may unfold again infinitely often in the future, and in inviting you to say 'Yes: I want it thus!' – i.e. Yes I'd like it all again *and* Yes I'd like exactly *those* things again – you seem, in effect, to be given the opportunity to will backwards, i.e. to exercise your will on the future recurrence of the past. You can't actually change anything in the past – you can't roll away the stone. But you can at least recuperate the stone as something you have *chosen*.

So that covers the present and the past. The future is now easy. First, since the future will one day be present it can be seen as prospectively weighty *now* since it, like every present, is destined to have a significance which can never be finally exhausted. And second, because the future, having been present, will become past, it is, as prospectively past, brought *permanently* within the ambit of the will – as something which one can decide *now* to say 'Yes' to, to choose. And of course the capacity thus to bring both future and past within the ambit of the will *now* adds precisely the sort of significance to the present which the Christian had enjoyed before the death of God. How much significance? Well it depends, presumably, on how much recurrence there is. The Christian's kind of significance was infinite: so better make recurrence infinite too. Better, in fact, make it eternal.[21]

So the thought of eternal recurrence, although hopelessly unsatisfactory as a test (for the reasons I have mentioned), seems to be Nietzsche's attempt to invent a this-worldly successor to Christianity – something that will do pretty much the same job as Christianity and will even do it in something like the same way, namely, through the redemption of the present via (a kind of) *weight*. But the question arises: regardless of the coherence or otherwise of eternal recurrence, is it the sort of thing that Nietzsche, given his other commitments, had any business to be proposing? Has it any *real* place in his thought?

5. Art and the love of fate

Book IV of *The Gay Science* opens with Nietzsche's finest expression of *amor fati*, the love of fate – 'I want to learn more and more to see as beautiful what is necessary in things', he says (GS 276) – and it closes with *The greatest weight* (GS 341) and *Incipit tragoedia* (GS 342), the section that reappears more or less unaltered at the beginning of *Zarathustra*. It is therefore reasonable to suppose that Nietzsche regarded the thoughts of eternal recurrence and of *amor fati* as intimately connected to one another – a supposition reinforced by the fact that both reappear in *Zarathustra*.[22] But if Nietzsche *did* regard them in this way, it seems to me that he was mistaken. Indeed, I suggest that the thought of eternal recurrence does nothing but undermine and cheapen the insight – and the inspiration – offered by the thought of *amor fati*.

To love fate is, at the limit, to say 'Yes' to even the most unpalatable necessities of existence. It is, in effect, to have become (genuinely) well disposed to (a naturalised conception of) oneself and life – something that may not, in fact, be possible: one may, as Nietzsche acknowledges, need a measure of art, of falsification, if one is to make life bearable (GS 107). But at the limit, one can see what the connection to eternal recurrence must be meant to be: in affirming the thought that everything will be repeated endlessly, one is necessarily affirming the repetition even of what is unpalatable – one is, in effect, saying 'Yes' to it. And indeed, Zarathustra, not at all unreasonably, reports this as having been his stiffest challenge:

> Alas, man recurs eternally! The little man recurs eternally!
>
> I had seen them both naked, the greatest man and the smallest man: all too similar to one another, even the greatest all too human!
>
> The greatest all too small! – that was my disgust at man! And eternal recurrence even for the smallest! that was my disgust at all existence!
>
> Ah, disgust! Disgust! Disgust!
>
> (Nietzsche, Z III, 'The Convalescent')

But it isn't at all clear that the littleness of 'even the greatest' is, or should be, the end or the worst of the matter. Nietzsche does, after all, insist on *as much honesty as possible* in the face of life after the death of God. And one might have thought that the following facts would be among those that one should be trying to cope with: the future is limitlessly open; the vastness of the future infinitely surpasses the scope of any finite will; the past is past; the past is a dead weight about which nothing can be done; the present and future are destined to become past; the will *cannot* 'break time and time's desire': what is past is done with; the pastness of the past is limitlessly voracious. These, and considerations like them, would appear to be inescapable truths about post-Christian living. And it is facts such as these that the lover of fate is supposed to be able – as far as he can – to say 'Yes' to, is supposed to learn to find as beautiful and to make as beautiful as possible. To simply deny them, wholesale, is surely to misrepresent to oneself the *kind* of fate of which one is to become a lover.

These, however, would appear to be exactly the truths that the thought of eternal recurrence denies. I have suggested that eternal recurrence is Nietzsche's attempt to reinvent the Christian's relation to the present – as not merely the junction of past and future, but as the site of decisive action on both. The Christian can view every present as maximally weighty with redemptive potential: the thinker of eternal recurrence, Nietzsche appears to hope, can, in a supreme moment of affirmation, bring the whole of the past and the whole of the future within the ambit of his will, and so accord to the present a weight which, in its character as transient happening, it entirely lacks. At such a moment – at such a present – the will is in effect to become omnipotent: it is, in effect, to 'break time and time's desire'. Or, to put it another way, the will is suddenly to find itself capable of *transcending* the 'de-deified' world – of step-ping outside of time, and of affirming the present from there. In his efforts to retrieve something of the Christian's relation to time, then, Nietzsche seeks – as the Christian seeks – to make the present transcendent. And in seeking to do that he is as false as he well could be to his own insistence on honesty, on the 'intellectual conscience': he finds himself, in a very blatant way, denying the real character of the fate which, under the sign of *amor fati*, he is committed to loving, to saying 'Yes' to. The thought of eternal recurrence, then, really does just turn out to be one of the dead God's shadows, a place of refuge for a soul that cannot, in the end, quite accept that God is dead. It is, in fact, an exercise in precisely the kind of 'bad intellectual conscience' that Nietzsche criticises in 'ethical teachers', in 'teachers of the purpose of existence' (GS 1).

Nietzsche's (Zarathustra's) greatest weight is not the thought suggested by the demon – it is not the prospect that 'This life as you now live it and have lived it, you will have to live once more and innumerable times more' – but rather has to do with the prospect that the demon might *not* 'steal after' him after all. What Nietzsche craves is something decisive: a test which, if one can but pass it, will somehow reintroduce the kind of comfort and consola-tion – the 'ultimate confirmation and seal' (something that Nietzsche has no business to be offering[23]) – that the death of God has taken away; and which will, as a result, make the burden of having to love fate a little more tolerable. But the real test, it seems to me, if one takes seriously what is best and deepest in Nietzsche's thinking, is to try to love fate without having to invent things like the thought of eternal recurrence (or indeed any *further* test at all).

What are the consequences of the foregoing for an understand-ing of *Zarathustra*? There would appear to be three main things to say. The first is that, to the extent that the falsifications embodied in the thought of eternal recurrence are falsifications that Zarathustra cannot bear to live without, the thought of eternal recurrence constitutes the 'style' that he gives to his 'character' (GS 290).[24] Zarathustra can be seen, that is, to be engaged in a cer-tain form of self-aestheticisation (although not, it has to be said, a notably modest one): and it is in this, if what I argued in section 3 is correct, that his claim to be considered an exemplar principally consists. The second thing to say is that, to the extent that this is what Nietzsche intended – and he surely *did* intend it – he shouldn't have done. Zarathustra exemplifies a style of character who, in his refusal to acknowledge some very fundamental features of the 'course of nature' and 'its conditions' (GS 1), Nietzsche should *not* consider exemplary – and, indeed, should regard as dishonestly attempting to evade precisely the kinds of necessity that a lover of fate should be trying to affirm. And this, I suggest, licenses a fairly negative overall assessment of the achievement that *Zarathustra* represents. It isn't great art (far from it); and it monumentalises a character who is so far from exhibiting a good 'intellectual conscience' that neither Nietzsche nor we should take him for an inspiring model. The figure of Zarathustra is altogether too much over-shadowed by the dead God.[25]

The final thing to say is that, these reservations notwithstanding, *Zarathustra* is indeed a terrific case study. Even if much of its headline news is (in my view) regrettable, its author – considered as a philosopher of art – shows through it, and shows in a very direct way, the kind and scale of significance that he considers art to have, certainly at this stage in his thinking. For in *Zarathustra* Nietzsche gives up doing philosophy, in anything *like* a normal sense, in favour of fiction; and he does so because of philosophical conclusions that he has drawn about what art has the power to *do*, about the capacity of art to invade and to colonize the soul in ways that are, he has come to suspect, simply unavailable to philosophy as ordinarily practised. He returned to (his version of) philosophy immediately afterwards; but the significance that he continued to attach to *Zarathustra* for the remainder of his life indicates that the philosophical conclusions that led him to write it still seemed to him to be good ones, and that, like the 'innovator' of GS 106, he never ceased to hanker after '[m]usic as an advocate'.

5

THE ART OF FREEDOM: AFTER *ZARATHUSTRA*

Whoever knows how seriously my philosophy has pursued the fight
against vengefulness and rancour, even into the doctrine of 'free
will' – the fight against Christianity is merely a special case of this –
will understand why I am making such a point of my own behaviour,
my *instinctive sureness* in practice.

(Nietzsche, *Ecce Homo*, 'Why I Am So Wise')

Introduction

If *Zarathustra* strikes, in many ways, as a failure, then the works
that Nietzsche produced in the final two or three years of his effective life more than make up for it. At least one – *On the Genealogy
of Morals* (1887) – is an out-and-out masterpiece; while the
remainder (*Beyond Good and Evil* [1886], Book V of *The Gay
Science* [1887], *Twilight of the Idols*, *The Anti-Christ*, *The Case of
Wagner* and *Ecce Homo* [all 1888]) are first rate by any standards,
including Nietzsche's own pre-*Zarathustra* standards.[1] Given
which, it may seem strange to be cramming them all into a single
chapter. But the reasons for that are simple: first, the late writings
are of a piece with one another, and so go naturally together; and,

second, Nietzsche's final thoughts about art are scattered throughout those writings, in a way that would make it self-defeating to try to treat them separately.

Nietzsche's chief preoccupation at this period is the critique of Christian or traditional morality, a morality whose values stand in need, he claims, of 're-evaluation'.[2] His reasons for claiming this are the ones that we should by now expect: that God is dead; that his shadow lingers on; and that our moral thinking is conducted in terms that mistake that shadow for part of the fabric of reality. One important effect of this latter state of affairs, Nietzsche holds, is that the *conditional* status of Christian morality is occluded: indeed, 'this morality resists' the thought that there might be other moralities 'with all its power: it says stubbornly and inexorably, "I am morality itself, and nothing besides is morality"' (BGE 202). But this morality *is* conditional, Nietzsche insists:

> Christianity is a system, a consistently thought out and *complete* view of things. If one breaks out of it a fundamental idea, the belief in God, one thereby breaks the whole thing to pieces . . . Christian morality . . . stands or falls with the belief in God
>
> (Nietzsche, TI IX.5)

A significant part of his task, then, is – as it had been throughout the 1880s – to find a way of making this point, and of spelling out its ramifications, that will allow it to have the sort of impact that he is convinced that it should have.

In *Zarathustra*, Nietzsche had tried to exploit the power of art so as to by-pass his readers' resistance and, as it were, implant his thought directly into their heads, hoping that it might take root there. In the post-*Zarathustra* writings, by contrast, Nietzsche's tactic is to reach, not inside his readers' heads, but inside the morality to which they are committed, and to try to show from there that *they themselves* have reasons to doubt the authority of their own morality. The decisive move here, as David Owen has shown (2003), is Nietzsche's connection of the 'intellectual conscience' – of the most rigorous kind of honesty – to Christianity itself, a connection that is first made explicit in Book V of *The Gay*

Science: 'This unconditional will to truth', Nietzsche asks, '– what is it?' And he answers:

> it is still a *metaphysical faith* ... – ... even we seekers after knowledge today, we godless anti-metaphysicians still take our fire, too, from the flame lit by a faith that is thousands of years old, that Christian faith which was also the faith of Plato, that God is the truth, that truth is divine.
>
> (Nietzsche, GS 344)

The 'only' virtue 'left to us' (BGE 227) – our honesty – is thus an explicitly *Christian* virtue; but it is also a virtue that must eventually turn itself back *against* Christianity. Nietzsche claims that:

> Unconditional honest atheism is the awe-inspiring *catastrophe* of two thousand years of training in truthfulness that finally forbids itself the *lie involved in belief in God* ... In this way Christianity *as a dogma* was destroyed by its own morality [i.e. by truthfulness]; in the same way Christianity *as morality* must now perish, too: we stand on the threshold of *this* event.
>
> (Nietzsche, GM III.27)

Nietzsche's thought, in other words, is that Christianity contains within itself the seeds of its own destruction; and that Christian morality, like the Christian God, must now submit to the scrutiny of its own flagship virtue, truthfulness – an encounter that it cannot hope to survive.

His new tactic, then, is to try to dispel the shadow of the dead God *from within*, rather than – as he had done previously – to attack and denounce it from the outside. And it is a brilliant tactic, whose details are both complex and fascinating. Most of those details, however, are not directly relevant to our purposes here, so I don't propose to go into them. Instead, and presupposing the brief outline just given, I propose first to explore Nietzsche's mature position on art in general (sections 1–3), and then to set out some of his final thoughts on art, agency and the self – thoughts first floated in the 1870s but which, in these late works, come together in a strikingly satisfying way.

1. The metaphysical position

Rather little needs to be said about Nietzsche's later metaphysics, since it is essentially the same as that which he had arrived at in the first four books of *The Gay Science* (see Chapter Three). He makes his position plain in the section of *Twilight of the Idols* called 'How the "Real World" at last Became a Myth' (TI IV),[3] where six stages in the 'History of an Error' are recounted. The fourth stage corresponds to his view in *Human, All Too Human*:[4]

> The real world – unattainable? Unattained, at any rate. And if unattained also *unknown*. Consequently also no consolation, no redemption, no duty: how could we have a duty towards something unknown?
>
> (The grey of dawn. First yawnings of reason. Cock-crow of positivism.)
>
> (Nietzsche, TI IV)

The fifth stage is arguably a reflection of his stance in Books I–IV of *The Gay Science*, and represents a development of the fourth:

> The 'real world' – an idea no longer of any use, not even a duty any longer – an idea grown useless, superfluous, *consequently* a refuted idea: let us abolish it!
>
> (Broad daylight; breakfast; return of cheerfulness and *bon sens*; Plato blushes for shame; all free spirits run riot.)
>
> (Nietzsche, TI IV)

And the sixth and final stage, which brings out what is implicit in the fifth, captures his late position: 'We have abolished the real world: what world is left? the apparent world perhaps? . . . But no! *with the real world we have also abolished the apparent world!*' (TI IV). What is left, in short, is just the world – 'this world, *our* world' (GS 344) – shorn of any metaphysical extravagances. As was the case in *The Gay Science*, therefore, art and science – and indeed every kind of human activity – are, metaphysically, on a par with one another.

We might leave it there, were it not for an aspect of Nietzsche's later thought that is a possible source of confusion. In *Beyond*

Good and Evil the term 'Dionysus' makes a come-back (BGE 295), and in *Twilight of the Idols* it is joined by the term 'Apollonian'. In *The Birth of Tragedy*, these terms had at least seemed to be intimately bound up with a metaphysics that posited a very strong distinction between appearance and reality; and their re-emergence now may well prompt the thought that something of the same metaphysics is being reintroduced at the same time. But it is not. However those terms can best be understood in *The Birth of Tragedy*, it is clear in the later writings that Nietzsche intends the 'Dionysian' and the 'Apollonian' to be construed in an exclusively psychological way – as 'forms of intoxication' (TI IX.10) – and that he has no metaphysical views in mind when he uses them.[5]

In his new usage, the 'Dionysian' kind of intoxication is referred to a good deal more often than the 'Apollonian'. Of the latter, we really learn only that it 'alerts above all the eye, so that it acquires power of vision. The painter, the sculptor, the epic poet are visionaries *par excellence*' (TI IX.10). Of the 'Dionysian', by contrast, we hear quite a lot. So, for instance, we are told that: 'The desire for *destruction*, change, and becoming can be an expression of an overflowing energy that is pregnant with future (my term for this is, as is known, "Dionysian")' (GS 370); Dionysus is distinguished by 'his explorer and discoverer courage, his daring honesty, truthfulness, and love of wisdom', as also by his lack of 'shame' (BGE 295); those who 'say *yes* to everything questionable and terrible in existence, they are *Dionysian*' (TI III.6); 'Saying yes to life even in its most strange and intractable problems, the will to life, celebrating its own inexhaustibility by *sacrificing* its highest types – that is what I called *Dionysian*' (TI X.5); 'In the Dionysian state . . . the entire emotional system is alerted and intensified: so that it discharges all its powers of representation, imitation, transfiguration, transmutation . . . conjointly' (TI IX.10); '"the most comprehensive soul, which can run and stray and roam farthest within itself; the most necessary soul that plunges joyously into chance; the soul that, having being, dives into becoming . . . ; the soul that loves itself most, in which all things have their sweep and countersweep and ebb and flood –." *But that is the concept of Dionysus himself*' (EH, 'Zarathustra', 6); and, finally, 'Have I been understood? – *Dionysus versus the Crucified.–*' (EH, 'Why I am a Destiny', 9).

These passages (and there are a good number like them) share more with each other in terms of rhetorical temperature than they very obviously do in terms of content. But we can at least extract a general flavour from them. The 'Dionysian' character is capacious, is alive in every fibre of his being, and takes joy in being himself; he is truthful and yet affirmative in the face of everything that is 'questionable', 'terrible', 'strange' and 'intractable'; he is full to overflowing with the powers and energies of existence. He is, in short, the exact opposite of (Nietzsche's version of) a Christian. He also represents, in these late writings, Nietzsche's ideal creator, his ideal artist.

2. The art of works of art

Works of art, ordinarily so-called, re-acquire some prominence in Nietzsche's work at this period.[6] 'Art is the great stimulus to life' (TI IX.24), he writes; in art there is the *'compulsion'* to 'transform [things] into the perfect' (TI IX.9). It is true that Nietzsche continues to invest considerable significance in an art of the self (of which more later), but he also – as he hadn't, arguably, since *Human, All Too Human* – pays some real attention to actual *works*, to the external embodiments of artistic activity.

The aim of art remains as it had been in the early books of *The Gay Science*, namely, to make existence bearable. The 'strength of a spirit should be measured', Nietzsche says, 'according to how much of the "truth" one could still barely endure – or to put it more clearly, to what degree one would *require* it to be thinned down, shrouded, sweetened, blunted, falsified' (BGE 39). The measure of the strength of a spirit, then, is just how *little* of art, of falsification, it requires. Concomitantly with that, Nietzsche remains firmly committed to the value of the intellectual conscience (regardless of its roots in Christian morality):

> At every step one has to wrestle for truth; one has to surrender for it almost everything to which the heart ... cling[s] otherwise. That requires greatness of soul: the service of truth is the hardest service. What does it mean, after all, to have integrity in matters of the spirit?

> That one is severe against one's heart, . . . that one makes of every
> Yes and No a matter of conscience.
>
> (Nietzsche, AC 50)

And he retains the distinction between the kind of falsifying that is done out of a good intellectual conscience and the kind that is done out of a bad one (see, e.g., GM III.25). So the basic backdrop is familiar.

Some differences in emphasis are noteworthy, however. In *The Gay Science*, the artist's falsifying role was characterised in deliberately modest terms: faced with nature, which is revealed by science to lack 'order, arrangement, form, beauty, wisdom, and whatever other names there are for our aesthetic anthropomorphisms' (GS 109), the artist does not keep his 'eyes from rounding off something and, as it were, finishing the poem' (GS 107). In *Twilight of the Idols*, by contrast, the matter is cast in a quite different register: 'Nature, artistically considered, is no model', Nietzsche says. 'It exaggerates, it distorts, it leaves gaps. Nature is *chance*' (TI IX.7). Artistically considered, that is, nature doesn't merely lack certain aesthetic qualities, it 'exaggerates' and 'distorts' – it gets things *wrong*. The significance of this shift is that it puts the artist's point of view, rather than the scientist's, in the front line: the basic facts remain the same, but the perspective from which they are presented is quite different. And this difference is carried over into Nietzsche's characterisation of artistry, which is now described in much more active terms. In place of the rather passive-sounding business of not keeping one's 'eyes from rounding off something', Nietzsche now invites us to think of artistry as 'intoxication', as springing from a 'feeling of plenitude and increased energy':

> From out of this feeling one gives to things, one *compels* them to take, one rapes them – one calls this procedure *idealizing*. Let us get rid of a prejudice here: idealization does *not* consist, as is commonly believed, in a subtracting or deducting of the petty and secondary. Instead, what is decisive is a tremendous drive to *bring out* the principal traits, so that the others disappear in the process.
>
> (Nietzsche, TI IX.8)

So, again, while the facts remain essentially the same, they are presented from a vantage point for which the observation that artistry is, above all, a form of *activity* – a (perhaps violent) kind of *doing* – is fundamental.[7]

Part of the reason for this change of emphasis lies in a parallel shift in Nietzsche's understanding of human motivation. At least from the time of writing *Daybreak*, he had, at any rate officially, regarded the 'drives' and 'instincts' of individual human beings as essential to any such understanding;[8] and yet, at the same time, he had tended to explain significant developments in human living and behaviour in rather passive terms, usually concerning 'the preservation of the species' (GS 1). But in the late works, although we do still hear a fair amount about 'the preservation of the species', we begin also to hear a good deal more in the following vein: 'A living thing seeks above all to *discharge* its strength', he says; 'self-preservation is only one of the indirect and most frequent *results*' of this (BGE 13). However,

> The now prevalent instinct and taste . . . would rather be reconciled to the absolute fortuitousness, even the mechanistic senselessness of all events than to the theory that in all events a *will to power* is operating . . . – to the detriment of life, as goes without saying, since it has robbed it of a fundamental concept, that of *activity*. Under the influence of the above-mentioned idiosyncrasy, one places instead 'adaptation' in the foreground, that is to say, an activity of the second rank, a mere reactivity . . . [Thus] one overlooks the essential priority of the spontaneous, aggressive, expansive, form-giving forces that give new interpretations and directions, although 'adaptation' follows only after this.
>
> (Nietzsche, GM II.12)

And increasingly, Nietzsche speaks of the *'instinct for freedom'* (GM II.17), of the 'instinct' for 'self-affirmation' (GM I.13), of the 'instinct' for *'life'* (TI IX.24) – and assigns to these a kind of explanatory primacy that he had not done previously (or certainly had not done as consistently). So again, there is a shift from a passive voice to an active voice, from a quasi-spectatorial standpoint to a standpoint that is, as it were, in the thick of the action.

This adjustment of perspective has two main consequences for Nietzsche's philosophy of art. The first is expressed through a critique of Kant's and Schopenhauer's notion that aesthetic experience should be *disinterested*. For Kant, such disinterestedness – the suspension of one's ordinary worldly desires and preoccupations – is a constituent of aesthetic experience; for Schopenhauer, disinterestedness is at least as importantly a *result* of aesthetic experience, an experience yielding a 'Sabbath of the penal servitude of willing'. To these accounts Nietzsche opposes Stendhal – 'a genuine "spectator" and artist' – 'who once called the beautiful *une promesse de bonheur* [a promise of happiness]'. For Stendhal, that is, 'the fact seems to be precisely that the beautiful *arouses the will* ("interestedness")', rather than, as Kant would have it, giving us 'pleasure without interest',[9] or, as Schopenhauer would have it, delivering us 'from the vile urgency of the will' (1969: 1: 196). Nietzsche clearly prefers Stendhal's conception, and attributes its superiority to Stendhal's having had 'refined first-hand experience' of the beautiful – 'as a great *personal* fact and experience, as an abundance of vivid authentic experiences, desires, surprises, and delights in the realm of the beautiful'. Stendhal's superiority, in other words, is a function of his being an *artist*, one who envisages 'the aesthetic problem from the point of view of the artist' rather than of 'the "spectator"', and so who knows at 'first-hand' what 'idealization' really involves and amounts to. Not for him, then, the Kantian claim 'that, under the spell of beauty, one can *even* view undraped female statues "without interest"', or the Schopenhauerian claim that beauty 'counteracts *sexual* "interestedness"', like lupulin and camphor'. No, for Stendhal beauty is a 'promise of happiness': it *'arouses the will'* (GM III.6).

Nietzsche is insistent on this theme, and even enlists Plato to the cause. Noting again that Schopenhauer values beauty 'especially as redeemer from the "focus of the will", from sexuality – in beauty he sees the procreative impulse *denied* . . . Singular saint!', Nietzsche asks: '*To what end* is there beauty at all in the sounds, colours, odours, rhythmic movements of nature? what *makes* beauty *appear?*'. And the answer he gives – with Plato's backing – is 'that all beauty incites to procreation – . . . precisely this is the *proprium* of its effect, from the most sensual regions up into the most spiritual . . . ' (TI IX.22).[10] What is fundamentally wrong with the aesthetics of Kant and Schopenhauer, then, is the misconstruction of the engagement with beauty as residing in a quite particular form of passivity ('disinterestedness') – the denial, in short, that that engagement is not only essentially *active* and wilful, but, indeed, that it derives from 'an erotic whirl' (TI IX.23).

The second consequence of Nietzsche's shift of emphasis is directly connected to this. He considers the doctrine of art for art's sake (*'l'art pour l'art'*), and asks:

> what does all art do? does it not praise? does it not glorify? does it not select? does it not highlight? By doing all this it *strengthens* or *weakens* certain valuations . . . Is this no more than incidental? an accident? Something in which the instinct of the artist has no part whatever? Or is it not rather the prerequisite for the artist's being an artist at all . . . Is his basic instinct directed towards art, or is it not rather directed towards the meaning of art, which is *life*? towards a *desideratum of life*? – Art is the great stimulus to life: how could it be thought purposeless, aimless, *l'art pour l'art*?
>
> (Nietzsche, TI IX.24)

In part this passage recapitulates Nietzsche's earlier account of 'idealization'; in part, too, it underlines the essential 'interestedness' of aesthetic experience. But it also draws the artist himself more fully into the picture, and portrays his activity in terms of 'instinct' – indeed in terms of the *sublimation* of instinct: 'For art to exist', Nietzsche claims, intoxication

> must first have heightened the excitability of the entire machine: no art results before that happens. All kinds of intoxication, however different their origin, have the power to do this: above all, the intoxication of sexual excitement, the oldest and most primitive form of intoxication. Likewise the intoxication that comes in the train of all great desires, all strong emotions; the intoxication of feasting, of contest, of the brave deed, of victory . . . ; the intoxication of cruelty; intoxication in destruction . . . ; finally the intoxication of the will, the intoxication of an over-loaded and distended will.
>
> (Nietzsche, TI IX.8)

The artist is not merely active, then; he is not merely given to something more energetic-sounding than rounding things off. He is, rather, a cauldron of (more or less thoroughly) sublimated desires that demand release – he is a 'living thing' who 'seeks above all to *discharge*' his 'strength'.

From one point of view, this new account of artistic creativity can be regarded simply as a supplement – perhaps as a useful, original supplement – to Nietzsche's general account of 'the art of works of art' (HH II.174). From another point of view, however, what Nietzsche is now saying threatens to set up a tension between two kinds of need that art might be required to answer to. On the one hand, there is the need to 'finish the poem' modestly, in line with the demands of the intellectual conscience. On the other hand, there is the (artist's) need to '*discharge* . . . strength'. Both can be seen as a matter of making existence bearable: the former takes the edges off the world, the latter allows the artist release. But they also threaten to pull in different directions. Specifically, the second sort of need stands in no necessary relation *whatever* to the demands of honesty, and so may be satisfied in ways that outrage, or that should outrage, the intellectual conscience. This is not, of course, in itself, an objection to Nietzsche's position. An account of the nature of artistic creativity is stronger rather than otherwise for being able to encompass, not only great art, but also art that might be considered bad or outrageous; and we will see in the next section how Nietzsche exploits this fact. But there is nevertheless a danger that, having insisted on the absolute priority in aesthetics of 'the point of view of the artist', Nietzsche may find himself tempted to privilege the second kind of need – the artist's need for the discharge of 'strength', with or without honesty – over the first kind of need, and to do so in a similarly absolute way. And this – as we will also see in the next section – is a temptation that Nietzsche cannot, in the end, quite resist.

3. Romanticism

In a well-known section of the final book of *The Gay Science*, Nietzsche announces that: 'Regarding all aesthetic values I now avail myself of this main distinction: I ask in every instance, "is it hunger or super-abundance that has here become creative?"' (GS 370). And he doesn't only ask this question with respect to aesthetic values: elsewhere, he attributes the values of 'noble morality' to a 'triumphant Yes said to *oneself* – it is self-affirmation, self-glorification of life . . . "its heart is too full"' (CW, Epilogue), while tracing those of 'slave' or Christian morality to hunger, to 'the *ressentiment* of natures that are denied the true reaction, that of deeds, and compensate themselves with an imaginary revenge'; slave morality's 'action is fundamentally reaction' (GM I.10). Broadly speaking, Nietzsche regards the values – whether aesthetic or moral – of 'super-abundance' as 'Dionysian', and contrasts them with those of 'hunger', which he takes to be symptomatic of an essentially *re*active, impoverished kind of life: and, in the aesthetic case, he aligns these latter values with Romanticism.[11]

Both the art of 'super-abundance' and the art of 'hunger' answer to particular kinds of need: indeed both 'presuppose sufferers and suffering'. But, Nietzsche claims, 'there are two kinds of sufferers: first, those who suffer from the *over-fullness of life* – they want a Dionysian art . . . – and then those who suffer from the *impoverishment of life*' (GS 370). Romantic art, then, which answers to the second kind of suffering, springs, no less than Dionysian art, from those 'great desires' and 'strong emotions' that, in the creative act, are experienced as forms of 'intoxication'. Romantic art *is* art, in other words, and the Romantic artist *is* a creator: it is just that the desires and emotions that stir him are different from those that stir the Dionysian.[12]

Within this basic dichotomy, however, Nietzsche traces a further distinction. There is art that is prompted by 'the desire for destruction, for change, for future, for *becoming*', on the one hand, and art that is prompted by 'the desire to fix, to immortalise, the desire for *being*', on the other – and he claims that there are Romantic and Dionysian versions of each of these. A Romantic art of '*becoming*' arises, he says, out of 'the hatred of the ill-constituted, disinherited, and underprivileged, who destroy, *must* destroy, because what exists, indeed all existence, all being, outrages and provokes them'. A Romantic art of '*being*', by contrast, expresses 'the tyrannical will of one who suffers deeply' and who 'would like to turn what is most personal, singular, and narrow, the real idiosyncrasy of his suffering, into a binding law . . . – one who, as it were, revenges himself on all things by forcing his own image, the image of his torture, on them, branding them with it'. On the other side, a Dionysian art of *'becoming'* is the 'expression of an over-flowing energy that is pregnant with future', while a Dionysian art of *'being'* is 'prompted, first, by gratitude and love; art with this origin will always be an art of apotheoses . . . , spreading a Homeric light and glory over all things' (GS 370).

It is clear from everything that he says that Nietzsche prefers the Dionysian to the Romantic, in either of their respective forms, and that he grounds that preference in the fullness of life, in the appetite for life, that he detects in the Dionysian. But the 'Dionysian', recall, is supposed to be connected, not only to 'super-abundance', but also to 'daring honesty, truthfulness and love of wisdom'. So we ought to expect that at least part of what makes Romantic art worse than Dionysian art is that (Nietzsche claims or implies that) Romantic art springs from some lack of that, from a version of the bad intellectual conscience, in other words. Can a case for this be made? I think it can be. The Romantic art of *'being'* is said, after all, to derive from a determination to as it were hyper-anthropomorphise: it is not just that the world is to be falsified in accordance with human needs, it is to be falsified by 'branding' it with one individual's 'image, the image of his torture'. The world is, in this much, potentially to be falsified *without regard* for its real nature, for the truth – since there may be all too much in any given person's 'suffering' that is 'singular', 'narrow' and idiosyncratic. And the same is still clearer when it comes to the Romantic art of *'becoming'*: since 'what exists, indeed all existence, . . . outrages and provokes them', Romantic artists are driven to negate, precisely, what is true – that is, to negate *whatever* it is about existence (the world) that constitutes its real character. So it looks plausible, at least, to say that part of what is wrong with Romantic art is that it proceeds from and expresses a bad intellectual conscience.

But what about Dionysian art? How good is *its* conscience? Perhaps, in the case of the art of *'being'*, not too bad. As the 'art of apotheoses', an art that spreads 'a Homeric light and glory over all things', it may be close enough in spirit to what I have called 'monumental' art to pass muster. If the Dionysian art of '*being*' is construed, in other words, as the art of rounding things off so as to bring out what is exemplary in them, then there need be no necessary tension between an art of that sort and the '*good* will to appearance' (GS 107).[13] But – and however that might be – the Dionysian art of '*becoming*' presents a far stickier problem. In section 370 of *The Gay Science* we are told only that the 'desire for *destruction*, change, and becoming' *can* 'be an expression of an overflowing energy that is pregnant with future' – which tells us nothing, except that Nietzsche approves of it when it *is* such an expression. It tells us nothing, that is, about the connection between this sort of Dionysian art and the intellectual conscience. And, when we turn elsewhere for evidence of what that connection might amount to, what we learn is not encouraging.

Much the most intense and revealing discussion of the Dionysian art of '*becoming*' is to be found, not unexpectedly, in *Twilight of the Idols*. First, Nietzsche offers the following thoughts about tragedy: rejecting Schopenhauer's claim that 'the great utility of tragedy' lies in 'its "evoking resignation"', he observes instead that tragic artists communicate a 'state *without* fear in the face of the fearful' – a state of '[c]ourage and freedom of feeling before a powerful enemy, before a sublime calamity, before a problem that arouses dread – this triumphant state is what the tragic artist chooses, what he glorifies' (TI IX.24).[14] And then, in the penultimate section of the book,[15] he elaborates:

> The psychology of the orgiastic as an overflowing feeling of life and strength, where even pain still has the effect of a stimulus, gave me the key to the concept of *tragic* feeling . . . Saying Yes to life even in its strangest and hardest problems, the will to life rejoicing over its own inexhaustibility . . . – *that* is what I called Dionysian, that is what I guessed to be the bridge to the psychology of the *tragic* poet. *Not* in order to be liberated from terror and pity, not in order to purge oneself of a dangerous affect by its vehement discharge – Aristotle understood it that way – but in order to be *oneself* the eternal joy of becoming, beyond all terror and pity – that joy which included even the joy in destroying. And herewith I again touch that point from

which I once went forth: *The Birth of Tragedy* was my first re-evaluation of all values.

(Nietzsche, TI X.5)[16]

It is quite true that this passage has the effect of returning us to
one aspect of Nietzsche's position in *The Birth of Tragedy*: the
tragic experience that Nietzsche now describes is, as Julian Young
notes, an experience of the 'transcendence of individuality'; 'one
loses one's identity as an individual and identifies instead with "the
will to life rejoicing over *its* own inexhaustibility"' (Young's ital-
ics). 'The tragic effect, in short, is, as it was in . . . *The Birth of
Tragedy*', to 'bring one the "metaphysical comfort" of feeling oneself to be at one with the "primal unity", or as Nietzsche says, "the
will to life"' (Young 1992: 136–137). And this amounts, as Young
points out, to something rather different from a courageous
acknowledgement of the truth 'in the face of the fearful'. There is
an immense 'difference of outlook between *The Gay Science* and
Twilight of the Idols'; and one way to bring this out

is to observe that in *Twilight* Dionysian man (or man in the Dionysian
state) has transformed himself into, in Nietzsche's terminology, a
being. The problematic character of our life, that is, its terror and
horror, is . . . attributed by Nietzsche to the fact that the world we
inhabit is a world of . . . *becoming*: being subject to change inexorably
entails, Nietzsche holds, being vulnerable to pain and death. This is
why becoming is the object of our deepest dread, why we yearn
above all for a state, a world of being . . . In *The Gay Science*
Dionysian man is conceived as loving his fate *as* an inhabitant of the
realm of becoming. In *Twilight*, however, in the Dionysian state, one
escapes becoming by transforming oneself, by becoming 'oneself
the eternal joy of becoming'. Dionysian man, in other words, identifies himself with the whole eternal process of becoming and, as
such, achieves immunity to the penalties of being *part* of that flux. He
has, in short, become a *being*. Whatever the merits of achieving
this state, to do so is not to show the courage that is involved in
facing one's habitation of the world of becoming. If one conceives
oneself as identical with the process of becoming . . . , then one's
'freedom of feeling before a powerful enemy, before a sublime

> calamity' ... does not really constitute 'courage' at all. For the
> 'enemy' is not experienced as an enemy.
>
> (Young, 1992: 138–139)

This is a brilliant diagnosis, it seems to me. And it shows with great
clarity how Nietzsche succumbs to precisely the temptation noted
at the end of the previous section: in giving absolute priority to
'the artist's point of view', and so to his need to *'discharge ...
strength'*, the requirement of honesty has gone missing without
trace. Indeed, so completely has it gone missing that we are here
squarely back in the territory, not of making life *'bearable'* by
turning it into 'an aesthetic phenomenon' (GS 107), but of claiming that 'as an *aesthetic phenomenon* ... existence and the world'
are 'eternally *justified'* (BT 5).[17]

The Dionysian art of *'becoming'*, then, to which Nietzsche
accords the highest status of all, represents a travesty of the intellectual conscience. And this fact is made all the more glaring, I
think, when one observes that the principal passage just given in
evidence ends with Nietzsche's invocation of himself as 'the last
disciple of the philosopher Dionysus – I, the teacher of eternal
recurrence' (TI X.5).[18] Here, in other words, Nietzsche is once again
touching ground with a current in his thought that, as I argued in
Chapter Four, is false to everything that is best in him, however
deep-running that current might be. Here – in short – he is again
busily engaged in denying 'the course of nature' and 'its conditions' (GS 1), in denying the 'fate' that he is supposed to be learning how to love; and the upshot of that is that his Dionysian art of
'becoming' emerges, in a very striking way, as a truly excellent
example of precisely the kind of art that Nietzsche labels, and condemns as, 'Romantic'.[19]

In *Twilight of the Idols*, the 'Romanticism' that is diagnosed in
Book V of *The Gay Science* is redescribed as 'decadence' (TI II.11);
and Nietzsche admits that he himself – like all of his contempo-
raries – is a decadent (TI IX.43),[20] which is all well and good. It
doesn't excuse his Dionysianism; but it does at least encourage the
thought that, as a self-acknowledged decadent, he might have
something to offer *against* decadence – perhaps the beginnings of a
remedy for it, constructed as it were from the inside (decadence is

one shape of the shadow of God, after all). And I suggest, and devote the remainder of this chapter to trying to show, that Nietzsche's later thoughts about art, agency and the self can indeed be understood in something like this way.

4. Becoming who you are

The key idea here is that of becoming 'who you are', which Nietzsche had begun to take seriously some years earlier. An aphorism in the 1882 edition of *The Gay Science* reads: '*What does your conscience say?* – "You shall become who you are"' (GS 270); and Nietzsche expands on the thought in a later section called '*Long live physics!*'. It is important, he says, not to take the deliverances of conscience at face value, as if their source somehow guaranteed their truth: 'Your judgement "this is right" has a pre-history in your instincts, likes, dislikes, experiences and lack of experiences'; indeed, 'that you take this or that judgement for the voice of conscience . . . may be due to the fact that you have never thought much about yourself and have simply accepted blindly that what you had been *told* ever since your childhood was right' (GS 335).

What is needed to rectify this '*faith*', he claims, is 'an intellectual conscience', a 'conscience behind your "conscience"'(ibid.) – a determination, precisely, to think about yourself, 'to scrutinize [your] experiences as severely as a scientific experiment – hour after hour, day after day' (GS 319). By these means we can

> become who we are – human beings who are new, unique, . . . who give themselves laws, who create themselves! To that end we must become the best students and discoverers of everything lawful and necessary in the world: we must become *physicists* in order become creators in this sense . . . So, long live physics! And even more so that which *compels* us to turn to physics – our honesty!
>
> (Nietzsche, GS 335)

Thus, it is our 'intellectual conscience', our 'honesty', that both says 'You shall become who you are' and also makes becoming who you are possible.

At one level, Nietzsche's thought here is straightforward. One becomes who one is by getting to know oneself, and by getting to know the conditions under which one operates ('everything lawful and necessary in the world'). One ceases, on the one hand, idly to accept falsehoods about oneself – for instance, that one has an infallible organ of judgement, one's 'conscience', whose deliverances are somehow independent of one's 'instincts, likes, dislikes, experiences' etc. – and one ceases, on the other hand, to accept falsehoods about the world – for instance, that it is governed by 'providential reason and goodness' (GS 277), or that it is somehow organized with human purposes in mind, or indeed with any purpose at all.[21] At this level, then, one becomes who one is by honestly acknowledging, first, that one is essentially just an animal, rather than a creature with supernatural capacities, and, second, that the world in which one has one's being, in which one must act and try to make sense of oneself, is a world without God. We necessarily misunderstand ourselves, Nietzsche holds, if we fail to acknowledge either kind of truth.

But we are more than *merely* animals. Unlike the other animals, we also have a 'second nature',[22] a nature produced by culture. And it is this that is expressed through our practices, including those practices in which various misunderstandings of ourselves are encoded. An animal without a 'second nature' could no more mistake itself for a transmitter of the 'voice of conscience', or for an inhabitant of a divinely ordered world, than it could enter into a contract, form a friendship, or go to war. Our 'second nature' is what makes us 'interesting', as Nietzsche later has it,[23] and the 'experiences' that are rooted there are pre-eminently among those to be subjected to the 'intellectual conscience'. In order to 'become who we are', then, we must be honest with ourselves not merely as pieces of nature, as animals in an undesigned world, but as pieces of 'second nature', as animals whose character and circumstances are significantly constituted by culture.

There are many ways in which we can misunderstand ourselves. We can, as it were, be factually wrong about some matter concerning nature or second nature. Or we can adopt, perhaps unconsciously, a perspective on such matters that systematically occludes or distorts them. Nietzsche is particularly interested in misunderstandings of this latter kind – in habits of thought that have the effect of making whole dimensions of ourselves and of our worldly circumstances obscure to us. The most famous example, of course, is the perspective that Nietzsche diagnoses under the label 'morality'.[24] But that is a diagnosis that advances along several fronts: here, I will focus on just one of these, and attempt to indicate how Nietzsche understands the relation – obscured, he holds, by 'morality' – between our becoming our own 'creators' and our being the 'discoverers of everything lawful and necessary in the world'.

Two passages from *The Gay Science* that we have visited before are helpful here. The first is the one where Nietzsche speaks of the 'great and rare art' of giving '"style" to one's character':

> It is practised by those who survey all the strengths and weaknesses of their nature and then fit them into an artistic plan . . . Here a large mass of second nature has been added; there a piece of original nature has been removed – both times through long practice and daily work at it. Here the ugly that could not be removed is concealed; there it has been reinterpreted and made sublime.
>
> (Nietzsche, GS 290)

For our present purposes, four points are worth making about this passage. First, what Nietzsche is here describing is a form of self-creation, that is, a version of becoming who you are; second, this form of self-creation depends upon self-understanding, upon surveying one's nature and identifying the strengths and weaknesses in it; third, weaknesses or uglinesses are sometimes removable; and fourth, irremovable uglinesses are to be concealed if they cannot be 'reinterpreted' and transformed. The first two points connect this passage directly to our discussion so far: becoming who you are depends upon the exercise of the intellectual conscience. And the remaining two points provide the connection to the second passage:

> I want to learn more and more to see as beautiful what is necessary in things; then I shall be one of those who make things beautiful. *Amor fati*: let that be my love henceforth!
>
> (Nietzsche, GS 276)

The connection comes to this: becoming who you are requires that you distinguish between what is and what is not necessary in things, including yourself (a job for the intellectual conscience). What is not necessary, and is weak or ugly, should be removed. What *is* necessary should, if weak or ugly, either be concealed ('*Looking away* shall be my only negation' [ibid.]) or else 'reinterpreted', so that one learns to see it as beautiful, as a strength.

A distinctive conception of the relation between self-creation and necessity – whether in nature, second nature or circumstance – is implicit in these passages, and it is this that Nietzsche regards as obscured by the perspective of 'morality'. He develops the point explicitly in *Beyond Good and Evil*. 'Morality', he claims, trades on an impossible notion of freedom. It encourages 'the desire to bear the entire and ultimate responsibility for one's actions oneself, and to absolve God, the world, ancestors, chance and society'. It encourages, that is, a quite peculiar conception of autonomy, according to which one is properly self-governing and properly responsible for one's actions only to the extent that what one does is the product of '"freedom of the will" in the superlative metaphysical sense', a freedom that is supposedly operative independently of one's nature, one's second nature or one's circumstances. But this, observes Nietzsche, 'is the best self-contradiction that has been conceived so far'; it involves the desire 'to pull oneself up into existence by the hair, out of the swamps of nothingness'. And – crucially – it encourages one to perceive in every necessity 'something of constraint, need, compulsion to obey, pressure and unfreedom' (BGE 21).

The truth, Nietzsche holds, is quite otherwise. As the self-stylization and the *amor fati* passages make clear, he treats necessities of various kinds as material to be exploited and, where possible, affirmed. Indeed, he treats them as *conditions* of effective action, rather than as impediments to it, and hence as integral to the possibility of freedom, rather than as limits upon it:

> one should recall the compulsion under which every language so far has achieved strength and freedom – the metrical compulsion of rhyme and rhythm. How much trouble the poets and orators . . . have taken . . . – 'submitting abjectly to capricious laws', as anarchists say,

> feeling 'free' . . . But the curious fact is that all there is or has been on
> earth of freedom, subtlety . . . and masterly sureness, . . . in thought
> itself . . . , in the arts just as in ethics, has developed only owing to the
> 'tyranny of such capricious laws'; and in all seriousness, the probabil-
> ity is . . . that this is 'nature' and 'natural' – and *not* that *laisser aller*.
>
> (Nietzsche, BGE 188)

So Nietzsche offers a picture of freedom that roots it explicitly in
the 'tyranny' of 'capricious laws', which is to say, in the necessities
that constitute our second nature.

Only someone who acknowledges the rules of language has the
capacity – the freedom – to communicate in it. Only someone who
acknowledges the laws of chess has the freedom to castle his king,
say. Only someone who acknowledges the norms and courtesies of
conversation has the freedom to engage in one. And so on, for any
human practice at all. To resent such 'necessities' as a threat to
one's '"responsibility"', to one's 'belief in' *oneself*, to one's 'personal right to [one's *own*] merits at any price' would be, quite
simply, to render oneself impotent (BGE 21). Yet it is precisely
such a resentment that 'morality', with its fantasy of freedom in
the 'superlative metaphysical sense', expresses. Nietzsche's point,
then, is that if we are to understand ourselves as actors in the
world as it is, we have to acknowledge that certain necessities are
integral to our agency, to our 'freedom' and 'responsibility'.[25] And
this is a form of self-understanding – a finding of the intellectual
conscience – that the peculiar perspective of 'morality' necessarily
occludes; which is one of the reasons why it stands in the way of
our becoming who we are.

When Nietzsche says, therefore, that we must become 'discoverers of everything lawful and necessary in the world' if we are to
become 'creators' of ourselves, part of what he means is that we
must determine *which* of the circumstances of our existence really
are necessities. Some of these circumstances, for instance 'morality', may appear to be or may present themselves as being necessities,[26] when in fact they are only contingent sources of
self-misunderstanding: such circumstances are uglinesses or weaknesses, and they should be removed. Other of our circumstances
really are necessities. And, of these, some will be ineluctably ugly,

and will have to be concealed or looked away from.²⁷ The remainder, however, are to be understood – perhaps *via* 'reinterpretation' – as conditions of the possibility of agency, of freedom. And it is through the acknowledgement and affirmation of these that the discovery, development and – perhaps – the perfection of one's capacities is to be realized. To the extent that those capacities *are* realized, one has succeeded in becoming who one is.

It is not surprising that Nietzsche should link this process to art and creativity. Artistry is law-like, in the sense that it is possible to go wrong, to make mistakes. Yet the laws against which these mistakes offend often declare themselves only in the moment at which they are breached, indeed *in* the breaching of them. And this is why getting something *right* feels like – is – getting what one was after all along, even when one could not have said in advance precisely what that was. In this way, successful artistry is also a form of self-discovery – it is the discovery, in the lawfulness of one's actions, of the innermost character of one's intentions:

> Every artist knows how far from any feeling of letting himself go his most 'natural' state is – the free ordering, placing . . . , giving form in the moment of 'inspiration' – and how strictly and subtly he obeys thousandfold laws precisely then, laws that precisely on account of their hardness and determination defy all formulation through concepts
>
> (Nietzsche, BGE 188)²⁸

– and this, in turn, is a large part of the reason why Nietzsche so consistently connects self-creation to having one's *own* laws. In becoming who we are, he says, we become 'human beings who are new, unique, incomparable, who give themselves laws, who create themselves!' (GS 335); self-stylists 'enjoy their finest gaiety . . . in being bound by but also perfected under a law of their own' (GS 290); 'the "individual" appears, obliged to give himself laws and to develop his own arts and wiles for self-preservation, self-enhancement, self-redemption' (BGE 262).

So artistry represents a limit case of Nietzsche's understanding of agency.²⁹ Like every kind of agency, artistry is possible only for those who acknowledge necessity as a condition of, rather than as a limit upon, their freedom to act. We misunderstand ourselves if we misunderstand this. But in artistry we also perpetually discover ourselves, as our actions express those 'thousandfold' unformulable laws which are, Nietzsche suggests, most truly our own. We become most fully who we are, as he puts it at one point, when we become the 'poets of our lives' (GS 299).

5. Art and the self

This gives some of the background against which *Ecce Homo* needs to be read, since much of it is devoted to explaining – or perhaps to dramatizing – how Nietzsche himself has become who he is. But Nietzsche does not merely present his life as a work of art; he presents it as a fully achieved work of art, one that exhibits 'masterly sureness' throughout – that shows at every point his *'sureness of instinct* in praxis' (EH, 'Why I Am So Wise', 6).

It is important to bear this latter point in mind, if the text is to stay in its proper focus. It can appear, for instance, that Nietzsche's conception of *amor fati* must have changed since 1882. In *The Gay Science*, as we have seen, *amor fati* involves learning 'to see as beautiful what is necessary in things' (GS 276), which leaves it open just how much *is* necessary in things (an indeterminacy that is vital if self-stylization, for instance, is to remain intelligible). In *Ecce Homo*, by apparent contrast, we read this: 'My formula for human greatness is *amor fati*: that you do not want anything to be different, not forwards, not backwards, not for all eternity. Not just to tolerate necessity ... – but to *love* it' (EH, 'Why I Am So Clever', 10), which may suggest that Nietzsche now regards *everything* as necessary.

But this is misleading. His claim, rather, is that a great human being is one who has learned to see as beautiful every circumstance of his life, has learned to treat every fact about himself and his world as necessary conditions of his freedom to act and to create himself under laws of his own. And *this* achievement may well require that quite a lot that is true of him now has only become true of him because of (unnecessary) things in his life that he has changed – for instance, that he has cast off certain weaknesses or uglinesses that masqueraded as necessities: examples that Nietzsche gives in his own case include ridding himself of the conviction that he is just 'like everyone else', of 'a forgetting of distance' between himself and others, an '"idealism"' (EH, 'Why I Am So Clever', 2). Or perhaps the great human being has altered one set of circumstances in his life so as to accommodate another, as Nietzsche reports himself to have altered his diet and his environs in order to accommodate his physiology (EH, 'Why I Am So Clever', 1,2). Nor does this mean that he must necessarily have cause to regret the *status quo ante*, to want things 'to be different . . . backward'. For he may well understand it as a condition of his having arrived where he is now that he had to overcome things as they were before: 'he uses mishaps to his advantage', Nietzsche says; 'what does not kill him makes him stronger' (EH, 'Why I Am So Wise', 2).

The best way to construe *amor fati* throughout Nietzsche's work, then, is as an ethical attitude towards the world, rather than as a (disguised) metaphysical thesis about how much of the world is necessary. Indeed, the only difference between 1882 and 1888 is that whereas in *The Gay Science* the presentation had been aspirational ('I want to learn more and more . . . '), in *Ecce Homo* the learning-process is presented as complete. He now (he claims) affirms *all* of his worldly circumstances: '*How could I not be grateful to my whole life?*' (EH, 'On this perfect day');[30] and, in this limiting case, he achieves 'masterly sureness' in every aspect of his existence – he has '*learned*', as Nietzsche elsewhere puts it, '*to love*' himself (GS 334).[31]

These points bring out another strong continuity between the work of the earlier and the later 1880s, a kind of naturalized theodicy that Nietzsche first airs in the section of *The Gay Science* that immediately follows the *amor fati* passage:

> *Personal providence.*– There is a certain high point in life: once we have reached that, we are, for all our freedom, once more in the greatest danger of spiritual unfreedom . . . For it is only now that the idea of a personal providence confronts us . . . – now that we can see how palpably always everything that happens to us turns out for the best . . . Whatever it is, bad weather or good, the loss of a friend, sickness . . .

> – ... it proves to be something that 'must not be missing'; it has a profound significance and use precisely for *us*.
>
> (Nietzsche, GS 277)

The 'high point', clearly enough, is attained when one has learned to affirm all of one's worldly circumstances, when one's *amor fati* is complete; and the 'danger of spiritual unfreedom' is posed by the temptation to believe that there must, as an explanation for this, be 'some petty deity who is full of care and personally knows every little hair on our head', a supernatural source of 'providential reason and goodness' in our lives (GS 277). The danger, in other words, is that one will start to misunderstand oneself (to become who one isn't) by believing that it is a condition of one's freedom that there be a God who ensures that all is for the best, in this, the best of all possible worlds.

The truth, of course, in Nietzsche's view, is that the condition of one's freedom is not a benevolent God, but nature, second nature, and one's attitude to these. If we are 'strong enough', he says, then 'everything *has to* turn out best' for us (EH, 'Why I Am So Wise', 2), for which the credit should be given, not to anything supernatural, but to 'our own practical and theoretical skill in interpreting and arranging events' (GS 277). As an example, Nietzsche describes how his illness has had 'a profound significance and use precisely for' *him*: sickness can

> be an energetic *stimulus* to life ... This is, in fact, how that long period of illness looks to me *now*. I discovered life anew, ... myself included, I tasted all good and even small things in ways that other people cannot do so easily ... [Indeed,] the years of my lowest vitality were the ones when I *stopped* being a pessimist.
>
> (Nietzsche, EH, 'Why I Am So Wise', 2)

Nietzsche's illness has turned out to be for the best, to be one of those things that '"must not be missing"'.

So if a traditional, more or less Leibnizian, theodicy seeks to show that every apparent evil is a necessary part of God's benevolent grand plan, Nietzsche's naturalized version of it urges us to find a perspective on our circumstances from which even the most grim-seeming of them can be regarded as indispensable *to us*. In place of Leibniz's ambition to redeem the whole world from a God's-eye point of view, that is, Nietzsche's hope is that individual lives might be redeemed from the point of view of those who live them, from a first-person perspective.[32]

This dimension of Nietzsche's thought is largely backward-looking. One is to look back and interpret one's past as having been for the best; but one is to do so from a present whose character – whose rightness – is partly to be constituted by one's success in this very enterprise. Of course, one's past might need a good deal of interpretation in order to bring this off. It is not as if one had been all along the deliberate architect of one's life – indeed, one must *not* be such an architect:

> you [must] not have the slightest idea *what* you are. If you look at it this way, even life's *mistakes* have their own meaning and value . . . [Here, *know thyself*] is the recipe for decline, . . . *misunderstanding* yourself, belittling, narrowing, mediocratizing yourself . . . – the threat that instinct will come to 'understand itself' too early. – In the meantime, the organizing, governing 'idea' keeps growing deep inside, – . . . it slowly leads *back* from out of the side roads and wrong turns, it gets the *individual* qualities and virtues ready [which] will prove to be indispensable as means to the whole . . . Looking at it this way, my life is just fantastic [– the product of] the lengthy, secret work and artistry of my instinct.
>
> (Nietzsche, EH, 'Why I Am So Clever', 9)

To have turned out well, from this point of view, is to be able to interpret one's development as the unconscious unfolding of one's latent potential, as the gradual, invisible piecing-together of a coherent self. And the 'happiness' of such a development lies, as Nietzsche puts it, 'in its fatefulness' (EH, 'Why I Am So Wise', 1).

In *Ecce Homo*, then, Nietzsche presents his life as a species of artistry, in several senses. First, his life as it now is is one that he can affirm in all of its circumstances; he has learned to treat everything about himself and his world as necessary to his freedom to act and to create himself under his own laws. Second, he has interpreted his history in such a way that everything in it is 'for the best', so that his past unfolds like a work of art. And third, he attributes that unfolding to the 'artistry' of his 'instinct', since much that contributed to its course was not (and perhaps could not have been) consciously chosen. In each of these senses, Nietzsche portrays himself as the poet of his life, and hence as one who has become who he is.

So what – in light of this – are we to make of *Ecce Homo*? I suggested in the Introduction to this book that Nietzsche's autobiography is not in any interesting or important way the product of insanity. But it may now seem as if the truth is if anything worse than that – that *Ecce Homo* is actually no more than a self-help manual, of a sort that endorses a peculiarly self-serving variety of positive thinking. It may seem, too, as if the demands of the 'intellectual conscience', upon which I have laid a good deal of weight, have disappeared without trace. One is, it appears, opportunistically to reinterpret one's past in a way that makes it seem providential. And one is to take seriously the thought – the fantasy, surely – that one might regard one's life as a work of art, and oneself as its moment-by-moment creator.

The first thing to say, and as I've already noted, is that Nietzsche remains fully committed at this period to the value of honesty and the intellectual conscience.[33] Sections 50–56 of *The Anti-Christ* contain one of the longest discussions of 'the service of truth' (AC 50) in any of Nietzsche's works, and he summarizes that discussion in *Ecce Homo*: 'How much truth can a spirit *tolerate*, how much truth is it willing to *risk*? This increasingly became the real measure of value for me ... [E]very step forward in knowledge comes from *courage*, from harshness towards yourself' (EH, Preface, 3). These are not the words of a witting fantasist, or of one bent on falsifying his past. Moreover, the positions – such as 'morality' – against which Nietzsche most consistently ranges himself in *Ecce Homo*, and which he labels 'idealism', he regards as 'errors' and as the products of 'cowardice' (ibid.).

But Nietzsche's objection to 'idealism' is not merely that it falsifies the world – by pretending that there is a God, for example, or by pretending that freedom in 'the superlative metaphysical sense' is possible. It is also that 'idealism' devalues the world, by according the highest value to its own inventions, at the world's expense and out of resentment against it – out of a 'deadly hostility to life' (EH, 'Why I Am a Destiny', 8). And this means that Nietzsche's own project also has two dimensions. One is to diagnose the errors of 'idealism'; the other is to suggest how life and the world might still have value for us once we have refused to resort to supernatural or metaphysical remedies. The thoughts canvassed a moment ago are an important part of Nietzsche's attempt to engage with the second of these issues. They are, in effect, an exploration of the intuition, mentioned earlier, that 'As an aesthetic phenomenon existence is still *bearable* for us' (GS 107).

It is true that nothing could correspond to living one's life, from moment to moment, as if it were a work of art. So in this sense, Nietzsche's self-presentation does have the air of fantasy about it. But two points are worth making. The first is that, as I have argued, Nietzsche understands artistry as a limit case of agency in general, a limit at which one is, as it were, perfectly intelligible to oneself. And while it is surely true that that limit is not occupiable indefinitely, it is at least visitable from time to time; and it seems plausible to say that one is better off, by and large, for being closer to it than otherwise. And if this is right, it is hard to see why one might not try to imagine, as Nietzsche does, what it would be like if, *per impossibile*, one could occupy that limit for the whole of the time – if only as a way of dramatizing a regulative ideal. The other point is that the expression of *Ecce Homo* is often hyperbolic. In part, of course, this is just to say that it is exaggerated, and to that extent the present point is the same as the first. But hyperbole is also a means of self-deflation, a form of deliberate over-statement that is meant to be seen through, if not at once then at least pretty quickly. And from this point of view, it is not implausible to read Nietzsche as debunking his aesthetic ideal, as admitting that it is not fully realizable, at the same time as he dramatizes its realization.

So one shouldn't worry about the essential honesty of *Ecce Homo*, I think. Nor is it very troubling to think that it might be taken as a self-help manual, as a promoter of positive thinking. Positive thinking is surely better than the reverse; and, if Nietzsche is right that supernatural or metaphysical remedies are hard to do without, it seems entirely reasonable to suppose that, in their absence, some self-help might be needed. Nor, finally, do the charges of self-servingness and opportunism seem well-directed. Nietzsche is explicitly out to serve the self; he says so repeatedly. And one can pointfully be charged with opportunism only when there are alternatives available to one. Confronted with some grim fact about one's past, one can of course try to forget it; indeed, Nietzsche speaks warmly and often about the value of forgetting.[34] But if that is not possible, it is scarcely opportunistic to try to see it instead as something that '"must not be missing"', that has 'a profound significance and use precisely for *us*'. To refuse to recuperate what one can out of life is to turn one's back on it. And that, according to Nietzsche, is exactly what 'idealists' do.

In my view, the foregoing represents the most valuable strand in Nietzsche's later aesthetics, as well as marking the culmination of a number of themes that had played a distinctive role in his thought since at least the mid-1870s. It is also, I think, a valuable corrective to that other strand in Nietzsche's work – the one that issues in the thought of eternal recurrence, and that finds expression in his notion of the Dionysian art of '*becoming*'. There, the role of art is to supply a (dishonest) fantasy that is to replace a reality that one cannot face – it is, in effect, to hold out the prospect of becoming an impossible (non-)self, a (non-)self that is insulated, as nothing can be insulated, from the very conditions of its own existence. In contrast to this, the art of exemplary agency, the art of becoming 'who one *is*', is, first, relatively modest, second, at least arguably possible, and, third, something that, if it *can* be done, can *only* be done with a good intellectual conscience. In each of these respects, therefore, this latter conception of art is not only preferable to the former, it seems to me, but is also authentically connected to the best and most distinctive of Nietzsche's contributions to philosophy as a whole. *Here*, in other words, is one way in which the shadow of the dead God might, at least potentially, be dispelled from within; and it is for this, surely, that Nietzsche should really have reserved the label 'Dionysian'.

APPENDIX
NIETZSCHE ON WAGNER

As I said in the Introduction, Nietzsche was a philosopher whose aesthetics were driven, to a more or less unique extent, by his actual experience of and obsession with art, Wagner's above all. It is perhaps unsurprising, in light of this, that his philosophy of art has not been terrifically influential. The highly *personal* quality of it, for one thing, limits its portability; and – for another – subsequent philosophical thinking about art has tended to be driven by priorities arising not so much from direct aesthetic experience as from other areas of philosophy, such as metaphysics and the philosophy of mind. And from the perspective of these concerns, Nietzsche's views are likely to seem peripheral at best. One can, of course, detect clear traces of Nietzsche in the aesthetics of, for example, Heidegger and Gadamer, but not (to this reader at least) to any very interesting effect. So if Nietzsche's thoughts about art can be said to have left a legacy behind them, it has not been to philosophical aesthetics. It has, rather, been to two areas much more central to his own concerns: to art itself, and to Wagner criticism. No other philosopher, so far as I am aware, has been translated into music by composers of the calibre of Mahler, Delius and Richard Strauss, for instance;[1] nor have many had so clear an influence upon writers and poets of the stature of D.H. Lawrence, Rilke, Yeats and Thomas Mann, to name but a few. Nietzsche's thought has spoken to artists, it seems, in a peculiarly direct voice; and those especially interested in this dimension of his legacy can do no better than to turn to Erich Heller's wonderful collection of essays, *The Importance of Nietzsche* (1988), which shows very vividly what it was about Nietzsche that so captured the artistic imagination. Here, though, I propose to concentrate on the other dimension – on Nietzsche's legacy to Wagner criticism.

I '"My judgement is *my* judgement"', Nietzsche wrote: 'no one else is easily entitled to it' (BGE 43). This remark encapsulates a major and recurrent theme in Nietzsche's writings about specific artists and works of art.[2] His view, in effect, is that we reveal and define ourselves most ineluctably through how we judge, and above all through how we judge aesthetically. Traditional morality, for example, is to be rejected for many reasons: but a dominant one is that it is (or should be) offensive to our *taste*. '[R]egarding all the moral chatter of some about others', Nietzsche remarks, 'it is time to feel nauseous. Sitting in moral judgement should offend our taste' (GS 335). And the same goes for Christianity: 'What is now decisive against Christianity is our taste, no longer our reasons' (GS 132). We put ourselves on the line whenever we judge *pro* or *con*; but we give ourselves away more thoroughly in our judgements of taste than in any other domain.

So we must expect that Nietzsche's writings on Wagner will tell us at least as much about Nietzsche as they do about Wagner. And Nietzsche himself would surely have agreed: that must have been part of the point, after all, in compiling a book called *Nietzsche contra Wagner* (rather than one called, say, *The Anti-Wagner*). And this point is general. His praise of Bizet, for example, as the composer of 'perfect' music, music which 'approaches lightly, supplely, politely. It is pleasant, it does not *sweat*. "What is good is light; whatever is divine moves on tender feet": first principle of my aesthetics' (CW 1); of Shakespeare – 'that amazing Spanish-Moorish-Saxon synthesis of tastes that would have all but killed an ancient Athenian of Aeschylus's circle with laughter or irritation. But we – accept precisely this wild abundance of colours . . . ; we enjoy him as a superb subtlety of art saved up especially for us'

(BGE 224); of Goethe, 'who fought against the separation of reason, sensibility, feeling, will', who 'disciplined himself to wholeness,' who '*created* himself . . . ' (TI IX.49); of Leonardo – one of 'those magical, incomprehensible, and unfathomable ones . . . , those enigmatic men predestined for victory and seduction', who arise when 'a real mastery and subtlety in waging war against oneself . . . has been inherited or cultivated' (BGE 200); of Raphael, who 'said yes', who '*did* yes', and 'therefore . . . was no Christian' (TI IX.9) – all of these critical celebrations contribute, as one might put it, to the mapping of Nietzsche's soul.

'[W]hat does all art do?', Nietzsche asks: 'does it not praise? does it not glorify? does it not select? does it not highlight? By doing all this it *strengthens* or *weakens* certain valuations' (TI IX.24). And criticism – articulate judgement – does the same. In showing us, through the patterns of his taste, who he *is*, Nietzsche also seeks to strengthen certain valuations, to awaken or to reinforce in his reader a particular sense of the good – and of the bad. For he wants to weaken certain valuations, too. When he attacks Brahms, for example – 'His is the melancholy of incapacity; he does *not* create out of an abundance, he *languishes* for abundance' (CW Second Postscript); or George Sand – 'false, contrived, windy, overblown . . . She wound herself up like a clock – and wrote . . . Cool, like Hugo, like Balzac, like all the Romantics once they started writing!' (TI IX.6); or Schumann, whose 'taste' was 'basically a *small* taste', who was 'a noble tender-heart who wallowed in all sorts of anonymous bliss and woe': 'this Schumann was already a merely *German* event in music, no longer a European one' (BGE 245) – these assaults are intended to weaken the valuations which, according to Nietzsche, the artists themselves were in the business of strengthening and glorifying. And this negative pattern, too, contributes to the mapping of Nietzsche's soul – nowhere more so than in his criticism of Wagner. For in the Wagner writings we have a uniquely fully evolved attempt to weaken the valuations that one particular artist, according to Nietzsche, sought to promote; and so – since '[his] judgement is [*his*] judgement' – we have a uniquely detailed portrait of Nietzsche himself, the general flavour of which should, I hope, emerge over the following pages.

II Some background may be helpful. The musical and dramatic explorations of Richard Wagner (1813–83) – from *Der Fliegende Holländer* (1841), his first fully characteristic work, through *Tannhäuser, Lohengrin,* the mighty *Ring* cycle (*Das Rheingold, Die Walküre, Siegfried* and *Götterdämmerung*), *Tristan und Isolde, Die Meistersinger von Nürnberg* to his final work, *Parsifal* (1882) – opened up auditory terrains that were to haunt, and to be haunted by, almost every significant composer since. His works also polarized opinion to an unprecedented degree: to the traditionalists, Wagner was an uncouth, unruly megalomaniac who wouldn't (or couldn't) root his art in the hallowed tradition of Haydn, Mozart, Beethoven and Schubert; to his followers, by contrast, he was a prophet – the revolutionary composer of the 'music of the future'.

When Wagner and Nietzsche first met, in 1868, both were already avid devotees of Schopenhauer. Wagner had originally discovered Schopenhauer's *The World as Will and Representation* in 1854, and the sheer grandeur of the vision expressed there, together with the remarkable role reserved in it for music (see Chapter One), appealed to Wagner immensely. Indeed, he found there a warrant for his own most extravagant estimation of music's capacities, for his conviction that music was *the* metaphysically significant activity, and became an ardent admirer – to the extent that his book about Beethoven, supposed to be ardently admiring of Beethoven, in fact refers to Schopenhauer about ten times as often as to its ostensible subject. The young Nietzsche fell wholly under Wagner's spell. In *The Birth of Tragedy*, as we have seen, he hailed his new hero as the modern incarnation of Aeschylus. Wagner, he claimed, is the first artist since antiquity to have penetrated the Apollonian veil of appearances so as to touch ground again with a Dionysian reality beneath – a reality so dreadful that it could be borne only in the kind of intoxicated state that Wagner's music was so capable of inducing. But it was not only Wagner's art that enthralled Nietzsche. It was also his personality, his intellect.

Wagner wrote a great deal, and these writings – for all their frequent obscurity and grandiloquence – represent by far the most sustained attempt by a musician of genius to express his hopes for and understanding of his own art (only Arnold Schönberg comes close to him in this regard). Two of his larger ideas should be enough to suggest the thrust of his thought. First, there is the conception of the *Gesamtkunstwerk* (the 'total work of art'). Wagner longed for a synthesis of the arts in a single work – a work in which the various arts would come together to yield a power and a totality of vision unavailable to any of them individually; and he sought, with a degree of success that is still the subject of debate, to realize that ideal in his own music dramas (for which he wrote both texts and music and, when he could, designed the sets). The second large idea concerns the relation of thought to feeling: 'Nothing should remain', he said, 'for the synthesizing intellect to do in the face of a dramatic work of art ... In drama, we must become *knowers* through *feeling*'.[3] Here, in all likelihood, Wagner felt that a sufficiently open-hearted response to his own works would be enough to bear him out. These two ideas are not unrelated. Historically, both kick against the most important trend in nineteenth century musical aesthetics. Music, it was increasingly coming to be held, was autonomous: it bore no natural allegiance to the other arts, did not depend on them or anything else for its significance, and was, in that sense, *pure*, that is, meaningful in a purely musical way.[4] The *Gesamtkunstwerk* ideal turns this on its head. Music, for Wagner, is to be seen as a mere ingredient, as just one force in a field of significance whose import exceeds, no doubt impurely, anything that music might achieve by itself. Add to this the claim that dramatic art operates on thought via feeling, so that music, in its dramatic capacity, is significant for reasons other than purely musical reasons, and the repudiation of musical autonomy is complete. This is a repudiation that Nietzsche inherited from Wagner wholesale.

The relationship with Wagner was unquestionably the most important of Nietzsche's life, even if, also unquestionably, it was an unequal one. Wagner was Nietzsche's senior by some thirty years, and was an established, if highly controversial, cultural figure. He was also extremely charismatic. Nietzsche, on the other hand, was an obscure young philologist, generally rather shy and quiet, and given, as in the dedication to Wagner in the first edition of *The Birth of Tragedy*, to calling the older man 'Master'. Wagner saw Nietzsche as a potentially handy propagandist on behalf of his music dramas; Nietzsche saw Wagner as his mentor, as a father-figure fit to be worshipped.

This state of affairs couldn't last. By the mid-1870s, Nietzsche was beginning to find Wagner's hold over him oppressive: the fourth of the *Untimely Meditations* (1876), supposed to be a cele-bration of Wagner, already shows clear signs of rhetorical strain. And shortly afterwards he broke with Wagner altogether. He later claimed that the reason for this was his discovery of the character of the composer's current work-in-progress, *Parsifal*, which he, Nietzsche, took to represent an outright capitulation to Christianity. But this can't be quite right: Nietzsche had been aware of *Parsifal*'s themes for some years before the break, and there is little sign that the issue had previously bothered him. No: the explanation is surely that Nietzsche needed to leave the nest, as it were, to spread his wings as an independent thinker in his own right. He needed, as he later had Zarathustra put it, to repay his teacher by becoming more than a pupil – by moving beyond him.[5]

In one sense, though, he never quite managed this. His break with Schopenhauer's thought, which happened at much the same time, was far cleaner, and indeed marks the decisive move into Nietzsche's all-too-brief philosophical maturity. But Wagner's influence proved altogether harder to shake off: Nietzsche's estima-tion of the significance of art, and of music in particular, was perma-nently conditioned by his experience of Wagner; and he returned to him again and again, as if to a peculiarly seductive sore – picking, squeezing, probing, hating, fond – for the remainder of his life.

III It had always been clear to Nietzsche that Wagner had to be understood as a cultural phenomenon, rather than as a merely artistic one. At the height of his enthusiasm, he had equated Wagner's art with the renaissance of a nobler form of civilization. And after the break he continued to regard Wagner as of peculiarly far-reaching significance – indeed, as a uniquely rich symbol of the deepest malaises of the culture that had made him possible. Nietzsche was among the first, for example, to put his finger on, and to be explicitly bothered by, the wider character of some of Wagner's artistic ambitions. The aspiration to totality of vision, to an all-encompassing interpretation whose authority was to be grounded on the primacy of feeling, seemed, on the later Nietzsche's diagnosis, to be symptomatic less of an artistic impulse than of a religious one. Founders and furtherers of religions, he held, set out to combat the dissatisfactions engendered by the immanent, contingent nature of human life. And they do this through what Nietzsche often terms 'idealism':[6] the invention of *complete*, and therefore transcendent, interpretations of existence – that is, interpretations which, because they offer to account for everything, to make sense of everything, remove that 'illusion' of contingency that dissatisfaction is caused by and feeds off; and the founders of religions exploit the passions of the dissatisfied in order to force those interpretations on them or, at any rate, to render them irresistible.[7] In this sense at least, Wagner's aesthetic turns out to be a kind of substitute theology, expressly designed to comfort the afflicted (the decadent – those who suffer from themselves[8]) and to foreclose the possibility of living in that honest acknowledgement of immanence and contingency that Nietzsche, as we saw in Chapter Five, associates with the love of fate and with becoming who one is.[9] Small wonder that, having made this diagnosis, Nietzsche withdrew his youthful identification of Wagner's art as the *re*birth of tragedy.

Of course, the situation was more complicated than this. For one thing, Wagner – under the influence of Schopenhauer – came to accord to music a far greater significance than was consistent with his original conception of the *Gesamtkunstwerk*. But this is offset by his acceptance of Schopenhauer's metaphysics, itself an 'idealism' – a totalizing interpretation of existence – driven, if the later Nietzsche is right, by the acutest feelings of dissatisfaction.[10] Thus, Wagner's aesthetic remains quasi-religious, in Nietzsche's sense, even if his conception of the precise character of the metaphysical task to be fulfilled by art, and by music in particular, changed. What is beyond doubt, though, is that in a century on which religion proper had started to lose its grip, art was increasingly seen as its natural successor; and of this new cult (which counted Berlioz and Liszt among its early adepts), few, including Wagner, seriously doubted that Wagner was to be high priest. Where 'religion becomes artificial', he wrote, 'it is the duty of art to save religion's essential core';[11] and when he opened the Festspielhaus at Bayreuth in 1876, built by him and specifically designed for the performance of his own works, its character as a temple and a place of worship was widely appreciated.

No one who is at all serious about life can remain indifferent to religion. Its claims and demands are unconditional; it abolishes, by fiat, the very possibility of neutrality. One must be for it or against it,[12] and so, for closely analogous reasons, and to an extent unequalled by any other artist, with Wagner. No one who is at all serious about music can be (or has been) indifferent to him; for the astonishing thing is that Wagner's art succeeds, to a remarkable degree, in realizing and giving form to the fundamental tenor of his aesthetic. The larger-than-life, mythic quality of the characters and actions of his dramas, the huge and yet somehow hermetically sealed worlds in which they unfold, offer, or appear to offer, totalizing interpretations as complete and as unconditional as those of any religion. And as for the music, when Wagner demanded that a dramatic work should leave 'Nothing . . . for the synthesizing intellect to do' – that 'we must become *knowers*' of his interpretations 'through "*feeling*"' – he neither overestimated the expressive capacities of his own music nor underestimated the radical power that such capacities might have. For its sheer extremism, his is the most expressive music ever written. In its effects – seductive and intoxicating to the admirer, cynical and manipulative to the detractor – its power to polarize is unprecedented. No other artist has inspired worshipful fervour as Wagner has, nor has any artist been so brutally vilified.

Tristan und Isolde – Nietzsche's favourite of Wagner's works[13] – is Wagner at his most Wagnerian. It is, as Michael Tanner has shown, his one fully religious work – not in the sense of having overtly religious subject-matter, but in the sense that it pushes so uncompromisingly at the limits of immanence and contingency that the only possible resolution of its dramatic impetus is transcendent – a possibility, moreover, of whose reality Wagner's music more than half persuades one. 'Every religion', as Tanner puts it, is 'a doctrine of extremes'; and in *Tristan*, 'so paralyzingly absolute in its demands', that doctrine is 'humanism pressed to its limits, then exploded into transcendent metaphysics' – a metaphysics set to and apparently embodied in 'music which has a compelling beauty of a kind that none other possesses' (Tanner 1996: 144–153). It is this sort of thing that makes neutrality in the face of Wagner an impossibility. Either one is prepared to be seduced by him, to be converted, however briefly, into a quasi-religious 'knower' through 'feeling', or else, because one suspects that this is what Wagner can do, and one refuses him the authority to do it, one must recoil from him and denounce the means through which his effects are attempted.

Neither of these, as critical options, has proved easy to pursue with any grace: the former tends to degenerate too readily into idolatry, while the latter – which requires that one first acknowledge the power of Wagner's music to do *to oneself* what one refuses it the authority to do – demands a level of integrity that few have found it possible to sustain (hence the proliferation of idle and self-serving efforts to show that Wagner's music can be written off because it is somehow proto-Nazi, or is anti-Semitic). It is no accident, in light of this, that many of Wagner's most insightful critics – Thomas Mann (1985) is a particularly striking example – have also been the most ambivalent, perpetually torn between gratitude and revulsion, never settling for long into either. And it is in this context that the later Nietzsche's critical achievement needs to be appreciated: for, as Wagner's most intimate critic, and as one shot to the core with ambivalence, his writings have set the bench-mark against which all subsequent Wagner criticism must be gauged.

IV   In the final year of his sane life, 1888, Nietzsche devoted a considerable amount of attention to Wagner. He put together a collection of aphorisms – *Nietzsche contra Wagner* – culled, occasionally with minor revisions, from his earlier works; he discussed Wagner at length in his autobiography, *Ecce Homo*; and he wrote a book about him, *The Case of Wagner*. Nietzsche's underlying ambivalence is signalled clearly: 'I must express my gratitude', he says, 'for what has been by far the most profound and cordial' relationship of my life, that with Richard Wagner (EH, 'Why I Am So Clever', 5). 'I know better than anyone else of what tremendous things Wagner is capable . . . ; and given the way I am, strong enough to turn even what is most questionable and dangerous to my advantage and thus to become stronger, I call Wagner the great benefactor of my life' (EH, 'Why I Am So Clever', 7). So Wagner is one of those things in Nietzsche's biography that 'must not be missing' (GS 277), despite his questionableness and dangerousness. He is one of the conditions of Nietzsche's having become who he is.

Indeed, Nietzsche makes a stronger claim than this. He suggests that, as a decadent, Wagner is 'indispensable', not merely for Nietzsche, but for every philosopher. 'Through Wagner modernity speaks most intimately, concealing neither its good nor its evil – having forgotten all sense of shame. And conversely: one has almost completed an account of the value of what is modern once one has gained clarity about . . . Wagner' (CW, Preface). So for a philosopher interested in modernity – and hence, Nietzsche insists, in decadence – Wagner is a *'windfall'* (CW, Epilogue). But he is also complex, multi-faceted and wide-ranging; and Nietzsche's treatment of him reflects that. Here, then, and not without a certain arbitrariness, I focus on only three aspects of Nietzsche's critique, in the hope that something of the general flavour will emerge through that. The issues that I focus on are style, 'idealism', and who Wagner *is*.

We have already seen that 'style' matters to Nietzsche. It is, after all, what one has to give to one's character if one is to create oneself under a law of one's own.[14] And Nietzsche's model of style – which is drawn, obviously, from art – is a conventional one: style is a 'higher lawfulness' (CW 8), he says, marked by the fact that 'life . . . dwells in the whole', with the parts being related to one another in an 'organic' way (CW 7); it is 'necessary' but gives 'the impression of freedom' (CW 9); it has its own sort of 'logic' (CW 2). It is, in short, precisely what one gets when an 'organizing "idea"' is at work (EH, 'Why I Am So Clever', 9). And style, according to Nietzsche, is what Wagner lacks: indeed, Wagner has an 'incapacity for any style whatever' (CW 7).

In part, Nietzsche's objection arises from his dislike of so-called 'endless melody', which *'wants* to break up all evenness of tempo', with the result that the listener finds himself 'Swimming, floating – no longer walking, dancing': there is a 'complete degeneration of the feeling for rhythm, *chaos* in place of rhythm . . . ' (NCW, 'Wagner as a Danger', 1). But chaos, to Nietzsche's ear, is endemic to Wagner's music: there is an 'anarchy of atoms', a 'disaggregation of the will'; 'Everywhere paralysis, arduousness, torpidity *or* hostility and chaos: both the more and more obvious the higher one ascends in forms of organization. The whole no longer lives at all.' Wagner 'gains small units', 'animates' them 'and makes them visible. But this exhausts his strength: the rest is no good.' He has an 'incapacity for giving organic form', and is 'admirable . . . only in the invention of what is smallest'; he is 'our greatest *miniaturist* in music' (CW 7).

In light of the huge scale of Wagner's works, it is perhaps unsurprising that Nietzsche should enjoy the charge of 'miniaturism'; he returns to it repeatedly. Wagner specializes, he says, in

> some very small and microscopic features of the soul, the scales of its amphibious nature, as it were –, yes, he is *master* at the very small. But he doesn't *want* to be! His *character* likes great walls and bold frescoes much better! . . . It escapes him that his *spirit* has a different taste and disposition . . . and likes best of all to sit quietly in the corners of collapsed houses – there, . . . hidden from himself, he paints his real masterpieces, which are all very short, often only a bar long . . . .
>
> (Nietzsche, NCW, 'Where I Admire')

But it is not just the (alleged) 'decline in organizing energy', 'the abuse of traditional methods without any ability to *justify* this abuse', the 'counterfeit in duplicating great forms' (CW, Second Postscript) or the 'miniaturism' that attracts Nietzsche's fire. It is the *content* of Wagner's 'small units', the fact that each one of them has been drawn from the 'drained cup' of 'human happiness', where 'the most bitter and repulsive drops have merged . . . with the sweetest ones' (NCW, 'Where I Admire'). Wagner's states are uniformly pathological; and strung together in a way that is at once *'brutal'*, *'artificial'* and *'innocent'*, they result, not in a style, but in something closer to a nervous condition: Wagner, says Nietzsche, *'est une névrose* [neurosis]' (CW 5).

What Nietzsche construes as Wagner's 'incapacity' for style, then, is the absence of an 'organizing "idea"' in his works, which is, in turn, symptomatic of a nervous and 'physiological degeneration (a form of hystericism, to be precise)' (CW 7). 'Wagner's art is sick', Nietzsche says (CW 5). It is a sign of 'declining life' (CW, Epilogue), of life that lacks the energy for itself – indeed, that suffers of itself. It is, in a word, decadent.

This connects directly to the second aspect of Nietzsche's critique, the one concerning 'idealism'. Wagner's audience, like him, are decadents, and so hunger for something that will call them 'back into life' (CW 5), for something 'sublime', 'profound', 'overwhelming' (CW 6). They do 'not *want* to gain clarity about' themselves (EH, 'The Case of Wagner', 3). Instead, they want 'intimations'. And Wagner obliges – 'Chaos induces intimations' (CW 6) – and turns his listeners into 'moon-cal[ves]' – into '"idealist[s]"' (CW, Postscript). But 'It was not *music* that Wagner conquered them with, it was the "Idea": – the fact that his art . . . plays hide-and-seek under a hundred symbols . . . – this is what led and lured them' (CW 10). Indeed, claims Nietzsche, Wagner's elusiveness is a major source of his power to corrupt:

> He has an affinity for everything equivocal, every ambiguity, everything in general that persuades the uncertain without calling their attention to *what* they are being persuaded of. Wagner is a seducer in the grand style. There is nothing tired, enervated, life-threatening or world denying in matters of spirit that his art fails to secretly defend – he shrouds the blackest obscurantism inside the light of the ideal. He flatters every nihilistic . . . instinct and disguises it in music, he flatters every piece of Christianity, every form in which religion expresses decadence. Just open your ears: everything that has ever grown on the soil of *impoverished* life, the whole counterfeit of transcendence and the beyond has its most sublime advocate in Wagner's art – *not* with formulas: Wagner is too clever for formulas – but by persuading sensuality which, for its part, makes the spirit brittle and tired again.
>
> (Nietzsche, CW, Postscript)

And – to Nietzsche's ears, at least – Wagner's relation to 'idealism' reaches its most intimate pitch in his final work, *Parsifal*. 'Did *hatred of life* gain control over him . . . ?', Nietzsche asks:

> Because Parsifal is a work of malice, of vindictiveness, a secret poisoning of the presuppositions of life, a *bad* work. – The preaching of

chastity remains an incitement to perversion: I despise anyone who
does not regard Parsifal as an attempt to assassinate ethics.
(Nietzsche, NCW, 'Wagner as Apostle of Chastity', 3)

So Wagner is a decadent; he lacks style, an 'organizing "idea"'; his
art stands in perilously close relations to 'idealism'. But who *is*
he? – *what* is he? Nietzsche canvasses several possibilities: 'Is
Wagner a human being at all?', he asks; 'Isn't he rather a sickness?'
(CW 5). Is he 'a dramatist'? No: 'He loved the word "drama" –
that's all' (CW 9). Is he even 'a musician'? Perhaps; but 'there [is]
something else that he [is] even more: namely, an incomparable
histrio', a 'first-rate actor' – that is 'who Wagner is' (CW 8).

To be an 'actor', in Nietzsche's sense, is to want 'effect, nothing but
effect' (ibid.).[15] And his claim in Wagner's case can be taken at two
levels. First, Wagner is an actor with respect to his art: he produces
the effect of art, but not its substance. He counterfeits style; he
mimics drama; his characters are forgeries. 'Wagner's music is never
true', Nietzsche says (CW 8). But second, and perhaps more importantly, Wagner is an actor with respect to life. He is made for the
modern age: 'in declining cultures . . . authenticity becomes super-
fluous, disadvantageous, a liability. Only the actor still arouses
great enthusiasm. Thus the *golden age* dawns for the actor' (CW
11). In a robust culture, the instincts are in good shape; people can
be seen to have 'turned out well' (CW, Epilogue), to have become
masters and creators of themselves. In a declining culture, by contrast, where the 'instincts are weakened' (CW 5), the resources
required for self-creation are largely absent. And hence the importance, the timeliness, of the actor. With him, one gets the *effect* of
personality, at least – even if the substance is entirely lacking.

'Is it any wonder', Nietzsche asks, 'that falseness has become
flesh and even genius in precisely our age? That *Wagner* "dwelled
among us"?' (CW, Epilogue). And he pursues the issue of Wagner's
falseness into his 'idealism'. He imagines Wagner addressing his
fellow composers:

Let us be idealists! – This is . . . certainly the wisest thing we can do. In
order to raise people up, we need to be sublime ourselves. Let us
wander over the clouds, haranguing the infinite, surrounding ourselves

> with great symbols! ... The 'heaving bosom' will be our argument,
> 'beautiful feelings' are our advocate. Virtue has rights even against
> counterpoint. 'How could anyone who improves us fail to be good
> himself?' this is how humanity has always reasoned. So let us
> improve humanity! – that will make us good.
>
> (Nietzsche, CW 6)

Wagner's 'idealism' is thus presented as a policy – as a policy that
he adopts, like an actor, exclusively for the sake of 'effect, nothing
but effect'. And in the face of this, Nietzsche suddenly becomes
rather warm about Christianity:

> The need for *redemption*, the quintessence of all Christian needs, ...
> is the most honest expression of decadence, it is the most convinced,
> most painful affirmation of decadence ... The Christian wants to be
> *rid* of himself. *Le moi est toujours haïssable* [The self is always hateful].
>
> (Nietzsche, CW, Epilogue)

There is at least some integrity in the Christian's 'idealism', then.
In Wagner's, by contrast, Nietzsche suspects that there is nothing
but mendaciousness – the absence of an intellectual conscience – all
the way down.

V One might summarize the aspects of Nietzsche's critique that I
have discussed here in the following way: Wagner lacked style, an
'organizing "idea"'; he was a decadent, he suffered from himself;
therefore he was drawn to 'ideals' that slander the world; but, since
there was, strictly speaking, no one who he *was* (no 'organizing
"idea"'), he became an actor; and he became an actor *even* in his 'idealism'. And this, in Nietzsche's view, is not only decadence taken to
the limit – the polar opposite of the conditions required for self-
creation, for becoming who one is – it is also symptomatic of modernity as such. The modern world simply lacks the energy for itself.

There is plenty of room to disagree with Nietzsche about any or
all of this – and, in my own view, quite a bit of that room should be
exploited. But what always distinguishes Nietzsche's best remarks
about Wagner, whether or not one agrees with them, is their
extraordinary combination of psychological insight, passion and

the unfailing sense that what is at stake is the right understanding of an entire culture. In this – with the possible exception of Thomas Mann (who knew his Nietzsche) – he remains unmatched. Nor is it any sort of coincidence that the most stirring and compelling *defence* of Wagner in the century or so since Nietzsche's death – Michael Tanner's big essay, 'The Total Work of Art' (1979) – is so thoroughly Nietzschean in spirit. For the truth is that Nietzsche engaged more deeply with and saw more deeply into Wagner than any philosopher has ever done with or into a great artist, with the result that his mapping of the critical terrain has remained more or less definitive. Whether pro- or anti- or caught agonizing in between, all of Wagner's most rewarding critics have mined the territory that Nietzsche opened up, and they have taken their bearings from him. And if it is true that 'one has almost completed an account of the value of what is modern once one has gained clarity about . . . Wagner' (and it is certainly tempting to think that it might be), that is a significant legacy indeed.

Two final remarks. The first has to do with the portrait of Nietzsche that emerges from his Wagner writings. For these show him at his most unmasked, at his least cunning and oblique. The usual themes are there – Christianity, culture, strength, decadence, affirmation, self-creation, etc. – but they are given in an unusually direct register, focussed, as it were, through the lens of his engagement with Wagner's art – focussed, in fact, by his taste. Nietzsche *is* how he judges, and he knew it. The other remark is that we have largely lost sight of this sort of truth. Contemporary philosophical aesthetics is chary about personalizing judgement in this way. It is chary about taking art and taste *that* seriously, and so espouses, or at any rate evinces, a kind of relativism of indifference. Nietzsche, on the other hand, although certainly a relativist in one sense – *this* kind of art is proper to *that* sort of person, that to this – marks the utter repudiation of indifference. For to him it matters – indeed is decisive – what sort of art is proper to us. And in this, it seems to me, he must have been right, whatever one might think about what he thought about Wagner. 'In the end', as he puts it, 'it must be as it is and always has been: great things remain for the great, abysses for the profound, nuances and shudders for the refined, and, in brief, all that is rare for the rare' (BGE 43).

Notes

1 Throughout this book, unless otherwise specified, I understand the term 'art' to refer indifferently to painting, music, literature, sculpture, drama, etc. Music is what Nietzsche was most conspicuously bowled over by; but – as will become clear – his chief philosophical concern was with 'art' construed quite generally.

2 Letter to Erwin Rohde, 20th November 1868.

3 Readers wanting to know more about Nietzsche's life should read the excellent Hollingdale 1999. For a fine account of his last sane year, see Chamberlain 1996.

4 Nor, I should probably say, have I made any effort to conceal the fact that Nietzsche's writings seem to me to be of sometimes uneven quality: where he strikes me as wrong, or as confused, or as unworthy of himself, I have not hesitated to say so. Some readers, perhaps, will find this approach off-puttingly judgemental. But my view is that what Nietzsche writes about is important enough to be worth taking sides over, and I can't find it in me to apologize for having done so in what follows.

5 The fact that he also ended up mad, and very shortly afterwards too, has of course encouraged speculation that his last works are already the products of derangement. This speculation has tended especially

to focus on *Ecce Homo*, which is undeniably an odd book in some ways. But it doesn't seem a mad book. And my own view is that it should be taken perfectly seriously as a part of Nietzsche's main philosophical corpus – as I attempt to do, with results that readers must judge for themselves, in the final section of Chapter Five of this book.

6   For a good, level-headed discussion of the nature and use of Nietzsche's unpublished writings, see Bittner 2003: ix-xv.

Chapter 1

1   There are, of course, many other approaches that might be taken to Nietzsche's first book, and it has been much discussed. Noteworthy recent discussions include: Porter 2000; Silk and Stern 1981; Soll 1998 and Nussbaum 1998.

2   The German word 'Wissenschaft', usually translated as 'science', has no exact English equivalent. The German notion encompasses, not only what would be called 'science' in English, but also scholarly work more generally. For Nietzsche's most sustained late discussions of the 'problem of science', see GS 343–349 and GM III.23–27.

3   The most impressive discussion of a reading of this sort is Staten 1990. This is by some margin the most powerful piece on *The Birth of Tragedy* that I have ever read, and it should be sought out by anyone with a serious interest in Nietzsche's first book. I return to Staten, with a degree of trepidation, in section 4, below.

4   This question is invited, I think – but should probably not be mistaken for the question posed by the so-called 'paradox of tragedy' (i.e. why, given that the events portrayed in tragedy are uniformly distressing, would any of us put ourselves through it?). Hume was certainly concerned with this latter question (in his short essay, 'Of Tragedy'), and Aristotle may have been (in the *Poetics*). But I doubt that Nietzsche really was. It seems to me that Nietzsche was primarily interested in tragedy as a *cultural* phenomenon, rather than as something that a given individual might or might not choose to experience at first hand. For a very good discussion that aligns Nietzsche's concerns more closely with Hume's, however, see Tanner 1993.

5   BT 3; drawn from Sophocles, *Oedipus at Colonus*, lines 1224ff.

6   One might have expected Nietzsche to say something rather different here, perhaps that the chorus is partly Apollonian: that it enacts – on

the spectator's behalf, as it were – the response of any 'individual' to the events of the drama. And yet that it is also Dionysian: the chorus responds as a collective; its response is not yours or mine, but somehow *ours*, a response that disindividuates the 'individual' even as he identifies with it. But this is a view that Nietzsche criticizes Schlegel at length for espousing (BT 7) – even if Schlegel's view certainly has the advantage over Nietzsche's in terms of ready intelligibility.

7   The original full title was *The Birth of Tragedy from the Spirit of Music*.
8   Non-rational aspects of the Apollonian, as I read Nietzsche, include, e.g., mere beauty, sensually beguiling appearances, etc..
9   Act II, Scene 2.
10 For an excellent discussion of Tristan and Isolde's merging of identities, see Scruton 2004: chapter 5.
11 Except (perhaps) as an interpretative last resort. In fact, though, it has more often been regarded as a first resort. Julian Young, for instance, remarks that it is 'a surprise to discover that the question of the nature and scope of the Schopenhauerian influence [on *The Birth of Tragedy*] is a matter of deep controversy', since, in his view, it is clear that '*The Birth* incorporates without modification Schopenhauer's metaphysics' (Young 1992: 26). If what I have just argued is correct, however, the one thing that *The Birth of Tragedy* seems unlikely to have taken over from Schopenhauer 'without modification' is, precisely, his metaphysics, certainly in anything like the full-blown form that we have been discussing.
12 Nietzsche remained disappointingly attached to this picture, together with the philosophy of language that it invites, throughout his life. See, e.g., GS 354, BGE 268, TI IX.26.
13 Maudemarie Clark notes Nietzsche's flirtation in this essay with a similar-seeming distinction, between things 'in-themselves' and the 'things themselves' (1990: 82). But since Nietzsche seems to regard the latter as also wholly unknowable, it is unlikely that the 'things themselves' to which he alludes correspond to the 'essence of things', for this appears, at least in principle, to be capable of being revealed.
14 How, then, is one to understand Nietzsche's handless painter, who expresses 'in song the picture before his mind'? One can only guess, of course, but perhaps the idea is that, since the song and the picture (two discrete objects) are in some sense identical to one another, their identity must be secured by their common origin in the same primal

'mass of images'. The painter reveals something of the *ur*-text, as it were, and so of the 'essence of things', by offering two 'stammering translation[s]' of it into two 'completely foreign tongue[s]'. This doesn't make a lot of sense, but it's hard to see what else Nietzsche might have had in mind.

15 It used to be quite fashionable to take 'Truth and Lies' seriously (Nietzsche makes some exciting-sounding postmodernish noises in it). But it seems to me that there is nothing in the essay that repays attention in its own right, and it would be nice to think that this is a fashion whose day is past.

16 Staten (1990) in fact presents himself as merely fine-tuning, in this respect, bipartite readings of *The Birth of Tragedy* offered by Paul de Man (1979) and Philippe Lacoue-Labarthe (1971) – readings with which he otherwise disagrees quite strongly, indeed compellingly.

17 And the same would go – *mutatis mutandis* – if one were to reject the arguments offered in section 3, above, and impute the strong version of the metaphysical thesis to Nietzsche: that thesis would inform the whole of *The Birth of Tragedy*.

18 That is, perspectives which the later Nietzsche himself develops reasons to repudiate: see, e.g., BGE 2 and GM *passim*.

Chapter 2

1 Designed and built by Wagner specifically for the performance of his own works.

2 For an indication of his reaction, see, e.g., EH BT 4 and EH HH 2.

3 In fact, Nietzsche had been present at a reading of the text of *Parsifal* in 1869, so its content can hardly have come as that much of a shock to him.

4 For a superb and conclusive refutation of Nietzsche's claims about *Parsifal*, see Tanner 1979: 205–218.

5 *Assorted Opinions and Maxims* and *The Wanderer and his Shadow* were subsequently republished as the second volume of *Human, All Too Human*.

6 For discussion of what Nietzsche's aphoristic style might be intended to achieve, see Chapter Four, section 2.

7 As I noted in Chapter One, the German word 'Wissenschaft' encompasses not only what would be called 'science' in English, but also

scholarly work more generally. Julian Young notes, rightly, that in embracing *Wissenschaft* in this way Nietzsche is here at his least 'untimely' – i.e. is most in tune with the general intellectual climate of his age. See Young, *Nietzsche's Philosophy of Art* (Cambridge: Cambridge University Press, 1992), p.59.

8 Nietzsche's naturalism has been the subject of a lot of discussion lately, some of it pegging him much too strongly, in my view, to contemporary understandings of the relation between philosophy and the *natural* sciences, specifically (Leiter 2002: chapter 1 is especially uncompromising in this respect). But the truth of the matter, I think, is much more modest, and is well captured by what Janaway calls a 'minimal' naturalism, one which 'includes within the "natural" not merely' the subject matters of physics and biology, say, 'but also many complex cultural phenomena and the psycho-physiological states of past individuals and projected types of individual' (2006: 350). For further discussion of Nietzsche's naturalism, see Cox 1999 and Green 2003; for a more general snapshot of contemporary understandings of naturalism, see De Caro and Macarthur 2004.

9 Boscovich 'defined atoms only as centres of force, and not as particles of matter in which powers somehow inhere' (Gillispie 1960: 455).

10 He mentions it earlier – but in a different context: Young 1992: 60.

11 Actually, one might worry a little even about this: HH I.19 ends with the claim that – while 'the laws of numbers' apply 'to the *concept of nature* which we are obliged to attach to nature (nature = world as idea, that is as error)' – to 'a world which is *not* our idea', by contrast, 'the laws of numbers are wholly inapplicable: these are valid only in the human world.' Assuming that by 'the laws of numbers' Nietzsche means mathematics, then, to the extent that he understood that modern science consists precisely in the mathematicization of nature, the scientific world-view must be, according to him, based on the 'error' of belief in 'things'. It is unclear, however, whether Nietzsche did in fact appreciate the indissoluble connection between mathematics and the kind of science that so impressed him.

12 See, e.g., HH I.10 and I.16.

13 See Chapter One, section 3 for discussion.

14 It must be recognised, Nietzsche holds, that 'everything has become: there are no *eternal facts*, just as there are no absolute truths.

Consequently what is needed from now on is *historical philosophizing*, and with it the virtue of modesty' (HH I.2).

15 No doubt keen to put as much distance as possible between himself and *The Birth of Tragedy*, Nietzsche's remarks about tragedy in Book I of *Human, All Too Human* are uniformly deflating (see, e.g., HH I.166 and I.169). Signs that he began to re-awaken to the significance of the tragic can, however, be found in Book II (see, e.g., HH II.23 and WS 124).

16 Indeed, he insists upon it, repeatedly. So, for instance, the 'Last Men' in *Thus Spoke Zarathustra* are would-be eliminators of suffering who are held up for our contempt on that very account. And, in a famous and apocalyptic passage from *Beyond Good and Evil*, he thunders: 'You want, if possible – and there is no more insane "if possible" – *to abolish suffering*. And we? It really seems that *we* would rather have it higher and worse than ever. Well-being as you understand it – that is no goal, that seems to us an *end*, a state that soon makes man ridiculous and contemptible – that makes his destruction *desirable*. The discipline of suffering, of *great* suffering – do you not know that only *this* discipline has created all enhancements of man so far?' (BGE 225).

17 In the *Republic*, Plato had argued that it was a limitation of art that it could only present the appearances of particulars, and could not take us behind those appearances to reveal deeper levels of reality.

18 A premonition, perhaps, of his genealogical method, developed some nine years later.

19 Again, it was part of Plato's critique of art in the *Republic* that it restricted its audience to, and encouraged them to remain within, peculiarly local, human perspectives on the world.

20 See also HH I.161.

21 See, e.g., HH I.146.

22 It is impossible to ignore the Hegelian aspects of this dimension of Nietzsche's thinking: the content is rather different, but the overall *point* of their respective historical speculations is really quite strikingly similar.

23 See, e.g., HH I.158 and II.115. I don't take up this theme in detail here, for two main reasons: first, Nietzsche's grounds for thinking that art is degenerating are extremely protean; and, second, it isn't at all clear to me that those grounds are *philosophically* very interesting (however intriguing they might be as indicators of the character of Nietzsche's artistic tastes). A third, subsidiary, reason is simply reluctance to be drawn into a kind of competitive grumpiness (if he thinks that things

were in decline *then* – i.e. while Brahms, Manet, Ibsen, Tolstoy, Bruckner, Dostoyevsky, Strindberg, Cézanne and Chekhov were all going strong, and before Mahler, Schoenberg, Stravinsky, Conrad, Debussy, Camus, Feininger, James, Sibelius, Modigliani, Messiaen, Mann, Bartok and so on had even begun – he should see what they look like *now* . . . etc.).

24 See, e.g., HH I.3, I.217, II.126, II.131, II.159, II.171.

25 Nietzsche is serious about this. Earlier, he asks whether science can really meet the needs formerly satisfied by religion and metaphysics (and, implicitly, by art), and answers in the affirmative: science's 'sum of unimpeachable truths', he says, 'can in time become so great . . . that on the basis of them one may resolve to embark on "everlasting" works' (HH I.22).

26 For a particularly unambiguous assault on this picture, see GM III.12.

27 As he would later put it: '" . . . the things of the highest value must have another, *peculiar* origin – they cannot be derived from this transitory, seductive, deceptive, paltry world, from this turmoil of delusion and lust. Rather from the lap of Being, the intransitory, the hidden god, the 'thing-in-itself' – there must be their basis, and nowhere else." This way of judging constitutes the typical prejudice which gives away the metaphysicians of all ages' (BGE 2).

28 See, e.g., HH I.155, I.156.

29 See also HH I.27.

30 A remark sometimes wrongly attributed to Thomas Carlyle, occasionally attributed to Dr. Johnson, but most frequently attributed, it seems, to Jane Ellice Hopkins.

31 Despite his official priorities at this period, Nietzsche in fact devotes at least four times as much space to art in *Human, All Too Human* as he does to science.

32 See also HH II.178.

33 Nietzsche also – and this time without qualification – approves of an 'antiquarian' art of performance: see HH II.126.

34 Nietzsche's inspiration here is undoubtedly Emerson, whom he greatly admired. His line of thought is almost exactly the same as that expressed in Emerson's essay, 'Uses of Great Men'.

35 Notice that assigning this role to art does not contradict Nietzsche's earlier insistence that art is epistemically inferior to science: to portray an exemplar is not to make a truth-claim, large, small, pretentious or otherwise. Cf. Young 1992: 76.

36 Young later notices Nietzsche's endorsement of 'critical' art: 1992: 80–81.

37 Young claims that Nietzsche explicitly equates the 'classical' and the 'great' in art, and cites HH II.144 as evidence (1992: 77) – a passage in which, as far as I can see, Nietzsche does nothing of the sort.

38 It is just about possible, I suppose, that someone might say that 'Richard Wagner in Bayreuth' (the fourth of the *Untimely Meditations*) in fact does this. But – if it does – it does it in a hollow, half-hearted way.

39 It will not have escaped notice that the predominantly sceptical tone about art adopted in Book I gives way to something altogether more positive in Book II: Nietzsche is starting to convalesce from the break with Wagner.

Chapter 3

1 Plausibly argued by Maudemarie Clark and Brian Leiter to be the first of Nietzsche's mature works (1997: viii).

2 It does, however, contain a reasonably large amount about the decline of music – as does *The Gay Science*; but, for the reasons given in the previous chapter, I don't intend to pursue that theme here.

3 Much the best account of the development of Nietzsche's understanding of the death of God, and of the reasons for that development, is given in Owen 2003. See also Owen 2002.

4 Eternal recurrence, for instance, will be looked at in Chapter Four.

5 Actually, I don't think that Nietzsche ever believed *this*. But Young appears to hold that it is what Nietzsche's 'perspectivism' (developed in 1887) amounts to. For correctives, see, e.g., Clark 1990 and Leiter 2002.

6 See Chapter Two, fn.13.

7 See TI IV; and Chapter Five, for discussion.

8 GS 107 is also the passage that Clark cites as evidence for Nietzsche's thought that all human beliefs are false.

9 Nietzsche is sometimes said to be a defender of a pragmatist conception of truth – i.e., crudely, one in which the true equals the useful. And – if that were right – the reading that I offer here of GS 112 would have to be scaled down rather. But see the discussion of GS 110, below, where it is clear that Nietzsche *contrasts* the true with the useful. I do not, then, see any reason to construe Nietzsche as a pragmatist, or, accordingly, to scale down my reading of GS 112.

10 For a similar point about mathematics, see GS 246.

11 Quite what he might think it depends on instead must remain a matter for conjecture. But we can at least guess why he rejects causal reasoning: causation, he may well have thought, is a relation that holds between things; and if there are no such things as things . . .

12 Clark, because she holds that Nietzsche regards all human beliefs as false in *The Gay Science*, views his position at this period as confused. On her reading, Nietzsche has indeed arrived (in GS 54) at the denial of the intelligibility of a world as it is in itself, conceived of as independent of any of its possible appearances; but he has not yet noticed that this makes the claim that *all* human beliefs might be false incoherent. On her reading, it is not until the *Genealogy* that he finally notices his mistake, and retracts the claim. If I am right, on the other hand, then in the original edition of *The Gay Science*, at any rate, Nietzsche makes neither the claim nor the mistake, and so leaves himself with nothing to retract.

13 Cf., e.g., GS 123.

14 See also, e.g., GS 319.

15 See, e.g., HH I.22 and I.222; see also section 2 of the previous chapter for discussion.

16 The point is present in *Human, All Too Human* – in, e.g., HH I.222 – but Nietzsche doesn't make very much of it there.

17 Our 'second nature', in this sense, is where a large part of the dead God's 'shadow' is to be found – see the Introduction to this chapter.

18 See, e.g., HH I.108, 128, 148.

19 Cf. GM II.7, where Nietzsche reprovingly notes that 'Today' – wrongly in his view – 'suffering is always brought forward as the principal argument *against* existence'.

20 In GS 24 Nietzsche connects this smallness to the removal of the possibility of progress, including scientific progress.

21 Notice that Nietzsche is not here claiming that *all* suffering is a good thing. He is simply distancing himself from two positions that he had held in *Human, All Too Human*: that the complete abolition of suffering would be tantamount to a 'modest' version of the 'eternal bliss' on offer from religion (HH I.128); and that it is always a bad idea to attempt to 'change the effect' that an ill 'produces on our sensibilities . . . by reinterpreting the ill into a good' (HH I.108).

22 Voltaire was the original dedicatee of *Human, All Too Human*.

23 Cf. BGE 227, where Nietzsche describes 'Honesty' as the one 'virtue from which we cannot get away, we free spirits' – and, indeed, as 'the only [virtue] left to us'.

24 See also, e.g., GS 245.

25 See HH II.174.

26 I return to some of the elided parts of GS 290 in Chapter Five.

27 Which *is* the one needful thing, a point made persuasively by Dylan Jaggard in 'Why Giving Style to One's Character is *not* the One Needful Thing: a Reading of *Gay Science* 290', unpublished essay.

28 For an attempt to spell out this thought in more detail, see Ridley 1998: 135–142.

Chapter 4

1 A striking impression of continuity between *The Gay Science* and *Zarathustra* is imparted by the fact that the final section of the 1882 edition of the former (GS 342) is more or less identical to the opening section of the latter (Z, Prologue, 1).

2 Zarathustra is (very) loosely based on the ancient Persian prophet, Zoroaster. The details of that connection, however, are not of any real significance, so far as I can see; so it is safe to treat Zarathustra as a fictional character of Nietzsche's invention. (For Nietzsche's own account of the connection, see EH, 'Why I am a Destiny', 3.)

3 Actually, this second paean appears in the penultimate section of Book IV; the very final section, 'The Sign', sees Zarathustra aspiring again to his '*work*!'

4 And, except in the quasi-autobiographical *Ecce Homo*, we barely hear of him again.

5 Nor, during his sane lifetime, would Nietzsche ever succeed in breaking that silence: his later works, including *Zarathustra*, were as universally ignored as the earlier ones.

6 This sort of thing used to be known as 'dramatic irony', a term that has since been hi-jacked so as to mean something considerably less interesting.

7 Nietzsche abandoned this tactic in his post-Zarathustra writings, and instead developed his genealogical method: but the problem he was trying to solve remained the same. For a superb discussion of this dimension of Nietzsche's thought, see Owen 2003. For another excellent

discussion, this time devoted to the ways in which the later Nietzsche's rhetoric seeks to persuade by working on his reader's affects, see Janaway 2003.

8 This passage is among the many places at which Nietzsche is keen to distance himself from Kant. Kant had regarded 'the moral law' as being revealed to us by the highest part of ourselves, the faculty of reason, which stands '*above* our own likes and dislikes'. Part of Nietzsche's point here, then, is that on Kant's conception of the matter we do not '*impose*' the law upon ourselves at our 'own discretion', but rather '*discover* it' or '*have it commanded to*' us.

9 As, apparently unaware of the Nietzschean path that she trod, Elizabeth Anscombe would later point out: Anscombe 1958.

10 GS 152 is, strictly, about the difference between the modern world and the ancient world: but the metaphor is clearly applicable as well to the kind of change that Nietzsche understands the death of God to constitute.

11 Nietzsche's emphasis on music in this context is, of course, due to the impact (for better or for worse) that he knew that Wagner's music was capable of having.

12 Which is not, of course, to say that it cannot be 'refuted' later.

13 Again, Janaway 2003 is relevant to this point.

14 See Chapter Two, section 4.

15 Although he or she can have a jolly good go. Wagner, for example, presents his exemplars in an almost impossibly over-powering way. But – to the extent that he does so by working on his audience's feelings – he is imposing from 'within', as it were; and even then the imposition can always be refused. Whether an audience decides to take the exemplar up really does lie in its '*own discretion*': see the Appendix to this book for further discussion.

16 Another layer of difficulty should be noted, however. In order for Zarathustra to be an exemplar of the right sort for Nietzsche's purposes, he needs to be exemplary in two separate respects. He must exemplify, not only an ideal mode of post-Christian living, but also the (prior) recognition that it is as a recommender rather than as a commander that he must reach his audience. And this latter consideration means that he is obliged, if he is to succeed in the former task, consciously and deliberately to *constitute* himself *as* an exemplar – an undertaking that is replete, clearly enough, with dangers of insincerity, inauthenticity and, indeed, self-parody. That Nietzsche recognised

these dangers (and perhaps also the fact that he had not steered entirely clear of them in *Zarathustra*) partly explains, I suggest, the hyperbolic, self-consciously parodic tone of his late attempt to constitute *himself* as an exemplar, in the quasi-autobiographical *Ecce Homo*.

17 The thought of eternal recurrence figures largest in *The Gay Science* and *Zarathustra*. It then drops out for three years or so before reappearing briefly in *Twilight of the Idols* and, with some ceremony, in *Ecce Homo*.

18 Michael Tanner notes, rightly, that 'The reason why people's imaginations are' often 'so gripped by the idea is that they' illicitly 'take up a perspective outside any one cycle, so that they can visualize it occurring again and again' (1994: 54–55). I find it puzzling that, having recognised this, Tanner is still inclined to say that it would 'need, to say the least, an unfeeling person to say that it does not matter' whether 'Auschwitz occurs' only once or 'occurs infinitely many times' (ibid.).

19 For some noteworthy efforts to salvage something from the thought of eternal recurrence see, e.g., Loeb 2006, Nehamas 1980.

20 Milan Kundera's phrase, taken from his novel of that name.

21 I am not claiming that this is the *only* sense that can possibly be attached to what Nietzsche is up to here. I am claiming, though, that what I have proposed, first, does make sense of what Nietzsche's motivations may have been, and, second, makes sense of them against the background – namely, the death of the specifically Christian God – that the place of *Zarathustra* in Nietzsche's corpus most naturally suggests.

22 For *amor fati* in *Zarathustra*, see, e.g., Z III, 'Of Passing By'.

23 As, earlier in *The Gay Science*, he had recognised – hence his repudiation of *The Birth of Tragedy*'s talk of giving an 'eternal justification' of life in favour of talk, merely, of making life 'bearable'.

24 See Chapter Three, section 4 for discussion.

25 Of course, Nietzsche makes it quite clear that Zarathustra is not himself an instance of the *Übermensch*, but only prophesies the *Übermensch*. But this isn't enough, it seems to me, to get either of them off the hook: Zarathustra should at least exhibit virtues *of the right general sort*. By comparison with most of the first four books of *The Gay Science*, that is, *Zarathustra* strikes me mostly as a kind of back-sliding – indeed, as a pretty well wilful self-misunderstanding on Nietzsche's part.

Chapter 5

1 Nietzsche also prepared a collection of aphorisms, *Nietzsche contra Wagner*, in his final year (1888); but these are all excerpts from his earlier works.

2 See, e.g., GM P6. For discussion, see Ridley 2005.

3 For an excellent discussion of this passage and its implications, see Clark 1990: 109–117.

4 It is unclear to which stage the metaphysics of *The Birth of Tragedy* belongs (stages 1–3 are occupied, respectively, by Platonism, Christianity and Kantianism).

5 Although there may be the odd exception to this claim – see section 3, below.

6 As Julian Young has rightly pointed out (1992: 117–118). My reading of Nietzsche in this and the next section is broadly consonant with Young's discussion, which I have found very helpful.

7 See also, e.g., GM II.17, where we hear of 'hammer blows and artists' violence'.

8 See, e.g., D 560.

9 Kant, *Critique of Judgement*, Bk. I, section 5, 1952.

10 See Plato, *Symposium* 206b–207a, 1951.

11 Thus 'Romanticism', in Nietzsche's usage, does not match the sense of that term as it is encountered in standard historical or critical contexts.

12 The putatively 'Apollonian' artist is nowhere in sight in all of this.

13 Cf. TI IX.49.

14 As in Chapter One, the issue here is not so much whether Nietzsche was right about Schopenhauer, as what Nietzsche *took himself* to have reason to repudiate in Schopenhauer. (For what it's worth, and despite Nietzsche's strictures, it seems to me that his views in this context are very probably either compatible with Schopenhauer's, or else a good deal closer to Schopenhauer's than he recognized.)

15 The final section is a quote from *Zarathustra*.

16 See also the preceding section, TI X.4.

17 We are, in fact, as Young also notes, back in the territory of the 'child's play' discussed in Chapter One.

18 The only references in *Twilight of the Idols* to eternal recurrence are this one, and one made in the (closely related) section that precedes it, TI X.4.

19 There is an extra irony to be brought out here. In Book V of *The Gay Science* and in the *Genealogy* Nietzsche diagnoses the scientism that underpinned *Human, All Too Human* and, arguably, the first four books of *The Gay Science* as a symptom of a less than perfectly good intellectual conscience, and concludes that faith in science must henceforth be strictly conditional (see, e.g., GM III.12). At the same time, however, he seems intent on ratcheting up the faith in art. From something that really *was* conditional in the 1882 edition of *The Gay Science*, he arrives, in *Twilight of the Idols* (and in *Zarathustra*), at a faith in it that appears to be absolute. So if scientism is dethroned, it seems that aestheticism is to take its place — a fact that tells us something about the internal economy of Nietzsche's own intellectual conscience.

20 For a detailed and provocative discussion of this aspect of Nietzsche's thought, see Conway 1997.

21 See, e.g., GS 109.

22 See, e.g., D 38.

23 See, e.g., GM I.6.

24 i.e. Christian morality — and, just as importantly, the reincarnation of that morality in Kant.

25 Cf. TI, IX.38.

26 See, e.g., BGE 202.

27 Cf. BGE 39.

28 This is, in effect, Nietzsche's version of Kant's claim that nature gives the rule to art, and does so via genius. The chief difference between the two is that, in Nietzsche's case, it is *second* nature that gives the rule.

29 For a more detailed discussion of this point, see Ridley 2007.

30 Inscription placed between the Preface and the first chapter.

31 GS 334 provides an essential hinge between the notions of *amor fati* and of becoming who one is.

32 Nietzsche does occasionally seem tempted by supra-mundane world-redemption, especially when he starts talking about 'eternal recurrence'. But, as I suggested in the previous chapter, eternal recurrence is different from *amor fati*, and it is the strand of his thought that stems from the latter that concerns us here.

33 The wobble discussed in section 3, above, notwithstanding.

34 See, e.g., EH, 'Why I Am So Wise', 2; GM II.1.

Appendix

1 See, or rather hear: Mahler, *Third Symphony*; Delius, *A Mass of Life*; and Richard Strauss, *Also Sprach Zarathustra*. All of these set or are inspired by passages from *Zarathustra*, so lending a bit of sideways weight, as it were, to Nietzsche's claim that 'the whole of *Zarathustra* may be reckoned as music' (EH, 'Zarathustra').

2 For further discussion of this passage, see Ridley 2003.

3 From Richard Wagner, *Opera and Drama*, quoted in Tanner 1996: 9. This is essentially the claim, discussed in section 2 of Chapter Four, that Nietzsche would later make about the power of music (GS 106).

4 Eduard Hanslick, a staunch opponent of Wagner (and satirized by him in *Die Meistersinger*), offers the seminal statement of this view in his *On the Musically Beautiful* (1854).

5 Z I, 'Of the Bestowing Virtue', 3. See also Chapter Four of this book for discussion.

6 In, e.g., CW, *passim*.

7 See, e.g., GS 1; GM III.11 and 13–17.

8 See, e.g., TI II.

9 A possibility also foreclosed, as we saw in that chapter and the preceding one, by Nietzsche's own Dionysian art of becoming and by his doctrine of eternal recurrence. At these moments, Nietzsche's critique of Wagner might very well be turned back against him. Indeed, it is tempting – perhaps more than tempting – to regard these as moments at which Nietzsche has (unwisely) set himself up in competition with Wagner, in the hope of achieving discursively what, in GS 106, he has insisted that only music can do. For further discussion of this point, see Ridley 1998: 157–160.

10 See, e.g., TI IX.21–24. (Schopenhauer's 'will' is an all-embracing principle that, once grasped, is supposed to alleviate pain by fostering renunciation – renunciation being a response to which Wagner had always attached great significance.)

11 From Richard Wagner, 'Art and Religion', quoted in Tanner 1996: 184.

12 Or perhaps both; but not neither.

13 Nietzsche remained under the spell of *Tristan* until the end of his life.

14 See Chapters Three and Five for discussion.

15 Cf. GS 361, where Nietzsche discusses what he calls 'the problem of the actor', a problem that he links to 'the dangerous concept of the

"artist'". The problem that Nietzsche sees has to do with the loss of self: 'Falseness with a good conscience; the delight in simulation exploding as a power that pushes aside one's so-called "character", flooding it and at times extinguishing it; the inner craving for a role and mask, for *appearance*; an excess of the capacity for all kinds of adaptations . . . – all of this is perhaps not *only* peculiar to the actor?' The worry, as Paul Patton has put it, is that 'what was hitherto a partic-ular mode of relating to one's roles (consciously, artistically)' might expand 'to become the only role'; and, if it does, that the 'artist-self' may collapse 'into a single role, and the individual' become 'just an actor' (Patton 2000: 178).

BIBLIOGRAPHY

Anscombe, E. (1958), 'Modern Moral Philosophy', in *Philosophy* 33: 1–19.

Bittner, R. (2003), Introduction to Friedrich Nietzsche, *Writings from the Late Notebooks*. Cambridge: Cambridge University Press.

Chamberlain, L. (1996), *Nietzsche in Turin*. London: Quartet Books.

Clark, M. (1990), *Nietzsche on Truth and Philosophy*. Cambridge: Cambridge University Press.

Clark, M. and B. Leiter (1997), Introduction to Friedrich Nietzsche, *Daybreak*. Cambridge: Cambridge University Press.

Conant, J. (2001), 'Nietzsche's Perfectionism: a Reading of *Schopenhauer as Educator*', in R. Schacht, ed., *Nietzsche's Postmoralism*. Cambridge: Cambridge University Press, pp.181–257.

Conway, D. (1997), *Nietzsche's Dangerous Game: Philosophy in Twilight of the Idols*. Cambridge: Cambridge University Press.

Cox, C. (1999), *Nietzsche, Naturalism, and Interpretation*. Berkeley: University of California Press.

De Caro, M. and D. Macarthur, eds. (2004), *Naturalism in Question*. Cambridge, Mass.: Harvard University Press.

Gillispie, C. (1960), *The Edge of Objectivity: An Essay in the History of Scientific Ideas*. Princeton: Princeton University Press.

Green, M. (2003), *Nietzsche and the Transcendental Tradition*. Urbana and Chicago: University of Illinois Press.

Heller, E. (1988), *The Importance of Nietzsche*. Chicago: University of Chicago Press.

Hollingdale, R.J. (1999), *Nietzsche: the Man and his Philosophy*. Cambridge: Cambridge University Press.

Janaway, C. (2003), 'Nietzsche's Artistic Revaluation', in J. Bermudez and S. Gardner, eds., *Art and Morality*. London: Routledge, pp.260–276.

Janaway, C. (2006), 'Naturalism and Genealogy', in K. Ansell-Pearson, ed., *A Companion to Nietzsche*. Oxford: Blackwell, pp.337–352.

Kant, Immanuel (1952), *The Critique of Judgement*, trans. J. Meredith. Oxford: Oxford University Press.

Kaufmann, W. (1967), Introduction to Friedrich Nietzsche, *The Birth of Tragedy*. New York: Viking.

Kaufmann, W. (1974), Introduction and apparatus to Friedrich Nietzsche, *The Gay Science*. New York: Viking.

Lacoue-Labarthe, P. (1971), 'Le détour', in *Poetique* 5, pp.53–76.

Leiter, B. (2002), *Nietzsche on Morality*. London: Routledge.

Loeb, P. (2006), 'Identity and Eternal Recurrence', in K. Ansell-Pearson, ed., *A Companion to Nietzsche*. Oxford: Blackwell, pp.171–188.

de Man, P. (1979), 'Genesis and Genealogy (Nietzsche)', in his *Allegories of Reading: Figural Language in Rousseau, Nietzsche, Rilke, and Proust*. New Haven: Yale University Press, pp.79–102.

Mann, T. (1985), *Pro and Contra Wagner*. London: Faber.

Nehamas, A. (1980), 'The Eternal Recurrence', *Philosophical Review*, 89: 331–356.

Nehamas, A. (1985), *Nietzsche: Life as Literature*. Cambridge, Mass.: Harvard University Press.

Nussbaum, M. (1998), 'The Transfigurations of Intoxication: Nietzsche, Schopenhauer and Dionysus', in S. Kemal, I. Gaskell and D. Conway, eds., *Nietzsche, Philosophy and the Arts*. Cambridge: Cambridge University Press.

Owen, D. (2002), 'Nietzsche's Event: Genealogy and the Death of God', *Theory and Event*, 6:3.

Owen, D. (2003), 'Nietzsche, Re-evaluation and the Turn to Genealogy', *European Journal of Philosophy* 11: 249–272.

Patton, P. (2000), 'Nietzsche and the Problem of the Actor', in A. Schrift, ed., *Why Nietzsche Still?* Berkeley: University of California Press, pp.170–183.

Plato (1951), *The Symposium*, trans. W. Hamilton. Harmondsworth: Penguin Books.

Pothen, P. (2002), *Nietzsche and the Fate of Art*. Aldershot: Ashgate.

Porter, J.I. (2000), *The Invention of Dionysus*. Stanford: Stanford University Press.

Ridley, A. (1998), *Nietzsche's Conscience: Six Character Studies from the 'Genealogy'*. Ithaca: Cornell University Press.

Ridley, A. (2003), 'Critical Conversions', in J. Bermudez and S. Gardner, eds., *Art and Morality*. London: Routledge, pp.131–142.

Ridley, A. (2005), 'Nietzsche and the Re-Evaluation of Values', *Proceedings of the Aristotelian Society*, Vol CV, pp.171–191.

Ridley, A. (2007), 'Nietzsche on Art and Freedom', *European Journal of Philosophy* 15.

Schacht, R. (1996), Introduction to Friedrich Nietzsche, *Human, All Too Human*. Cambridge: Cambridge University Press.

Schopenhauer, A. (1969), *The World as Will and Representation*, trans. E.F.J. Payne, in 2 vols. New York: Dover Publications.

Scruton, R. (2004), *Death-Devoted Heart: Sex and the Sacred in Wagner's Tristan and Isolde*. Oxford: Oxford University Press.

Silk, M.S. and J.P. Stern (1981), *Nietzsche on Tragedy*. Cambridge: Cambridge University Press.

Soll, I. (1998), 'Schopenhauer, Nietzsche, and the Redemption of Life through Art', in C. Janaway, ed., *Willingness and Nothingness: Schopenhauer as Nietzsche's Educator*. Oxford: Oxford University Press, pp.79–115.

Staten, H. (1990), '*The Birth of Tragedy* Reconstructed', in his *Nietzsche's Voice*. Ithaca: Cornell University Press, pp.187–216.

Tanner, M. (1979), 'The Total Work of Art', in P. Burbidge and R. Sutton, eds., *The Wagner Companion*. London: Faber, pp.140–224.

Tanner, M. (1993), Introduction to Friedrich Nietzsche, *The Birth of Tragedy*. London: Penguin Books.

Tanner, M. (1994), *Nietzsche*. Oxford: Oxford University Press.

Tanner, M. (1996), *Wagner*. London: Harper Collins.

Young, J. (1992), *Nietzsche's Philosophy of Art*. Cambridge: Cambridge University Press.

INDEX

activity 118–19, 121, 122
actor 153–54, 170
Aeschylus 142, 144
'aesthetic phenomenon' 32, 80, 84, 85,
    127, 139
aestheticism 169
aesthetics 4–7, 91, 121, 122, 140, 141,
    145, 155
affirmation/affirmative 36, 102, 109,
    117, 119, 123, 133, 155
agency 114, 128, 132, 133, 139, 140
altruism 4
amor fati (love of fate) 83, 108–10, 130,
    131, 134–36, 167, 169
Anscombe, E. 166
Anti-Christ, The (AC) 112, 117–18,
    138
'antiquarian' art/history 51, 52, 55, 162
aphorisms 35, 99–100, 149, 168
Apollo/Apollonian 13–17, 19, 20, 25,
    116, 144, 157, 158, 168
appearance 14, 16–20, 28, 37, 39–41, 43,
    47, 65–66, 68–69, 116, 144, 161, 164,
    171
Aristotle 157
art and the self 58–60, 83–88, 101, 117,
    130, 134–40
art for art's sake 121
art of works of art 6, 58–59, 85, 86, 117–
    22
artistry 6, 25, 35, 50, 118–19, 133, 137,
    139
atheists 63, 92
atom/atomistic 38, 39, 65, 66, 70, 150,
    160
Attic tragedy/Greek tragedy 10, 12, 13,
    15, 16, 18, 20
audibility, problem of 92, 94, 96–98
audience 46–49, 63, 89, 92–94, 96–102,
    152, 161, 166

Balzac, H. de 143
Bartok, B. 161
Bayreuth 35, 147, 163

beautiful/beauty 4, 13, 14, 37, 54–55, 58–59, 79, 83–85, 87–88, 108–9, 118–21, 130–31, 134, 148, 158
becoming, art of 116, 123–27, 140, 170
becoming who one is 128–34, 140, 147, 154, 169
Beethoven, L.v. 45, 50, 144
being, art of 123–25
beliefs 44, 70–72, 74–76, 163, 164
Beyond Good and Evil (BGE) 5, 6, 38, 66, 68, 87, 112, 113, 114, 116, 117, 119, 121, 131, 132–33, 142, 143, 155, 158, 159, 161, 162, 165, 169
Birth of Tragedy, The (BT) 1, 3, 4, 6, 7, 8, 9–33, 34, 35, 37–39, 40, 41, 42, 43, 44, 62, 65, 80, 92, 97, 116, 126, 144, 145, 157, 158, 159, 161, 167, 168
Bittner, R. 157
Bizet, G. 142
blood 99–100
Boscovich, R. 38, 65–66, 70, 160
Brahms, J. 143, 162
Bruckner, A. 161

Camus, A. 161
Carlyle, T. 162
Case of Wagner, The (CW) 2, 7, 112, 123, 142, 149, 150–54, 170
causes/causation 19, 21, 26, 43, 70–72, 75, 76, 102, 164
Cézanne, P. 161
Chamberlain, L. 156
chaos 5, 66, 68, 76, 150–51, 152
character 4, 15, 16, 17, 19, 51, 59, 83, 84, 87, 88, 110, 111, 129, 130, 148, 150, 153, 165, 171
Chekhov, A. 161
child, playing 31–33, 168
chorus 15, 16, 157
Christian/Christianity 3–4, 10, 11, 12, 16, 35–36, 46, 64, 73, 76, 82, 92, 95, 105–10, 113–14, 117, 142, 146, 154, 155, 167, 168, 169
Clark, M. 37, 40, 65, 68, 69, 159, 163, 164, 168
commanding 94–96, 100–102, 166
composer 1, 97, 141, 142, 144, 146, 153
Conant, J. 57
Conrad, J. 161
conscience, intellectual 72–78, 79–82, 86, 87–88, 95, 110, 111, 113, 117–18, 122, 124–27, 128–31, 132, 138, 140, 154, 169
Conway, D. 169
Cox, C. 160
'critical' art/history 51, 52, 54, 58, 163, 168
criticism 141–42, 143, 149, 155
cultural/culture 3, 4, 5, 10–11, 12, 14, 15, 31, 35, 41, 45, 46, 48, 55, 62, 64, 71, 73, 76, 82, 129, 146, 153, 155

Daybreak (D) 3, 61, 64, 75–76, 84, 92, 94, 105, 119, 168, 169
De Caro, M. 160
Debussy, C. 161
decadence 147, 150, 152–53, 154, 155
degeneration 45, 150, 151, 161
Delius, F. 141, 170
Dionysus/Dionysian 13–14, 15, 16, 17–21, 27, 29–30, 31, 116–17, 123–28, 140, 144, 157, 170
disciple 89, 91, 92, 94, 95–96, 97, 127
discretion 94–95, 101, 166
disinterestedness 35, 46, 120–21
distortion 45, 53, 118, 129
doctrine 97–100
Dostoyevsky, F. 161
drama 10, 13–14, 15, 35, 102, 145, 146, 148, 153, 156, 157
drives 81, 84, 118, 119

Ecce Homo (EH) 6, 62, 99, 112, 116, 134–35, 136–39, 149–50, 152, 156, 159, 165, 166, 167, 169, 170

Emerson, R.W. 162

Enlightenment 3

epistemic/epistemology 22, 37, 41, 45, 46, 71–72, 162

errors 38–39, 41, 43, 66–67, 69, 70, 72, 73–74, 75–76, 78, 97, 115, 138–39, 160

'essence of things' 22, 24, 26, 27–28, 41, 158

eternal recurrence 33, 64, 90, 102–11, 127, 140, 163, 167, 168, 169, 170

ethical teachers 76, 81–83, 86, 88, 110

exemplar/exemplarity 18, 51, 53–54, 57–58, 60, 83, 100–101, 111, 125, 140, 162, 166

faith 73, 75, 76, 78–80, 81, 87

falsification 5, 68–69, 71, 79–80, 81–84, 87–88, 108, 110, 117–18, 124, 138

feeling 17, 18, 44–45, 48, 75–76, 118, 125–26, 132, 133, 143, 145, 147, 148–49, 154, 166, 167

Feininger, L. 161

fiction 53, 93, 111, 165

form 28, 54, 57, 66, 67, 79, 80, 118, 119, 133, 151

freedom 64, 119, 125, 131–34, 135–36, 137, 138, 150

future 4, 10, 42–43, 51, 53, 55, 59, 62, 75, 78, 83, 95, 105–9, 116, 123, 124, 125, 144

Gadamer, H.-G. 141

Gay Science, The (GS) 5, 6, 43, 60, 61–88, 89, 91, 92, 93, 95, 97, 98, 101, 102, 103, 108, 110, 111, 112, 114, 115, 116, 117, 118, 119, 122, 123, 124, 125, 126, 127, 128, 129, 130, 133, 134–36, 139, 142, 150, 157, 158, 163, 164, 165, 166, 167, 169, 170

Genealogy of Morals, On the (GM) 4, 58, 77, 87, 112, 114, 118, 119, 120, 123, 157, 159, 162, 164, 168, 169, 170

genius 46–51, 144, 153, 170

Gillispie, C. 160

God 3, 81, 86, 90, 105, 113, 114, 129, 131, 136–37, 138

God, death of 35, 62–64, 82, 84, 86, 89, 90, 92–93, 95, 96, 98–99, 102, 103, 104, 105, 107, 109, 110, 111, 113, 114, 140, 163, 166, 168

God, shadows of 62–64, 93, 102, 103–4, 110, 111, 113, 114, 128, 140, 168

gods, Olympian 15

Goethe, J.W. 143

'good will to appearance' 79–80, 83, 125

greatness 17, 49, 53, 56, 117, 134

Greeks, the 16–17, 30, 42

Green, M. 160

grumpiness, competitive 161

Hanslick, E. 170

happiness 4, 14, 58, 77–78, 82, 94–95, 120, 137, 151

health 3, 5, 10, 11, 14

Hegel, G.W.F. 161

Heller, E. 142

Heidegger, M. 141

history/historical 16, 36, 43, 51–56, 76, 115, 128, 137, 145, 160, 161, 168

Hollingdale, R.J. 156

Homer 42, 124

honesty 67, 73–74, 75–76, 79, 80, 82–84, 87, 109, 110, 111, 113–14, 116, 122, 124, 127, 128–29, 138, 140, 147, 165

Hopkins, J.E. 162

horse, getting on to 2

horticulture 88
Hugo, V. 143
Human, all too Human (HH) 3, 5, 6,
    34–60, 61, 62, 64–66, 67–68, 73, 75,
    76, 78, 79, 83, 84, 87, 101, 115, 117,
    122, 159, 160, 161, 162, 163, 164,
    165, 169
human beings 13, 37, 41, 47, 68, 72, 95,
    119, 128, 133
human world 25, 71, 160
Hume, D. 157
hyperbole 139, 166

Ibsen, H. 161
idealism/idealists 135, 138–39, 140, 147,
    150, 152–54
idealization 118, 120, 121
images 22, 23, 25–26, 29, 32, 53, 55, 57,
    124, 158
immodesty 82
individuality 13–14, 17–18, 26, 30, 126
Ingres, J.-A.-D. 42
inspiration 41, 46–51, 108, 133, 162
instinct 11, 81, 119, 121, 128, 129, 134,
    137–38, 152, 153
intellect 70, 71, 72, 73, 144, 145, 148
intentions 133
intoxication 17, 18, 80, 116, 118, 123
irony 165, 169

Jaggard, D. 165
James, H. 161
Janaway, C. 36, 160, 165
Johnson, Dr. 162
judgement 17–18, 50, 69, 74, 75, 128–
    29, 142–43, 155, 156
justification 32–33, 76, 80, 167

Kant, I. 11, 21–22, 120–21, 166, 168, 169
Kaufmann, W. 10, 70–71
Kundera, M. 167

Lacoue-Labarthe, P. 159
language 65, 69, 97, 131–32, 159
'Last Man', the 90
law/laws 39, 83, 94–95, 124, 128–29,
    130, 131–34, 137, 150, 160, 166
Lawrence, D.H. 142
Leibniz, G.W. 136–37
Leiter, B. 160, 163
Leonardo 143
Life of Brian, The 95
Loeb, P. 167
love, sexual 18

Macarthur, D. 160
madman, the 63, 92–93, 98–99
Mahler, G. 141, 161, 170
de Man, P. 159
Manet, E. 161
Mann, T. 142, 149, 155, 161
mathematics 160, 164
melody, endless 150
Messiaen, O. 161
metaphysical thesis 19, 20, 22–23, 30,
    33
metaphysical thesis, strong 23, 27, 28,
    159
metaphysical thesis, weak 23, 27, 28, 29,
    30, 32
metaphysics 11–12, 17, 19–20, 21–33,
    36, 37–41, 42, 45–48, 50, 51, 64–72,
    73, 75, 91, 114, 115–17, 126, 131,
    132, 135, 138, 139, 141, 144, 147,
    148, 158, 162, 168
miniaturism 151
modernity 16, 90, 150, 154
modesty 42, 46, 79–80, 83, 87, 88, 110,
    118, 122, 140, 160
Modigliani, A. 161
'monumental' art/history 51–58, 59,
    101, 111, 125
morality 4, 11, 36, 64, 78, 92, 94, 113–

14, 117, 123, 130, 131–32, 138, 142, 169

music 10, 15, 16–17, 18, 19, 28, 29–30, 31, 97–99, 141–55, 156, 158, 163, 166, 170

Napoleon 42

naturalism 36, 41, 47, 64, 67–68, 69, 72, 74, 82, 86, 90, 92, 108, 135, 136, 160

nature, course of 81–84, 88, 111, 127

nature, second 50, 76, 85, 128–32, 136, 164, 169

nausea (and suicide) 67, 73, 75, 79, 80, 82

necessary/necessities 11–12, 29, 52, 66, 67, 78, 83–84, 87, 107, 108, 111, 128–29, 130–35, 137, 150

Nehamas, A. 7, 167

neo-classicism 57

Nietzsche contra Wagner (NCW) 1, 7, 142, 149, 150, 151, 152–53, 168

noumena/noumenal 19, 21–23, 25–27, 28, 30, 37, 40

number 38, 160

Nussbaum, M. 157

'On Schopenhauer' (OS) 8, 21–23, 27

Othello 42

Owen, D. 113, 163, 165

painter, handless 26, 158

Parsifal 35, 144, 146, 152–53, 159

passivity 118, 119, 121

past, the 51, 53, 56, 105–7, 109

perfect/perfection 47, 50, 58, 80, 117, 133, 142

perspective 11, 19, 32–33, 93, 118, 120, 129, 130, 131–32, 136–37, 159, 161, 163, 167

phenomena/phenomenal 21, 23–26, 29, 30, 36, 47

philology 2, 3, 10, 36, 145

philosophy 3, 10, 41, 42, 46, 75, 97, 111, 140, 141, 158, 160

Plato 1, 43, 44, 54, 114, 115, 120, 161, 168

plot 4, 15, 16, 17, 19, 90

poetry/poets 33, 53, 85–86, 90, 100, 116, 125, 131, 134, 138, 142

Porter, J.I. 157

positivism 6

postmodernism 159

Pothen, P. 7

present, the 53, 105–10

primal/primordial 14, 15, 17, 18, 23, 25, 27, 29, 30, 31, 33, 126, 158

principium individuationis 19, 27, 29, 30, 38, 39

principle of sufficient reason 19, 21, 27

progress 5, 43, 76, 164

prophet 89, 91, 95, 102, 144, 165, 167

psychological thesis 17, 18, 19, 20, 23, 27, 30, 31

psychology 14, 19–20, 29, 36, 76, 116, 125, 154

Raphael 48, 143

rationalism, Socratic 10, 11

rationality 17, 18

reactivity 119, 123

reality 15, 19, 20, 31, 37, 39, 40, 44, 65, 69, 79, 82, 113, 116, 140, 144, 161

reason/reasons 16, 76, 77, 78, 79, 80, 81, 85, 86–87, 115, 129, 136, 142–43, 166

recommending 94–95, 100–102, 166

redeem/redemption 10, 12, 32, 33, 68, 73, 105–8, 109, 115, 120, 133, 137, 154, 169

relativism 155

religion/religious 5, 36, 41, 42–43, 48, 75, 81, 147–49, 152, 162, 164, 170

renunciation 170
revenge 123, 124
rhetoric 96, 104, 117, 146, 165
Ridley, A. 165, 168, 169, 170
Rilke, R.M. 142
Rohde, E. 156
Romantic/Romanticism 9, 12, 33, 45, 46, 49, 50, 122–24, 127, 143, 168

salvation 86, 95, 105
Sand, G. 143
Schacht, R. 36
Schlegel, F. 157
Schoenberg, A. 144, 161
Schopenhauer, A. 2, 3, 7, 11–13, 15, 19–20, 21–23, 27, 28, 33, 34, 38, 120–21, 125, 144, 146, 147, 158, 168, 170
Schulpforta 2
Schumann, R. 143
science 5, 11, 35, 36, 37–46, 50–51, 65–67, 68–72, 73, 75–76, 77–80, 157, 159, 160, 162, 169
scientific man 46, 50
scientism 169
Scruton, R. 158
self-creation/-stylization 6, 86–88, 130–31, 133–34, 153, 155
self-discovery/-understanding 18, 130, 132–33
selflessness 4
self-preservation 25, 119, 133
sexuality 120–21
Shakespeare, W. 48, 142
Sibelius, J. 161
sick/sickness 136, 152, 153
Silenus, wisdom of 15, 16, 20, 27, 33
Silk M. 157
Socrates 16, 97, 100
Soll, I. 157
Sophocles 42, 157

soul 47, 53, 54, 55, 58, 86, 105, 110, 111, 116, 143, 151
spectator 13–14, 15–16, 33, 47, 106, 119–20, 157
spritual/spirituality 121, 135–36
Stalin, J. 54, 55, 56, 57, 101
Staten, H. 27–29, 157, 159
Stendhal 58, 120
Stern, J.P. 157
Strauss, R. 141, 170
Stravinsky, I. 161
strength/strong 5, 6, 45, 52, 53–54, 56, 57, 85, 87, 117, 119, 122, 127, 130, 131, 136, 149, 151
style 85–86, 87, 88, 110–11, 130, 150, 151, 152–53, 154, 165
sublimation 18, 121–22
sufferers/suffering 5, 14, 43, 44, 51, 72–78, 86, 123–24, 147, 152, 154, 161, 164

Tanner, M. 91, 94, 95, 148–49, 155, 157, 159, 167, 170
taste 119, 142–43, 151, 155, 161
theodicy 135–36
thing-in-itself 23, 26, 28, 158, 162
things, no such things as 38–41, 43, 65, 66, 70, 71–72, 75, 160, 164
thinker 70, 74, 109, 146
Thus Spoke Zarathustra: see *Zarathustra*
time 19, 21, 63, 70, 106–7, 109–10
Tolstoy, L. 161
tragedy/tragic 4, 5, 9–33, 38, 43, 108, 125–26, 147, 157, 161
transcendence/transcendent 22, 28, 33, 36, 37, 106, 110, 126, 147, 148, 152
translate/transpose 24, 68, 97–98, 141, 158
tree 84, 88, 97–100
Tristan und Isolde 18, 144, 148, 158, 170

truth 4–6, 7, 9–10, 13–14, 16, 44, 70–71, 73–76, 80, 82, 83–84, 87, 114, 117, 124, 126, 138, 163
'Truth and Lies in a Nonmoral Sense, On' (TL) 8, 23–27, 159
truthfulness 73, 114, 116–17, 124
Twilight of the Idols (TI) 58, 59, 112, 113, 115, 116, 118, 119, 121, 125, 126–27, 143, 158, 163, 168, 169, 170

Übermensch 90, 167
Untimely Meditations (UM) 3, 6, 34, 51–58, 101, 146, 163
untruth 67, 72–73, 79, 80, 82

value 11, 16, 41, 46, 73, 74, 79, 82, 92, 101, 103, 105, 113, 122, 138, 139, 155, 162
values, re-evaluation of 4, 113, 126
violence 119, 168
virtue 50, 83, 87, 114, 137, 154, 160, 165, 167

Voltaire 78, 164

Wagner, R. 2, 3, 6–7, 10–13, 17, 18, 19–20, 27, 29, 30–32, 34–35, 46, 97, 141–55, 159, 163, 166, 170
weakness 85–86, 87, 130–31, 134
will 19–20, 22, 23, 27–30, 32, 38, 74, 75, 90, 106–7, 109, 114, 116, 119, 120, 121, 123, 125–26, 131, 143, 151, 170
Will to Power, The (WP) 4
Wissenschaft 72, 78, 157, 159
Wittgenstein, L. 1

Yeats, W.B. 142
Young, J. 7, 37–40, 54–57, 65–70, 73, 79, 126–27, 158, 159, 160, 162, 163, 168

Zarathustra, Thus Spoke (Z) 1, 6, 7, 88, 89–111, 112, 113, 161, 165, 166, 167, 168, 169, 170